VYANKATESH MADGULKAR

Vyankatesh Madgulkar (1927–2001) was one of the pioneers of modernist short fiction (nav katha) as well as 'rural' (grameen) fiction in Marathi in the post-World War II era. He wrote eight novels, two hundred short stories, several plays, including some notable 'folk plays' (loknatya), screenplays and dialogues for more than eighty Marathi films. This book offers a comprehensive understanding of Vyankatesh Madgulkar's work by analysing selections from his major creative fictions and nonfictions. This is augmented with important writings on him by his contemporaries, as well as critical writings, commentaries and reviews by present-day scholars. It situates Madgulkar in the context of Marathi literary tradition and Indian literature in general.

Part of the Writer in Context series, this book will be useful for scholars and researchers of Indian literature, Marathi literature, English literature, comparative literature, postcolonial studies, cultural studies, global south studies and translation studies.

Sachin Ketkar is a bilingual writer and translator. He is Professor in English, Faculty of Arts, The Maharaja Sayajirao University of Baroda, Gujarat, India.

Keerti Ramachandra is a teacher, freelance editor and translator of fiction and nonfiction from Marathi, Kannada and Hindi into English.

WRITER IN CONTEXT
Series Editors
Sukrita Paul Kumar
Critic, poet and academic
Chandana Dutta
Academic, translator and editor

The Writer in Context series has been conceptualized to facilitate a comprehensive understanding of Indian writers from different languages. This is in light of the fact that Indian literature in English translation is being read and even taught extensively across the world with more and more scholars engaging in research. Each volume of the Series presents an author from the post-Independence, multilingual, Indian literature from within her/his socio-literary tradition. Every volume has been designed to showcase the writer's oeuvre along with her/his cultural context, literary tradition, critical reception and contemporary resonance. The Series, it is hoped, will serve as a significant creative and critical resource to address a glaring gap in knowledge regarding the context and tradition of Indian writing in different languages.

Sukrita Paul Kumar and Chandana Dutta are steering the project as Series Editors with Vandana R. Singh as the Managing Editor.

So far, twelve volumes have been planned covering writers from different parts and traditions of India. The intent is to facilitate a better understanding of Indian writers and their writings for the serious academic, the curious researcher as well as the keen lay reader.

AMRITA PRITAM
The Writer Provocateur
Edited by Hina Nandrajog and Prem Kumari Srivastava

MAHASWETA DEVI
Writer, Activist, Visionary
Edited by Radha Chakravarty

VYANKATESH MADGULKAR
A Villageful of Stories and a Forestful of Tales
Edited by Sachin Ketkar and Keerti Ramachandra

For more information about this series, please visit: www.routledge.com/Writer-In-Context/book-series/WIC

VYANKATESH MADGULKAR

A Villageful of Stories and
a Forestful of Tales

Edited by
Sachin Ketkar and
Keerti Ramachandra

LONDON AND NEW YORK

First published 2024
by Routledge
4 Park Square, Milton Park, Abingdon, Oxon OX14 4RN

and by Routledge
605 Third Avenue, New York, NY 10158

Routledge is an imprint of the Taylor & Francis Group, an informa business

© 2024 selection and editorial matter, Sachin Ketkar and Keerti Ramachandra; individual chapters, the contributors

The right of Sachin Ketkar and Keerti Ramachandra to be identified as the authors of the editorial material, and of the authors for their individual chapters, has been asserted in accordance with sections 77 and 78 of the Copyright, Designs and Patents Act 1988.

All rights reserved. No part of this book may be reprinted or reproduced or utilised in any form or by any electronic, mechanical, or other means, now known or hereafter invented, including photocopying and recording, or in any information storage or retrieval system, without permission in writing from the publishers.

Trademark notice: Product or corporate names may be trademarks or registered trademarks, and are used only for identification and explanation without intent to infringe.

British Library Cataloguing-in-Publication Data
A catalogue record for this book is available from the British Library

ISBN: 978-0-367-72129-9 (hbk)
ISBN: 978-0-367-74740-4 (pbk)
ISBN: 978-1-003-15931-5 (ebk)

DOI: 10.4324/9781003159315

Typeset in Sabon
by Apex CoVantage, LLC

CONTENTS

List of Figures — *x*
Preface to the Series — *xi*
Preface — *xiii*
Acknowledgements — *xv*

Introduction: Situating Vyankatesh Madgulkar — 1
SACHIN KETKAR AND KEERTI RAMACHANDRA

SECTION 1
Chitrakathi: Selections from Madgulkar's Creative Writing — 23

Short Stories — 25

1 The Black-faced One (*Kalya Tondachi*) — 27
   TRANSLATED BY SHANTA GOKHALE

2 Deva Satva Mahar — 32
   TRANSLATED BY SUDHAKAR MARATHE

3 Dharma Ramoshi — 40
   TRANSLATED BY CHINMAY DHARURKAR

4 Vyaghri — 45
   TRANSLATED BY VIKRAM BHAGWAT

5 Way to the Bazaar (*Bajarachi Vaat*) — 53
   TRANSLATED BY KEERTI RAMACHANDRA

CONTENTS

Excerpts from the Novels — 61

6 The Village Had No Walls (*Bangarwadi*) — 63
   TRANSLATED BY RAM DESHMUKH

7 Whirlwind (*Vavtal*) — 67
   TRANSLATED BY SACHIN KETKAR

8 Tender Days (*Kovale Divas*) — 70
   TRANSLATED BY SACHIN KETKAR

9 Transfer of Power (*Sattantar*) — 73
   TRANSLATED BY SACHIN KETKAR

Excerpts from the Plays — 77

10 Oh, You Silly Potter (*Tu Veda Kumbhar*) — 79
    TRANSLATED BY SHANTA GOKHALE

11 Sati — 84
    TRANSLATED BY VRUSHALI DESHPANDE

12 Oh, The Husband Has Gone to Kathewadi
    (*Pati Gele Ga Kathewadi*) — 87
    TRANSLATED BY CHINMAY DHARURKAR

SECTION 2
When The Brush Was Not Enough — 93

13 Presidential Address at the 57th Akhil Bharatiya Marathi
    Sahitya Sammelan, Ambejogai on 4 February 1983 — 95
    TRANSLATED BY MANALI SHARMA, SACHIN KETKAR AND
    CHINMAY GHAISAS

14 A Conversation with Vyankatesh Madgulkar — 110
    VIDYADHAR PUNDALIK
    TRANSLATED BY MEERA MARATHE

CONTENTS

15 My Life as a Hunter   119
   VYANKATESH MADGULKAR
   TRANSLATED BY SACHIN KETKAR AND PUNIT PATHAK

16 Vyankatesh Madgulkar's Work in the World of Art,
   Writing on Art, and His Art   124
   VASANT SARAWATE
   TRANSLATED BY WANDANA SONALKAR

17 Madgulkar's Drawings and Illustrations   133
   VYANKATESH MADGULKAR

SECTION 3
Between the Regional and the Universal   137

3.1 Critical Reception and Legacy   139

18 The Course of the New Short Story and Madgulkar's Story   141
   SUDHA JOSHI
   TRANSLATED BY MEERA MARATHE

19 The Regional and the Rural Reality in Vyankatesh
   Madgulkar's Short Stories   145
   RAVINDRA KIMBAHUNE
   TRANSLATED BY MANALI SHARMA AND SACHIN KETKAR

20 Limitations of Language in Rural Literature and the
   Way Forward   149
   ANAND YADAV
   TRANSLATED BY NADEEM KHAN

21 Plays of Vyankatesh Madgulkar: Some Observations,
   Some Questions   158
   ANAGHA MANDAVKAR
   TRANSLATED BY CHINMAY DHARURKAR

22 Vyankatesh Madgulkar (Vyama): Depiction of Dalit Life   168
   GO MA PAWAR
   TRANSLATED BY MADHURI DIXIT AND DEEPAK BORGAVE

vii

CONTENTS

23 Female Characters in Vyankatesh Madgulkar's Narrative Prose   186
    VANDANA BOKIL-KULKARNI
    TRANSLATED BY VRUSHALI DESHPANDE

24 Reconnoitring Caste, Language and Folklore in the Novels
    Vavtal by Vyankatesh Madgulkar and *Fakira* by
    Anna Bhau Sathe   192
    BALIRAM GAIKWAD

25 Nature of Political Consciousness in Vyankatesh
    Madgulkar's Writings   197
    BHASKAR L. BHOLE
    TRANSLATED BY MADHURI DIXIT

26 Tatya: A Tribute   208
    VINAY HARDIKAR
    TRANSLATED BY CHINMAY DHARURKAR

27 The Inseparable Relationship between Man and
    Water-culture As Seen in Madgulkar's Writings   215
    RAJANISH JOSHI
    TRANSLATED BY NADEEM KHAN

28 Vyankatesh Madgulkar's Nature Writing – A Love
    and a Passion   219
    SUHAS PUJARI
    TRANSLATED BY MEERA MARATHE

3.2 Remembering Tatya   223

29 Loving Yet Detached   224
    DNYANADA NAIK
    TRANSLATED BY MEERA MARATHE

30 Dear Tatya   230
    RAVI MUKUL
    TRANSLATED BY CHINMAY DHARURKAR

CONTENTS

31 The Rustic Journey of Bangarwadi   235
    AMOL PALEKAR
    CURATED BY SAMIHA DABHOLKAR

32 Memorabilia and Image Photo Gallery   238

SECTION 4
Biochronology and Bibliography   247

33 A Biochronology   249
    VYANKATESH MADGULKAR
    COMPILED BY CHINMAY DHARURKAR AND SACHIN KETKAR

    Vyankatesh Madgulkar: A Select Bibliography   *255*
    List of Contributors   *259*
    Index   *263*

FIGURES

17.1	Kaziranga 1975	133
17.2	A tiger and a fox	134
17.3	Vyankatesh Madgulkar's brother and renowned Marathi writer G. D. Madgulkar	135
17.4	Brother G. D. Madgulkar who never turned his back on the sufferings of his siblings	136
32.1	'Chitrakathi', Madgulkar's Art Studio	238
32.2	Vyankatesh Madgulkar (a photo on the cover of his books published by Mehta Publication House, Pune)	239
32.3	Maharashtra Gaurav Puraskar for *Bangarwadi*	240
32.4	'My Life as a Hunter', Madgulkar's Gun	241
32.5	Sahitya Kala Akademi Award	242
32.6	Cover of the German translation of *Bangarwadi*	243
32.7	Vyankatesh Madgulkar accepting an award at the hands of Shri Sharad Pawar	244
32.8	Vyankatesh Madgulkar with the renowned actor and director Shri Amol Palekar	244
32.9	Vyankatesh Madgulkar's horoscope in Marathi	245

PREFACE TO THE SERIES

The conceptualisation and making of the Writer in Context series must in itself be seen in the context of a historical evolution of literary studies in English in India. It was as late as the mid-80s of the 20th century, decades after the independence of India, that the angst to redefine English literary studies in the universities manifested itself in thoughtful discussions amongst scholars. In 1986, the Kenyan writer Ngugi wa Thiong'o published his well-known book *Decolonizing the Mind*, which had a widespread appeal amongst the academia and people in general who were struggling to shed their deep-set colonial hangover. Soon after, English departments of the Indian universities and the Centers of South Asian Studies abroad began to incorporate Indian literatures in translation into their syllabi. This encouraged more translations of Indian literatures into English, even though translation studies never picked up as a popular academic discipline. Other than the translations of a few critical texts from Indian languages, the creation of appropriate critical material for an understanding of the comprehensive context of the writers remained minimal. There still remains an impending need to place Indian writers within the context of their own literary as well as sociocultural linguistic traditions. Each language in India has a well-developed tradition of creative writing, and the writings of each writer require understanding from within that tradition, even if she/he may be writing against the tide. Readers, translators, editors, and publishers ought to be able to acknowledge and identify these writings from within their own intimate contexts. Familiarity with the oeuvre of the writers, with their times, as well as the knowledge of their critical reception by the discerning readers of their own language, facilitate an understanding of certain otherwise inaccessible nuances of their creative writings. Apart from getting an insight into the distinctive nature of the specific writer, this would also add to the sense of the fascinating diversity in Indian literatures.

Each volume in this series is designed to provide a few extracts from the creative and other prose writings by the author in focus, followed by the English translations of selected critical essays on the author's works. For better insights into the writer's art and craft, self-reflexive essays and articles by the author about the creative process and her/his comments on the writerly environment are also included. Much of this material may be available as scattered correspondence, conversations, notes, and essays that lie untranslated and locked – as it were – in different *bhashas*. A discreet selection of such material has also been included in each of the volumes in this series.

In the making of this series, there has been an ongoing exchange of ideas amongst the editors of different volumes. It is indeed intriguing that while the writers selected belong to more or less the same times, the contexts vary; and, even when literary conventions maybe similar in some languages, the author stands out as unique. At times, the context itself creates the writer, but many a time, the writer creates her/his own context. The enquiry into the dialectic between the writer and the context lends a significant dimension to the volume. While the distinctive nature of each volume is dictated by the uniqueness of the author, all the volumes in the series conform to the shared concept of presenting an author from within the literary context of her/his language and culture.

It is hoped that the Writer in Context series will make it easier for the scholar to, first, examine the creative interventions of the writer in her/his own language and then help study the author in relation to the others, thus mapping the literary currents and cross-currents in the subcontinent. The series presents fiction writers from different Indian languages of the post-Independence era in their specific contexts, through critical material in translation and in the English original. This generation of 'modern' writers, whether in Malayalam or Urdu, Assamese or Hindi, or for that matter in any other Indian language, evolved with a heightened consciousness of change and resurgence fanned by modernism, postmodernism, progressivism, and other literary trends and fashions, while rooted in tradition. Highly protective of their autonomy as writers, they were freely experimental in form, content, and even the use of language. The volumes as a whole offer a vision of the strands of divergence as well as confluence in Indian literature.

The Writer in Context series would be a substantial intervention, we believe, in making the Indian writers more critically accessible and the scholarship on Indian literature more meaningful. While the series would be a creative attempt at contextualising Indian writers, these volumes will facilitate the study of the diverse and multilingual Indian literature. The intent is to present Indian writers and their writings from within their socio-literary context to the serious academic, the curious researcher as well as the keen lay reader.

Sukrita Paul Kumar and Chandana Dutta
Series Editors

PREFACE

'*Naal sapadli mhanun ghoda ghetla.*' 'You find a horseshoe so you get a horse.' The saying is exemplified by this book on Vyankatesh Madgulkar. A story by him, *Maaza Guni Janawar* ("My Virtuous Beast"), read and translated many years ago, came to mind when Chandana suggested that I edit the volume on a Marathi writer for the Writer in Context series, and Sukrita made me the offer. It has been a journey of discovery into the many worlds of Vyankatesh Madgulkar, who is primarily known for his *grameen* short fiction.

As Sachin Ketkar and I delved into his works, we found not only his short stories and novels, his writings on the jungles with detailed accounts of their biodiversity and ecological wealth, word pictures of people he admired and was inspired by and the numerous screenplays and scripts for movies, but also plays which he wrote and were performed by well-known drama companies of the day. But Madgulkar was more than a writer. He was an excellent sketcher of animals and birds, portraits and some landscapes. He was a hunter, first with a double-barrelled rifle, but soon exchanged it for a camera and binoculars which took him into the jungles to study wildlife.

Going by the number of editions most of his books have gone into, Madgulkar is clearly very popular among the readers. Vishwas Patil, himself a novelist who writes about the people on the margins, said he was indirectly influenced by Madgulkar's *Mandeshi Manse* (variously referred to as Mandeshi Manasa in Marathi and Mandeshi Folks or The People of Mandesh in English) and could recite whole passages from it! It was very surprising, therefore, to find that so little academic research, analysis of his work or critical essays are available.

Except for the novels *Bangarwadi* ("The Village had No Walls" by Ram Deshmukh 2008), *Vavtal* ("Whirlwind" by Pramod Kale 1985) and a collection of 18 (out of about 200) short stories, "Sweet Water and Other Country Stories" by Sudhakar Marathe (2011), there are no other translations in English.

To establish that Madgulkar is more than just a '*grameen*' writer, we have introduced as much of Madgulkar's other writings in translation as

PREFACE

the structure of the series permitted. Madgulkar's ear for the musicality of language is evident in all his writing, especially his plays, owing to the influence of the oral and folk traditions. This *'laya'* or rhythm is very obvious in the original, so for a translator to capture it in English is an exciting creative adventure. We hope that this book will generate enough curiosity in his work and inspire students and scholars to study, examine and assess Vyankatesh Madgulkar's contribution from a multidisciplinary perspective and establish his place in the context of Indian literature and more.

In all the essays and articles that were read and all the people spoken to about Tatya, as Madgulkar was fondly called, we found an affectionate, indulgent tone. What endeared him to everyone was his compassionate nature, amiable temperament, joie de vivre and impeccable appearance. Tatya was a deeply private person and reticent about his private life. A man of few words, he disliked inane chatter but waxed eloquent when the subject was the relationship between man and Nature. He believed that Man was as much an inseparable part of Nature as the animals and plants that inhabit the earth. It was a bond that must be respected and nurtured. The physicist Jagadish Chandra Bose also believed in the essential Unity of all forms of life and non-life. Bose's was an articulated scientific-philosophical belief. Madgulkar's was a lived, instinctive faith.

Madgulkar's daughter recalls what he told her a few days before he passed away. 'Whatever I have written in my life has always been true to myself and to my experience. I am proud of it. I am content.' All his work is invested with these two values: honesty and integrity. It makes Vyankatesh Madgulkar a very special human being and a very special writer!

Another Marathi proverb, *Untavarun shelya hakaycha* . . . meaning herding sheep from a camel's back and that is exactly what we did, Sachin Ketkar from Baroda and I from Bangalore. But we held our flock together. We now present it to you.

Keerti Ramachandra
Sachin Ketkar
Editors

ACKNOWLEDGEMENTS

We would like to express our sincere gratitude to family, friends, and acquaintances who set the book off on its journey with suggestions, advice and contacts.

Our thanks to the copyright holders, Ms Dnyanada Naik and Shri Anil Mehta, Akhil Mehta, and most importantly, the late Sunil Mehta, Shri Mohan Madgulkar, Smt Sujata Pawar, Smt Jyoti Kimbahune, Dr. Krishna Kimbahune, Ms Manjiri Sarawate, Dr. Randhir Shinde, Smt Vijaya Bhole, Smt Sudha Joshi and Smt Usha Tambe, Shri Vinay Hardikar, Shri Rajanish Joshi, Shri Suhas Pujari.

The Loksatta Group for permission to use Ravi Mukul and Dnyanada Naik's articles.

Shri Anand Yadav, Shri Vidyadhar Pundalik, Shri Vasant Sarawate, and Shri Ravi Mukul, whose essays we have used. Our esteemed translators, Shanta Gokhale, (late) Sudhakar Marathe, Meera Marathe, Wandana Sonalkar, Nadeem Khan, Ram Deshmukh, Vikram Bhagwat, Yashodhan Parande, Dr. Madhuri Dixit, Manali Sharma, Chinmay Ghaisas, Punit Pathak, Dr. Deepak Borgave, Vrushali Deshpande, Samiha Dabholkar, Chinmay Dharurkar, and Meera Taralekar.

Shri Amol Palekar, Baliram Gaikwad, Vandana Bokil-Kulkarni, Anagha Mandavkar, Shri Rajanish Joshi, and Dr. Suhas Kulkarni, who readily agreed to write for the volume.

Shubhada Sahasrabuddhe for making several visits to Ms Dnyanada Naik's home to collect memorabilia, etc.

Smita Chaturvedi for all her help.

Chinmay Dharurkar for his invaluable assistance throughout this project.

Prof. Sanjay Karandikar, Dhiren Parmar, and Sabbir Galariya for their assistance.

To all of you, a heartfelt thank you.

Shoma Choudhury at Routledge and her team have been wonderfully supportive and patient. Thank you for facilitating this project.

And the biggest thanks to Sukrita and Chandana for being the perfect guides and handholders!

INTRODUCTION
Situating Vyankatesh Madgulkar

Sachin Ketkar and Keerti Ramachandra

A *Villageful of Stories and a Forestful of Tales* by Vyankatesh Digambar Madgulkar (5 April 1927, August 2001) in the series Writer in Context is in line with the overall objectives of the series, namely, to make a modern Indian writer like Madgulkar more critically accessible and the scholarship on Indian literature more relevant by presenting the writers and their writings from within their socio-literary context to the serious academic, the curious researcher as well as the keen lay reader. These objectives are the results of the cultural and academic needs produced by the disciplinary developments of English studies and comparative literary studies after the mid-1980s, where efforts are being made to shed the deep-set colonial hangover by incorporating modern Indian literatures in English translation in syllabi and research projects.

Vyankatesh Madgulkar is one of the pioneers of modernist short fiction (*nav katha*) as well as 'rural' (*grameen*) fiction in Marathi in the post-World War II period. Madgulkar's oeuvre is extensive and varied. He wrote eight novels, two hundred short stories, several plays, including some notable folk plays (*loknatya*), popular screenplays and dialogues for Marathi films, as well as translations and memoirs. He was among the first few writers who dealt sensitively, realistically and evocatively with marginal geocultural spaces (Mandesh, the region near river *Man* in Western Maharashtra) and the lives and everyday struggles of those who occupy them. His stories incorporated several languages and dialects of the *dhangars* (itinerant shepherds) and the Dalits of rural Maharashtra. His short story collections like "Folks of Mandesh" (*Mandeshi Manse*, 1949) and novels like "The Village had No Walls" (*Bangarwadi*, 1955) are acknowledged as classics of Marathi literature. One of his most powerful novels, "Transfer of Power" (*Sattantar*, 1984) which deals with the power struggle in colonies of monkeys, is based on his research and experience as a trekker and hunter. This generation of 'modern' writers, in most Indian languages, evolved with a heightened consciousness of change and resurgence fanned by modernism, postmodernism, progressivism and other literary trends and fashions, while rooted in tradition. However, modernity in south Asian languages and literatures

DOI: 10.4324/9781003159315-1

has a longer history compared to the modernist literatures in the same languages that seems to emerge prominently only after World War II. Modernist avant-garde impulses in Marathi were clearly visible initially in poetry in the form of '*navakavya*' and short fiction in terms of '*nav katha*'. The modernity as well as modernist literature in Marathi has to be understood in a wider Indian and South Asian modernist impulse as well as larger world literary phenomenon described by Andreas Huyssen as 'modernism at large' (2007) and Susan Stanford Friedman as 'planetary modernisms' (2015). Both scholars have emphasized the importance of the contemporary context of cultural globalization after the 1990s in producing the 'planetary turn' in the modernist studies and its attention to broader geographies of modernism beyond the European and American modernisms. This is also the period in which the notion of world literature came to be freshly theorized.

Modernity in Marathi Literature

Modern Marathi literature, like most modern literatures in south Asia, emerged in the middle of the nineteenth century along with the modern cultural institutions, discursive practices and epistemologies. Precolonial Marathi literature was largely performative, oral and 'recitative' even in its written forms. The emergence of the print sphere, the introduction of western models of education, the establishment of the modern nation state, industrial capitalism and urbanization that followed colonialism played a foundational role in the development of modern Marathi literature as it did in numerous other South Asian literatures. Modern literary genres like novels, travelogues, polemical tracts, short stories, lyrics, literary essays and criticism began to appear regularly in periodicals and journals and were not simple imitative derivations of their western counterparts but were implicated in the regional cultural and artistic histories, ideological and literary agendas.

In Maharashtra, ideological polemics of social reforms spear-headed by Gopal Hari Deshmukh 'Lokahitwadi' (1823–1892), Mahatma Jotiba Phule (1827–1890), Gopal Ganesh Agarkar (1856–1895) and anti-colonial nationalism led by Vishnu Shashtri Chiplunkar (1850–1882) and Bal Gangadhar Tilak (1856–1920) characterized this period, and modern Marathi literature participated in these discursive conflicts, directly or indirectly.

Marathi society and culture also started undergoing significant shifts in the period between the world wars. After the death of Tilak (1920), the news of the Russian revolution (1917) and the entrance of M. K. Gandhi (1915) in the second decade of the twentieth century profoundly influenced the social and cultural environment of western India. With the Morley Minto reforms (1909), the Census of 1911, the Montague-Chelmsford Government of India Act 1919 and the Government of India Act 1935, electoral politics of representation based on numbers altered the way politics was done on the subcontinent. It transformed the dynamics of identity politics based on region, religion, class, caste and language.

The anti-Brahmin movement started by Mahatma Jotiba Phule entered the mainstream national freedom struggle under Gandhi, and the period saw the rise of Dr. Babasaheb Ambedkar (1891–1956) as the leader of the Dalits and one of the sharpest critics of Brahminism and the Indian National Congress under Gandhi. Dr. Ambedkar's critiques of 'modernity' as it was understood in Marathi, however, could never be what Toral Gajarawala calls 'casteless modernities'.

The other forces that began to influence discourse in the region were the Hindu Mahasabha under the leadership of Vinayak D. Savarkar (1883–1966) and the trade union movement which was influenced by the ideas of Marxism and the Russian revolution.

While providing a historiography of modern Marathi literature, renowned Marathi novelist and short story writer Vishnu S. Khandekar (1898–1976) divides the period between 1874 and 1934 into three parts. According to him, the period between 1874 and 1894 saw the rise of new social, cultural and political thought. The two decades between 1894 and 1914 were a continuity with the earlier period. After 1914, though, a significant shift took place. Khandekar points out that the thoughts of the earlier period, the *vichar*, began to get established as *aachar*, as behaviour and lifestyle. Echoes of international happenings after World War I were heard in Marathi literature, giving rise to new concerns like the rise of socialism, Freud's research on the unconscious, and the idea of New Woman. "Many people thought that Goddess Saraswati had cut her hair short, and instead of the *veena*, she is walking with a tennis racket in her hands", as Khandekar puts it.

While the ideological influences on Marathi literature, especially the novels after World War I ranging from Gandhianism, Marxism, Freudianism and Socialism to Hindu nationalism, in the domain of literary criticism and theory, the fundamental questions regarding the nature and function of art and literature gained prominence. The debate between the proponents of the 'Art for Art's sake' (*Kale sathi Kala*) school and the promoters of the 'Art for Life's sake' (*Jeevana sathi Kala*) became significant. While Narayan S. Phadke (1894–1978) and V. S. Khandekar held completely opposing views, they were both extremely prolific, hugely popular and widely read.

Important short story writers of the period between the World Wars include Vitthal S. Gurjar (1885–1962), who wrote hundreds of short stories and was also a translator. He is credited for reducing the didacticism in Marathi fiction and taking it closer to N. S. Phadke's art for art's sake and formalist position along with the short story writer and economist Vaman K. Chorghade (1914–1995), who was involved with the Gandhian struggles of 1930 and 1942 and deeply influenced by Gandhian thought. In addition, one of the most important and influential women writers of this period was Balutai Khare who wrote under the pseudonym of 'Vibhavari Shiroorkar'

(1905–2001) and came to be known as Maltibai Bedekar after her marriage to well-known Marathi playwright, novelist and filmmaker Vishram Bedekar (1906–1998). While many contemporary critics attacked her for her ignorance of the craft of fiction, later critics believe that her emphasis on internal emotional states instead of crafted and plotted incidents make her the precursor of the modernist short story (*nav katha*) that would emerge a decade later. A popular group of poets who called themselves Ravi Kiran Mandal, led by poets like Madhav T. Patwardhan, alias 'Madhav Julian' (1894–1939), wrote poetry marked by aestheticism and formalism. Their poetry was often a reaction against the social didacticism of the Keshavsut generation.

The Marathi authors of the post-war period like Chorghade, Gurjar, Phadke, Julian, Shiroorkar and Khandekar, who were brought up reading and admiring the important authors of the pre-war generations like Hari Narayan Apte (1864–1919), Keshavsut (1866–1905) and his followers, Shripad Krishna Kolhatkar (1871–1934) and Ram Ganesh Gadkari (1885–1919), displayed continuities on the one hand and also sought to go beyond their predecessors in several ways. The canon of world literature in Marathi expanded to include Ibsen, Luigi Pirandello, the Russian novelists and Bengali writers, among others. There was a growing emphasis on formalistic and aesthetic dimensions of literary art, as revealed in the critical writings of this period.

Vyankatesh Madgulkar and Emergence of Modernism in Marathi

The major writer who brought about a modernist shift in Marathi literary sensibility is Bal Sitaram Mardhekar (1909–1956). His landmark Marathi collection *Kahi Kavita* (1947) reveals the poet's response to the historical conditions of the period. Mardhekar, the aesthete of the decadent Ravi Kiran Mandal school, who wrote his early poems collected in *Sishiragam* (1939), fails to reconcile himself to the massive and mindless violence and despair of World War II and the Partition of India. The very first poem in *Kahi Kavita* is built on the paradox and irony of evoking the Lord as one who rots the dried leaves, fans fires and cremates the Earth in the bhakti idiom that characterizes existentialist modernist preoccupation that would be found in many later important Marathi poets like Arun Kolatkar (1932–2004) and Dilip Chitre (1938–2009). Both Kolatkar and Chitre engage with and evoke bhakti in order to deal with the contemporary existential crisis. Many of Mardhekar's poems expressed darkness and urban angst, broke the conventions of sentimental Marathi poetry and used a hybridized-anglicized poetic diction. The modernist writers discovered in bhakti poetry demotic anti-establishment attitudes and existentialist outlooks that appealed to their own sensibility. This modernist rereading of bhakti became very influential.

INTRODUCTION

As Vinay Dharwadkar notes in the context of modernist poetry in Indian languages, "The nation-wide movement that started in the 1930s and continued to affect writers and readers until the end of the 1970s was the Indian counterpart of Anglo-American modernism." He further points out that they concentrated on themes such as

> the disintegration of traditional communities and familiar cultural institutions, the alienation of the individual in urban society, the dissociation of thought and feeling, the disasters of modernization, the ironies of daily existence, and the anguish of unresolved doubts and anxieties. This new sensibility found its earliest expression in the Bengali poetry of Jibanananda Das (1899–1954) in the thirties and Mardhekar in Marathi
>
> (189)

These modernist writers rebelled against the dominant paradigm of poetry, which the editors of *Vibhava*, an anthology of modern Indian writing, termed the 'Tagore Syndrome'. They remark,

> In terms of both style and ideology, one can notice a surprising similarity among the father-figures of different Indian literatures. Cultural nationalism, romantic love, nature, mysticism, metaphysical leanings, and an ideal of nation building formed the common ethos of the Tagore Syndrome and the concoction they produced had become a little too sweet and stale. The dominant form in poetry was the lyric and the fiction writer's creed was realism
>
> (Anantha Murthy et al., 1992, 1–2)

Vyankatesh Madgulkar's own oeuvre belongs to these broader historical impulses which Dharwadkar and Anantha Murthy describe.

Modernism found a strong expression in the Marathi short story and the development of what was known as '*nav katha*' – the New Short Story, which is critical to the evolution of modernist Marathi literature. Along with Vyankatesh Madgulkar (1927–2001), Gangadhar Gadgil (1923–2008), Arvind Gokhale (1919–1992), P. B. Bhave (1910–1980), D. B. Mokashi (1915–1981), Sadanand Rege (1923–1982) and K. J. Purohit 'Shantaram' (1923–2018) are some of the pioneers of the *nav katha* movement. Mardhekar's own experimental fictions, *Ratricha Divas* (1942), *Tambdi Mati* (1943) and *Pani* (1948), deal with the impact of World War II and 'development' on the lives of Marathi people. These novellas use the modernist 'stream of consciousness' mode of narration and often deal with the questions of the region and history.

In the domain of Indian fiction, the *nav katha* and *navakavya* movement is analogous to the *prayogwaad* and *nayi kahani* movement and its practitioners like Nirmal Verma (1929–2005), Mohan Rakesh (1925–1972), Kamleshwar (1932–2007) and Bhisham Sahni (1915–2003), among others in the Hindi speaking region. The *navyathe* and *navina* movements in the south were led by writers such as Gopalkrishna Adiga (1918–1992) and U. R. Anantha Murthy (1932–2014). *Adhuniktawadi* literature in Gujarati was represented by the fiction of Suresh Joshi (1921–1986), Madhu Rye (1942–) and Kishor Jadhav (1938–2018).

Unlike most of the modernist writers of the period who were urban and wrote about urban life, Madgulkar's modernist vision is deeply rooted in the rural and regional spaces of Maharashtra. It is useful to bear in mind that the term '*grameen*' lacks a clear equivalent in English and has been variously translated as provincial, country or rural by writers in this volume. Essentially, the word *grameen* refers to the literature of and about the rural space or the countryside in contrast to the urban space that remained hegemonic in Marathi until the 1970s.

Until the period after World War II, when Vyankatesh Madgulkar started writing short stories, the Marathi literary world was dominated largely by the urban and upper-caste elite, sometimes referred to as the 'Sadashiv Pethis' (a term popularized by renowned Marathi sociologist and novelist S. V. Ketkar), that is, by and for Pune-based Brahmins. The so-called '*grameen sahitya*' or rural fiction that existed at that time took a largely condescending view of village folk and village life, often presenting characters as stereotypes and situations guaranteed to create humour. It was fiction written from the 'outside', so to speak.

Most of the mainstream fiction in Marathi of this period dealt with the clichéd themes of romantic love. But a distinctive shift toward literary representation of specific regions, something of a 'regional turn', is noticeable in Marathi literature in the 1940s. For instance, N. S. Pendse's novels depict the Konkan region, while Mandesh figures prominently in Vyankatesh Madgulkar's fiction. The emergence of this turn is correlated with the rise of the Samyukta Maharashtra Movement after the late 1940s which brought to the fore questions of linguistic and regional identity. This movement was part of a larger social and political process leading up to the reorganization of the states on a linguistic basis.

The emergence of the questions of 'region' in Marathi parallels the emergence of regional literatures in other South Asian languages like Gujarati with Pannalal Patel (1912–1989) and Jayant Khatri (1909–1968) and Hindi with Phanishwar Nath 'Renu' (1921–1977), after World War II. Critics like Ravindra Kimbahune, whose essay is included in this book, hold that Madgulkar is able to create a literary semiotics of *grameen* writing from an authentic 'insider's' knowledge of the village and the visual artist's detachment and exactness, which is 'universal' precisely because it is regional and specific. A feature that is found in other writers on the Indian subcontinent as well.

INTRODUCTION

In this scenario, Madgulkar's 'insider' fiction broke new ground as he brought in a modern existential, sociological, psychological and humane perspective to the people and their lives in the village. His deep familiarity and understanding of Marathi society and culture, plus his use of dialects, makes his fiction rooted in the soil of that region. Madgulkar's foremost contribution as a writer of fiction is that he introduces a whole range of characters from all strata of rural society. He depicts the challenges they have to deal with in the face of drought, poverty and deeply entrenched caste and gender discrimination with empathy and sensitivity.

Vyankatesh Madgulkar: A Brief Overview of His Life and Works

Neither India nor Maharashtra could escape the massive global transformations unleashed by World War II. The immediate economic impact was the price rise, the boost to industrialization, especially the textile industries (as had happened after World War I), and the consequent escalation in urbanization and the rise of the trade union movement. The War also brought home the fact of the real possibility of political independence and power for the national political players. Gandhi launched his Quit India Movement in 1942 with the slogan *'karenge ya marenge'* ('Do or Die'). The 16-year-old Madgulkar, fired by revolutionary zeal and the nationalist spirit, joined the Quit India Movement in 1942. He was considered a criminal and was forced to be on the run, hiding from the government authorities. He was a participant, witness and victim of this period of history and would go on to write about it in his semi-autobiographical novel, *Kovale Divas*, 1971, where he revisits this phase of his life.

Madgulkar was a talented visual artist and deeply desired to be a painter; hence, he went to Kolhapur to learn drawing and painting. Unfortunately, his involvement in the Quit India Movement brought his formal education and training as an artist to an end. His life in this phase was also marked by much instability, and he had to take up odd jobs like painting milestones on the roads to earn a living.

As if in response to sceptical people around him, who doubted his abilities since he had discontinued his education, Madgulkar turned towards writing fiction. Until then, he probably had no noticeable inclination to be a writer. His success as a writer grew, and he described himself as *'chitrakathi'*. The term was first used in one of the earliest books in Maharashtra called the *Manasollasa*, which describes the storyteller who uses drawings and illustrations to tell his tale. Thus, Madgulkar admits that the visual artist in him was inseparable from the verbal story teller. His fictional writing, which tends to rely heavily on his own passion for drawing, wandering and exploring the forests and observing wildlife, lends a strong element of authenticity to his work. The essays by Vasant Sarawate and Ravi Mukul in the book examine Madgulkar the artist at a greater length.

Madgulkar's very first short story, *Kalya Tondachi*, included here as "The Black Faced One", was published by *Abhiruchi*, a prestigious journal, in 1946 and got him early acclaim. The story speaks about the plight of a dog with a black face, which was considered inauspicious and a bad omen. After moving to Pune in 1947, Madgulkar heard of the anti-Brahmin riots that had exploded after the assassination of Mahatma Gandhi. Some houses and buildings in Pune were burnt, and a curfew was imposed. He started out for his village with his friends after the curfew was lifted, and the journey and his experiences of anti-Brahmin rioting in the villages are described in his novel *Vavtal* ("Whirlwind") which was published in the Diwali special issue of the renowned periodical *Mauj* in 1964. All the eight houses of Brahmins in his village were reduced to ashes. In Madgulkar's own words, "*Vavtal* is not a novel, it is history. Only the names have been changed. There is no scope for imagination in history"(*Pravas: Ek Lekhaka-cha*, 46–47).

In 1948, Madgulkar left Kolhapur and went to Mumbai. As he had no place to stay, he shared accommodation with Gajanan Kamat, an assistant editor at *Satyakatha* who was studying for his master's degree. He met some renowned Marathi writers, like Vishram Bedekar, Gangadhar Gadgil, P. B. Bhave, Sadanand Rege, and B. S. Mardhekar, there. Though he had very little formal education, he was very well-read in Marathi. The exposure to world literature came while in Mumbai, with the works of Liam O'Flaherty, John Steinbeck, Maxim Gorky, Maupassant and Gogol, among others. Their impact is visible on his theory and practice as a writer. In a conversation with Aruna Dhere (Dhere, 133), Madgulkar says that he and his friends used to read paperback novels published by Penguin and also anthologies like "African New Writings", etc. So when Gajanan Kamat was writing an article on B. S. Mardhekar's poetry for *Mauj*, Kamat took the expression 'new writings' and coined the Marathi word '*navakavya*' which was subsequently adopted for the short story as well (Dhere, 133). It was in 1949 that Madgulkar's famous collection of short stories about the rural folks of Mandesh, *Mandeshi Manase*, was serialized in *Mauj*.

In order to understand the apparent contradiction between the *nav katha* and *grameen* literature, it is important to understand Madgulkar's modernist vision and his practice in the context of the cultural history of Maharashtra. Madgulkar, in the modernist spirit, seems to recast the whole 'Art for Art's sake' versus 'Art for Life's sake' debate that was taking place in Marathi before World War II. The understanding of both 'artistic beauty' and 'life' in these debates was fairly conventional. Madgulkar's poetics critically undermined the debate by deliberately blurring and complicating the distinction between actual lived 'life' and 'art' that underlay such debates. He did this by using his own unconventional life as primary source

INTRODUCTION

material for most of his writings, thus introducing a whole new world of the Mandeshi village populated by marginalized and oppressed castes like the Ramoshis (nomadic tribes), the Dhangars (itinerant shepherds) the Mahars (the untouchables) and the small rural Muslim communities into Marathi literature.

As he states in his Presidential Address at the 57th All India Marathi Literary Meet held at Ambejogai on 4 February 1983 (included in this book), his house was surrounded by homes of people from diverse 'low-caste' communities like Ramoshis, Mulanis, Momins, Mahars and Nhavis, many of whom belonged to the *alutedar-balutedar* social system[1] of a typical Marathi village. He grew up befriending boys from these communities and acquiring their indigenous knowledge of the rural world and the wilds nearby. He learnt from them how to hunt, fish, graze cattle and gather all sorts of edible material from the forests. He picked up his love for hunting from his companions and the traditional custom of the entire village participating in a hunt on two or three occasions every year. Listening to vivid narrations of stories and tales from the villagers and watching a range of traditional 'folk' performers from itinerant communities like Vasudev, Balsantosh, Bharadi, Vaghye, Ramdasi and Bhorpi were a major part of his childhood. Not only that, Madgulkar's mother told him stories from religious texts. His father, he says, was also a great story teller, but since his job entailed travelling, he was rarely at home. Also, the many transfers did not allow the family to actually settle down. Besides, the family's financial condition was quite straitened. This entire repository of experiences was what Madgulkar drew upon as a creative writer, and that makes his modernist fiction unlike that of many others of his contemporaries whose modernity was, in Toral Gajarawala's phrase, 'casteless modernity'.

After passing the seventh standard Marathi Vernacular Final examination, Madgulkar found himself a job as a teacher in the nearby Nimbwad village. The school had one teacher and hardly any students. His older brother, G. D. Madgulkar, who later became an immensely popular poet, film lyricist and script-writer, also taught in a nearby 'single teacher' school in a Dhangar community. From him, Madgulkar got many stories about life in the village. All these experiences went into the making of his well-known short story collections "Mandeshi Manase" ("The Folks of Mandesh") and *Gavakadchya Goshti* (1949). His famous novel *Bangarwadi* (1955), "The Village Had No Walls", was showered with praise by scholars like Irawati Karwe, Malti Bedekar and T. S. Shejwalkar who averred that it was a valuable document of the cultural history of Maharashtra written from 'below' unlike the usual histories written from 'above', that is from the point of view of the kings (Madgulkar in *Pravas Ek Lekhakacha*, 35).

Madgulkar's sensibility, shaped by the performative folk traditions of the village, is evident in his plays like *Bin Biyanche Jhaad* (1955), *Tu Veda Kumbhar* (1961), *Pati Gele Ga Kathewadi* and *Sati* (1968). Madgulkar is credited with bringing the authentic ethos of a Marathi village into theatre for the first time. As someone who had grown up in a Marathi village and explored rural Maharashtra with keen observation and an adventurous spirit, Madgulkar had developed a sharp ear for the dialects and idiolects of that society with their phonological distinctiveness, intonations and rhythm patterns. This marks the effectiveness and richness of the texture and tonality of his fiction and his plays. It is also one of the reasons why he was so successful as a dialogue writer, screenplay writer and playwright. And yet, Madgulkar the playwright has not received the critical attention that is his due. Anagha Mandavkar's essay in this book seeks to address this lack. She notes that Madgulkar's play writing spans two decades, from 1955 through to 1976, to be precise. Madgulkar also contributed to All India Radio through his writings in the form of full-length and one-act radio-plays.

Mandavkar classifies the plays written by Madgulkar as adaptations, folk plays, independent plays and auto-adaptations of his short-stories. Tragic (*Sati*), melodramatic (*Nama Satpute, Tu Veda Kumbhar*), comic (*Pati Gele Ga Kathewadi*), and folk plays are the several thematic genres that Madgulkar wrote. The sources of these themes and genres are western literature, play-films, folklore, historical facts and his own stories. *Devaajine Karunaa Keli*, *Gaurai*, and *Bikat Vaat Vahivaat* are the adaptations he did of western plays. His *Devachya Kathila Avaj Nahi* was based on an idea from a western film that touched him. Vyankatesh Madgulkar also falls into this tradition of local-global or domestic-foreign sensibilities. This ability engenders quality in his literature and in his playwriting. Madgulkar's plays are of a specific time, a specific region and a specific socio-cultural context. But their content transcends these particular frames of reference. Hence, they have a timelessness and universal appeal.

Another important contribution of Madgulkar's dramas, according to Mandavkar, is that Madgulkar had been handling the genre of folk theatre since 1955. While contemporary Marathi theatre was influenced by Ibsenian realist techniques, most of Madgulkar's plays, both in content and form, were rooted in the local soil. According to the eminent theatre and film director Jabbar Patel (quoted by Mandavkar), Madgulkar's adapted plays are influenced by western literary trends. But the influence of these currents is not seen in his independent playwriting. They represent the soil of Mandesh and its people. Madgulkar's plays, rooted in the soil, instilled flexibility, simplicity, rural wisdom, etc. in Marathi theatre, until then represented by the middle class white-washed world, and brought the real rural world to the Marathi theatre. The excerpts from three of his popular plays, "Oh You Silly Potter!" (*Tu Veda Kumbhar*), *Sati* and "The Husband has gone to Kathewadi" (*Pati Gele Ga Kathewadi*), included in this book will provide a glimpse into Madgulkar's prowess as a playwright.

INTRODUCTION

Vyankatesh Madgulkar's Poetics of Fiction

Commenting on the questions of purpose and commitment as a writer, Madgulkar argues that as language is the most 'social' of all artistic mediums, the questions of social purpose of literary art and social commitment keep cropping up every now and then in the literary field. The same question is not generally asked of musicians, singers or painters. The purpose and the objective of art is a social need. Madgulkar points out that the triangular relationship between the literary, 'writer-literature-connoisseur' and 'writer-propaganda-reader' has existed from earliest times. It is necessary to realize that all writing is not literary, all readers are not connoisseurs, and all writers are not literary writers. Literary work is always rare. Madgulkar's theory of poetic creation seems romantic, almost Keatsian, as can be seen in his quotation of Henry David Thoreau's remark that, like a pumpkin to the creeper, great poetry is produced in a true writer.

The purpose of art, according to Madgulkar, is the same as the purpose of a flower in nature. A rose does not bloom so that people can make *gulkand*, a jam, from its petals. He tells of his experience when he was wandering in the Thar Desert in Rajasthan. He came across an orb of golden flowers in the middle of the desert in the month of January. A botanist might view it from its morphological features, species and usefulness, but an ordinary person would be delighted at the mere sight of the flowers. The purpose of the flowers' existence would not enter their mind. Similarly, good literature, which is as natural as the flower, is rare. Good literature, according to Madgulkar, is a habit, and like all good habits, it helps man to cover himself. If he does not have these habits, he is naked. And once upon a time, man was naked.

In the context of Madgulkar's own poetics and politics mentioned previously, it is pertinent to note an insightful analysis of William Faulkner's rural modernism by Jolene Hubbs. Faulkner, like Madgulkar, was a 'bioregional' writer of rural life and one of the most important American modernists. Hubbs notes that western modernism is largely perceived as an urban phenomenon, Faulkner's rural modernism "critiques the conflation of the urban and the modern, in part by revealing how the country is used as a foil against which urban modernity is defined" and understanding Faulkner's engagement with rural life redefines the relationship of Faulkner's work to literature and politics of its Depression-era context, "exposes the social and aesthetic import of rural obsolescence, and suggests a means of rethinking modernism writ large" (461). Hubbs also points out that though political, Faulkner's political engagements were neither reactionary nor radical like Pound's fascism and E. E. Cummings's interest in communism. He also eschews the documentary impulse to document the sufferings of the poor or critique capitalist institutions. Hubbs notes that the socio-politically significant aesthetic form of rural modernism facilitates the rethinking of literary modernisms in several ways (473). These insights are significant for understanding rural modernisms in Indian literatures like the fiction of Vyankatesh Madgulkar or Phanishwarnath 'Renu'.

'Life' for Madgulkar did not mean human life alone. He did not believe man is a zoon, politically only. Man cannot be separated from nature. In all his fiction, the boundaries between the human and the animal or environment are constantly blurred. His very first short story, "The Black-faced One", is written from the perspective of a dog. His stories like *Marut Raya* and the novel "Transfer of Power" stress the inseparability of humans from the environment. The monkeys of Madgulkar are not tropes or metaphors for human behaviour, they are an inseparable part of humanity. The vivid and evocative descriptions of flora and fauna one finds in almost all his works indicate a kind of communion and a continuum between the human, animal and plant world. This intense engagement with nature is pervasive, and his literary imagination is essentially bioregional and environmental.

The huge body of his non-fictional prose, which includes travel writing, is considered a brilliant example of nature writing. Given his enthusiasm for trekking and exploring the jungles across Maharashtra, Madgulkar had formally purchased a gun in the fifties and used it for hunting for almost two decades. In 1970, when he gave up *shikar*, he says, he carried his notepad, black ink pens and his camera on his expeditions. As he was passionate about animals and birds, he travelled widely, studying wildlife and nature and spent much time visiting several sanctuaries. This provided him the material which went into his books like *Ranmeva* (1976) and *Nagzira* (1979) and the semi-fictional "On the Trail of the Tiger", *Vaghachya Magavar* (1962) and *Janglatil Divas* (1984).

Madgulkar's biographical sketches of people who influenced him include writers from other languages. Being himself a naturalist, Madgulkar admired people like Jane Goodall and Jim Corbett and translated their works into Marathi. As a result, his descriptions of the landscape of rural Maharashtra, rich with flora and fauna, and the sharp portraits and sketches of his characters present an evocative picture of the large spectrum of Marathi society and the vast geocultural landscape that had been left out of literary engagement before his own intervention as a writer. His poetic and precise engagement with environmental diversity and bioregional imagination will be of great interest to researchers and scholars using ecocritical ideas to read literature, based on contemporary eco and geo-critical theories as his writings emerge from the postcolonial cultural spaces of Global South that are peripheral to the mainstream environmental discourse and have only recently started getting attention (see Scott Slovic, Swarnalatha Rangarajan and Vidya Sarveswaran eds. *Ecocriticism of the Global South*, 2015). More contemporary Marathi academics like Rajanish Joshi and Suhas Pujari, included in this book, have explored these bioregional and ecological dimensions of Madgulkar's works. Rajanish Joshi has explored the bioregional relationship between water-culture and human life in Madgulkar's fiction, while Suhas Pujari focuses on more general aspects of the man-nature relationship in Madgulkar.

Madgulkar's novels and short stories avoid overt didacticism or escapist romanticism of the established Marathi fiction of that period. They carry an unmistakable stamp of his deep knowledge of the lives of the people in the village. This depiction of the village differs significantly from the Gandhian notions of the village as an idyllic repository of 'authentic' Indian culture. Madgulkar's fiction reveals the village as a site of exclusion, deprivation, poverty and violence, more akin to the Ambedkarite, anthropological and sociological view of village life rather than the Gandhian idealization. However, he also depicts his characters as resigned and stoic who often passively accept their oppression. His unsentimental and unromantic 'modernist' vision offers a contrast to the modern romantic notions of Indian culture and literature that were pervasive in Marathi before World War II. This anti-romantic and unsentimental attitude to the village and society is also found in Madgulkar's vision of nature, not as a site of some divine benevolence but of violence, struggle for survival and cruelty, as his novel "Transfer of Power" (*Sattantar*) reveals.

Though he was never a literary critic or scholar like B. S. Mardhekar, Gangadhar Gadgil or Arvind Gokhale, Madgulkar sought to locate himself in the tradition of Marathi fiction and theorize his own craft in his presidential addresses, interviews and speeches. For instance, in the presidential address at the Gomantakiya Marathi Literary Meet in April 1975, he begins by quoting the presidential addresses of a couple of his predecessors. One of them was P. K. Atre, a leading playwright, journalist, educationist and political leader who had asked why contemporary literature did not reflect the occupational diversity existing in the society and why it was that the problems of farmers and the questions of villages did not feature in the literature of the times (Nasik 1942). Madgulkar then refers to Shripad Mahadev Mate's address at the Sangli literary meet (1943) in which Mate insisted that writers should intensely engage with the wider social questions and asked why literature of the time did not engage with the lives of the *dhangars*, the untouchables, and the barbers.

The scenario in Marathi, notes Madgulkar, has changed for the better three decades after Mate's and Atre's speeches and writers from diverse castes, regions and professions like Narayan Surve, Namdeo Dhasal, Baburao Bagul, G. V. Pantavane, R. R. Borade, Shankar Patil, Charuta Sagar, Sakha Kalal and Anand Yadav are vigorously writing excellent literature. Madgulkar claims that, in a way, all these writers, including himself, have taken Shripad Mate's work as a point of departure, even though his "The Diary of an Untouchable" (*Eka Asprushtachi Diary*) no longer holds the same fascination that it did earlier. However, the themes of human estrangement and loneliness that feature most prominently in contemporary writing seem to begin with Mate. Madgulkar quotes Turgenev's statement that we all come out from Gogol's 'Overcoat' to underline the fact that the sufferings of a very ordinary person, for example, a small clerk, become the theme of fiction for the first time in Gogol. Madgulkar and his contemporaries, he admits, are indebted to Mate in a similar way (*Paritoshik*, 3–4).

Madgulkar goes on to briefly analyze stories by Shankar Patil, Mirasdar, Udhav Shelke, R. R. Borade and Anand Yadav, who are all associated with *grameen* literature, and Arvind Gokhale and Gangadhar Gadgil, who are connected to the *nav katha* movement, and points out that in spite of diversity of locations, the artists and the settings of their stories, they are all concerned primarily with loneliness, alienation and estrangement of ordinary people. This deep loneliness is a by-product not only of human destiny but also often imposed on them by society. Poverty, caste distinction, ignorance and superstition have been around almost eternally in our society and have started appearing like destiny. Once they are accepted as Fate, there is hardly any scope for complaint! People are rarely aware of this. This depiction of the existential predicament of the people living on the margins of society allows Madgulkar to find a common ground between the *grameen* literary movement and the modernist *nav katha*. It is interesting to note here that Madgulkar emphasizes the existential condition of loneliness in these writers rather than the questions of social oppression that many of them highlight.

Madgulkar evokes Frank O'Connor's influential theory that a short story is a product of "intense awareness of human loneliness" and cites Chekhov's "Misery" as an illustration. Madgulkar goes on to explain the fascination and development of the short story as a literary genre based on sociology. He points out that monolithic society as an organic totality does not exist in India, and what we have is fragmentation. The novel works well in a monolithic society, while the feeling that we are all alone and we have to die alone comes easily in the fragmented Indian society. Therefore, the short story is far more successful and has almost become the 'national art form' of India. It is so rich that it can stand in comparison to any short story in the world. The same cannot be said about the novel in India.

Madgulkar notes that the distinction between the short story and the novel is not of length, and there can be a novel of seventy-five pages and a short story of two hundred pages. The novel very often sets up the individual against the society, and episodes of the individual's journey and development are required for the novel. He uses the analogy of a full-strength orchestra to describe the novel and the soloist performer to describe the short story. Madgulkar also acknowledges the vital role played by periodicals like *Abhiruchi*, *Mauj* and *Satyakatha* in the development of the Marathi short story (*Paritoshik*, 11–15).

Madgulkar's poetics of fiction reveal his modernist temperament, deeply influenced by modernist world literature, and yet it does not indulge in

INTRODUCTION

experimentation for its own sake. Madgulkar's realistic modernism is evident in his deep understanding of the complexities of human existential psychology and the sociological dimensions of the human predicament, especially of those who were marginal to the mainstream cultural history of Maharashtra. Sudha Joshi's essay included in this book assesses the place of Madgulkar's fiction in the *nav katha* trend. She draws attention to the context of Madgulkar's migration and displacement to the city and the impact of modernist world literature on him while in Mumbai. She adds that his fiction does not deal with urban life, which is one of the characteristics of modernist literature, and his style of narration, though deceptively simple and easy, avoids direct commentary but relies on implicature and indirection to reveal his philosophical and moral vision. This is a typical modernist technique.

Modernist writing in Marathi transformed the very basis of Marathi literature by changing the beliefs of what emotions, experiences, sensibilities and elements should go into literature, and thus expanded the experiential horizons of literature. These changes were not merely quantitative but qualitative as well, and Madgulkar, according to Joshi, played a key role in the modernist movement in Marathi. Madgulkar's modernist vision of existential formalism that is simultaneously influenced by the global crisis of modernity, the local histories and politics, as well as the modern tradition of literary poetics, finds its expression in the narrative strategies and modes. His realism is based on using 'reality effects' (to use Roland Barthes's term), which are achieved by a deliberate blurring of the boundaries between fiction and non-fiction, nature and man. They abandon the 'well-structured' plot for a more loose episodic and anecdotal structure and a fluid, unselfconscious narration. Deliberate erasure of the boundaries between autobiographical realism and fictional narration makes it difficult for scholars to categorize his writings.

Reception, Legacy and Influence of Vyankatesh Madgulkar

Critical reception of Madgulkar, a Brahmin writer in Marathi, as reflected in the third section of this book, is deeply ambivalent and reveals more about cultural politics in Marathi literary culture than about Madgulkar. It is related to new cultural politics of literacy, literature and reading that emerged in Maharashtra and India during the late fifties and sixties. The social and cultural history of modern Maharashtra after Independence and the formation of the Maharashtra State has been characterized by vigorous identitarian movements like the Dalit, *grameen*, feminist, *Adivasi*, '*janwadi*' and Marathi Muslim movements, and so on. A widely-held explanation for this phenomenon is found in R. B. Mancharkar's discussion regarding the rise of the new literary trend. Responding to the formalist objection to 'labels' like Dalit, *grameen*, feminist, *Adivasi* and so on, Mancharkar says that though one can think about 'literature' without any labels in abstract terms, literary historiography always has to rely upon some form of classification and labelling while dealing with concrete texts. Hence, there is nothing wrong, in principle, in using labels like Dalit or *grameen*.

Mancharkar goes on to argue that the literary world before Independence was dominated by a numerical minority section of the society, mostly white-collared, urban, upper-caste and male, and hence remained constricted and homogenous. This section largely controlled the print and writing-centric notion of literature and became predominant due to colonial modernity. As a result, it successfully displaced the oral and performative literary practices that were more inclusive.

With the spread of education and literacy, 'the new reader' discovered that he and his life experiences were excluded from this literary field, and due to this dissatisfaction, the new reader turned into 'the new writer'. Besides, the history of the freedom struggle, reformism, industrialization, urbanization and other processes of modernity resulted in 'the explosion of democratization' and resulted in the heterogenization of the literary culture. Drawing upon Nemade, Mancharkar argues that this contemporary phenomenon resembles the thirteenth-century bhakti period, when writers came from diverse social and cultural backgrounds, and concludes that part of the tradition of rebellion was started by Namdeo, Janabai and Chokhamela long ago ("Nave Vangmay Pravah", 137–156).

The processes of democratization of Marathi literary culture have to be understood in the wider context of the evolution of democracy and its relation to modernity in India. While the systemic caste and gender-based discrimination have longer histories on the subcontinent, these movements are distinctively modern and contemporary developments. One leading reason is that the nature of the colonial and postcolonial states, which is one of the key institutional contexts of literature and cultures, differs significantly (with certain continuities, of course) from the pre-colonial states in South Asia.

In this context, Sudipta Kaviraj's discussion of politics in India after Independence is pertinent. Kaviraj suggests a major rupture between the Nehru and Indira Gandhi years. During the Nehru years, Indian democratic politics resembled politics as it was practised in the West, where the fundamental political identifications were on either class or ideological lines. At the same time, the prevalent belief as embodied in Ambedkar and Nehru's position, stemming from Enlightenment belief, was that traditional ideas and practices were erroneous, and to rescue people from the tradition, all that was needed was to present a modern option. People's inherent rationality would do the rest. After Nehru's death, democratic awareness spread to the lower strata of society, and formerly excluded groups began to voice their expectations. By the 1970s, the intermediate castes, those between the upper caste

INTRODUCTION

and the scheduled castes, started to form alliances and coalitions, altering the dynamics of caste politics (34–35). A fairly large portion of Madgulkar's creative life, like many major writers of the modernist phase in Indian languages, falls in the Nehruvian period of internationalism.

However, Madgulkar's perception of his own craft does not sit comfortably with the reading of the new reader as the new writer that cultural historians like Mancharkar offer. For him, a certain kind of deep historical orality as an aesthetic as well as an epistemological mode held a deep fascination and inspired his art. In his Presidential Address (included in this book), he says:

> These days people ask me whether I am drawn towards folk arts and since when. We people are not natural readers, but natural listeners. We use the term 'bahushrut' (one who has listened to many things) for the English term 'well-read'. We have heard the tales of Aditya and Ranubai at home. We have heard the Harikatha in temples. In our courtyard, we have seen and heard folk-performances of the Gondhalis, Jagars, Tamashas and Lalits. Considering our love for listening, wandering folk-singers and performers like Vasudev, Balsantosh, Bharadi, Vaghe, Ramdasi and others would sing and perform the devotional and didactic compositions of the saints for us and we would give them food grains and flour in return.

Nevertheless, Madgulkar's influence on later *grameen* and Dalit writing was significant. As G. M. Pawar, better known as Go Ma Pawar, in the same essay states, Vyankatesh Madgulkar was largely perceived as a *nav kathakar* when he began in the mid-1940s and his place in Marathi literature as a precursor to the later *grameen* and Dalit literatures was emphasized when these movements gained momentum. Pawar adds, "Anand Patil confesses that influenced by Madgulkar's 'The People of Mandesh' which he read while studying for the B.A. course, he too felt that he should delineate people from the village and consequently wrote 'The Soil below the Soil' ". Pawar also points towards Bandhumadhav, one of the earliest Dalit writers in Marathi, who confesses that Vyankatesh Madgulkar's advice shaped his writing:

> I grew up hearing stories read out loudly and started writing my youthful, romantic narrative dreams as love stories. They began to be published in recognised, popular magazines and weeklies. Gradually I began to gain identity and fame as an author. Meanwhile I happened to meet my friend Madgulkar in Sangli. At that time, he was writing his character sketches from "The People of Mandesh" in the periodicals, *Mauj* and *Satyakatha*. He was also gaining name and fame as a provincial short story writer. He had only read my romantic love stories in different magazines and weeklies. Hence

> in our meeting he said something like this: "What is this? Why are you writing only love stories? Write about your fellow Dalit men just as I am writing about my Mandeshi people." His advice pushed me to reconsider my writing and since I was also thinking in that direction, I started introspecting. Thus, my first provincial story, nay the first Dalit story, titled "The Poisoned Bread" based on the real life of my own grandfather Yetala became the first Dalit story written by me.
>
> (Quoted by G. M. Pawar)

Pawar's argument in the essay is that the leader of these movements seems to marginalize or even forget Madgulkar's contribution to the development of these movements. However, literary and cultural politics in Maharashtra and elsewhere in India took an identitarian turn in the 1960s, and as the essay by Bhaskar Bhole in the book indicates, Madgulkar's poetics were increasingly being seen as politically conservative and status-quoist. Responding to Pawar, Bhole argues that though Madgulkar's writings reveal his deep and compassionate first-hand knowledge of Dalit life and though they seem technically superior to many of the Dalit writers, his writings are not a part of any social and political movement and not written with the ideological agenda of Dalit politics. He critiques G. M. Pawar's analysis of Madgulkar's representation of Dalit life as being a precursor to the Dalit literary movement. Bhole argues that while Madgulkar escaped imbibing the constraints of the Brahminical upbringing, his representation of Dalits, as well as his vision of politics, is status-quoist, neo-Darwinian and almost fascist and hence does not visualize the possibility of revolutionary social change. This is in contrast to the Ambedkarite Dalit ideology, whose politics are based upon such a possibility, and hence, ideologically, Madgulkar cannot be considered as a precursor to the Dalit literature.

Pawar also draws attention to Madgulkar's authentic and realistic use of a range of languages, registers and idioms of the castes and communities he is writing about. Pawar says that Madgulkar absorbs almost all the nuances of languages that are spoken by members of different castes in his literary representation and goes on to add that

> The tone of persuasion found in the language of the Mahar or Mang caste is not there in the language of the nomadic castes. Nomadic language does not have the plural form used to show respect. "Have you ever eaten an owl?" – This is the innocent question asked by Mithu Shipayi to the author. "No space to turn this way, there was a thicket everywhere, to both the sides, to my back, even on my head; and he suddenly occurred right in front of me", this is how Govinda Katkari narrates. Bhau Vaid's language is totally different from all of them. His original language is similar to southern

INTRODUCTION

languages like Tamil or Telugu. Hence, he always misplaces the genders while speaking Marathi. Madgulkar has certainly enriched the narrative language of Marathi literature by using a very wide range of languages used by the upper caste Brahman or Maratha people, touchable Balutedar castes, and the beggar nomadic castes.
(See G. M. Pawar's essay in this book.)

Madgulkar's linguistic repertoire and his sociological understanding of the language ecology of the region pose special challenges for the translators translating into English. These problems of translation are, of course, ubiquitous to the translators translating the richly diverse linguistic landscape of South Asia. Each translator very often is left to develop their own translational strategies and negotiate this linguistic complexity and diversity at various levels. This is true even in the editorial processes and influenced by one's own literary and linguistic abilities and translational competence. The current book provides a sample from reputed literary translators like Ram Deshmukh, Sudhakar Marathe, Shanta Gokhale, Keerti Ramachandra and Sachin Ketkar as an illustration of how translating Madgulkar has developed over a period of time.

Nevertheless, this question of Madgulkar's language is also critical to the later Dalit and *grameen* writers who saw him as their precursor. The noted 'rural' writer and theorist of '*grameen*' literature, Anand Yadav (essay included in this book), would praise Madgulkar for moving away from the tendencies to entertain the audience, preach to the reader or 'explain' rural life to the audience found in the earlier 'rural' writers like G. L. Thokal, R. S. Dighe and S. M. Mate and for accurately capturing the social and cultural realities of Marathi village life. Nonetheless, Yadav would state that his influence on the later *grameen* writing would be thin and merely on the surface, as he was influenced by formalist and aesthetic aspects of modernism, while the later writers would be neo-literate villagers who would not be exposed to the elite movements like modernism. He is also 'a bridge' between the earlier generations of *grameen* writers and the later generation of writers like him. Yadav also notes that while the generation of writers like Madgulkar used the standard language for narration and dialect for dialogues, the later writers used the rural dialect more prominently. However, unlike the language of the Mate-Thokal generation, Yadav notes, Madgulkar's 'standard' dialect is not purist and is inflected with regional influences. Baliram Gaikwad's essay in this book compares writings of the famous Dalit contemporary fiction writer Anna Bhau Sathe (1920–1969) with those of Vyankatesh Madgulkar with an emphasis on literary style, theme and language.

Madgulkar, in his Presidential Address included in this book, is critical of the division of literature on political and sociological lines as these political categories are themselves symptomatic of the dominance of the political in literature. He quotes Anatole France's remark that art is one man's gift to humanity. Therefore, instead of classifying literature as *grameen*, Dalit, middle class and so on, we should classify it on literary lines as conventional, fantasy, realistic, existential, psychological and surreal. Such a formal classification, then, is no longer specific to any society and culture but international literary poetics.

Madgulkar would ask that if we were keen on creating a caste-less, inclusive society, such distinctions would only perpetuate social divisions. He goes on to point out that the poetics of *grameen* and Dalit literature are freer and more authentic versions of realism. A work that embodies natural qualities acquires a proper context which makes it stand apart, very much like a great tree in a flat plain or a hillock against the vast horizon. Madgulkar's views about creative writing are obviously formalistic, and looking at the metaphors in his rhetoric, also ecological and naturalistic. Nevertheless, in spite of writing about the marginalized communities with empathy and understanding without being condescending or prejudiced, Madgulkar's own work and contribution slowly became side-lined by scholars when the authors and critics from these communities started writing about their own lives. However, his popularity among the wider readership in Marathi remains unabated.

The Structure of the Current Book

The first section of the book, 'Chitrakathi', provides a selection of Madgulkar's creative writing in translation. It includes his important short stories, *Deva Satva Mahar*, "Way to the Bazaar", *Vyaghri*, "The Black-faced One" and *Dharma Ramoshi*, excerpts from his novels "The Village had No Walls", "Whirlwind", "Transfer of Power" and "The Tender Years", as well as excerpts from his plays "Oh You Silly Potter!", "Oh the Husband has gone to Kathewadi" and *Sati*. These stories and excerpts are selected as they not only played a crucial role in establishing Madgulkar's reputation as a writer but also revealed cultural and social histories of the period, Madgulkar's distinctive style of narration and his vision as an artist.

One of the key objectives of the Writer in Series is to provide better insights into the writer's art and craft, self-reflexive essays and articles by the author about the creative process and his comments on the writerly environment. In line with that, the second section of the book titled 'When the Brush was not Enough' focuses on Madgulkar the man, and it consists of Madgulkar's non-fictional writings on his life as a writer, visual artist, and environmentalist. It includes the Presidential Address at the 57th Akhil Bharatiya Marathi Sahitya Sammelan, 1984, his interview with noted Marathi writer Vidyadhar Pundalik and his write-up on his fascination for hunting. This section also includes essays on Madgulkar the visual artist by well-known Marathi artist Vasant Sarawate. These writings are extremely important for understanding the author in his historical context. There is also a small sample of Madgulkar's drawings and illustrations.

Section three of the book titled 'Between the Regional and the Universal' consists of significant Marathi critical articles by renowned Marathi critics like Sudha Joshi, G. M. Pawar, Ravindra Kimbahune, Anand Yadav, Bhaskar Bhole, Anagha Mandavkar, Baliram Gaikwad, Vandana Bokil-Kulkarni, Vinay Hardikar, Rajanish Joshi and Suhas Pujari that reveal his reception in Marathi and add to our understanding of his oeuvre. These essays are not selected keeping chronology in mind but because they illuminate certain crucial aspects of Madgulkar's writing, like the depiction of the Mandesh region, Madgulkar's place in literary and cultural history, his narrative style as a modernist writer, as well as some very important questions regarding representation of caste and gender. They reveal how Madgulkar was read, how he was critically appreciated and how his legacy was understood in Marathi. The recent essays by Rajanish Joshi and Suhas Pujari explore the environmental imagination in Madgulkar which shows the more contemporary approaches to Madgulkar's fiction.

In section four, 'Remembering Tatya', we have included tributes to Madgulkar the man by distinguished filmmaker and actor Amol Palekar, Madgulkar's daughter Dnyanada Naik and the artist Ravi Mukul. Memorabilia from the Madgulkar museum in his home, Akshar, Pune are testimony to his multifaceted personality and interests as a writer. Through these, Madgulkar leaves an unmistakable imprint on the memory of a literary culture and helps the reader to establish a personal connection with the writer, giving a glimpse of the man behind the writer. The last section of the book provides a biochronology and bibliography. Biochronology provides a chronological overview of the significant events in Madgulkar's life, important to contextualize his life and writings.

Apart from English studies, comparative literary studies, ecocriticism and South Asian studies, the book will hopefully also contribute significantly to modernist studies, which are re-emerging as a vibrant discipline in the twenty-first century. It has turned its attention to 'geographies of modernism' and 'planetary modernisms' outside or on the peripheries, like modernities and modernisms in South Asia or Global South, beyond the traditional Eurocentric histories of modernity. It will also enable universities to include Madgulkar's work when courses are designed for Literature in Translation studies at the undergraduate and postgraduate levels.

Works Cited

Anantha Murthy, U. R., Sharma, Ramachandra, and Nagraj, D. R. eds. *Vibhava: Modernism in Indian Writing*, 1992, Bangalore: Panther Publications.

Friedman, Susan Stanford. *Planetary Modernisms: Provocations on Modernity Across Time*, 2015, New York: Columbia University Press.

Gajarawala, Toral. *Untouchable Fictions Literary Realism and the Crisis of Caste*, 2013, New York: Fordham University Press.

Hubbs, Jolene. "William Faulkner's Rural Modernism" *The Mississippi Quarterly*, Summer 2008, Vol. 61, No. 3, Special Issue on Faulkner, Labor, and the Critique of Capitalism (Summer 2008), pp. 461–475.

Huyssen, Andreas. "Geographies of Modernism in a Globalizing World" *New German Critique*, Winter 2007, No. 100, Arendt, Adorno, New York, and Los Angeles, pp. 189–207.

Kaviraj, Sudipta. *The Trajectories of the Indian State: Politics and Ideas*, 2012, New Delhi: Permanent Black.

Khandekar, V. S. *Saha Bhashane*, 1996, 2nd ed., Pune: Mehta Publishing House.

Lande, Sumati, ed. *Vangmayeen Chalvali Ani Drushtikon*, 2008, Shrirampur: Shabdalay Prakashan.

Madgulkar, V. M. *Paritoshak. Katha: Vyakti: Smarane*, 1982, 1st ed., Pune: Utkarsha Prakashan.

Madgulkar, V. M. *Pravas Ek Lekhakacha*, 2012, 4th ed., Pune: Mehta Prakashan.

Mancharkar, R. B. "Nave Vangmayeen Pravaha" in Lande, Sumati ed. *Vangmayeen Chalvali Ani Drushtikon*, 2008, Shrirampur: Shabdalay Prakashan, pp. 137–156.

Slovic, Scott, Rangarajan, Swarnalatha, and Sarveswaran, Vidya eds. *Ecocriticism of the Global South*, 2015, London: Lexington Books.

Notes

1 A system of various occupations like ironsmith, carpenter, potter and leather worker called 'balutedars' serving the village that emerged in the precolonial Deccan, largely in response to the lack of monetization. Scholars point out that unlike the *jajmani* system prevalent elsewhere where the individual peasant families employed the servants, the entire village as a whole was the employer in the balute system in the Deccan. It also included 'untouchable' castes like the Mahars.

Section 1

CHITRAKATHI
Selections from Madgulkar's
Creative Writing

Short Stories

1

THE BLACK-FACED ONE (*KALYA TONDACHI*)

Translated by Shanta Gokhale

It was a bright, moonlit night. A cold breeze whistled over the clods of the ploughed field. A hundred sheep or more sat crammed together in the pen beside the gate, body against body, clinging, susurrating, creating in that small space an unbelievable warmth against the bitter cold outside. Beyond lay remnants of fodder, trampled down and soiled with dung and mud. Shivya, seeking warmth, lay curled up in the mess. He was being true to his master's bread, guarding that solitary settlement, miles away from the nearest village. His ears, intentionally cut to shorten them, stood erect to catch any sound while his sleepy eyes were alert to any movement on that endless stretch of moonlit land that suggested an animal might be creeping up to pounce on the sheep. Gusts of wind sliced at the body like sharp knives, carrying with them the strong, stale stink of sheep droppings across the field. The field lay silent like a painting, its silence broken only by the wind that pushed through the *nepthi hingna* trees surrounding it.

Shivya heard a movement. He sat up, ears erect, head raised, looking around fearfully. Far away, in the distance, a pure white shape had crossed the Dhulbaji embankment and was trotting across the field. Dried palm fronds crackled. The sheep, crowded together in the pen, shifted and quickly rose. They raised their lowered heads and looked around with pounding hearts. Shivya was bounding towards the embankment, roaring like a lion. Some sheep pulled their little ones closer to themselves. Others bleated piteously. Their fluffy little kids pushed into their mothers' sides, emulating the sound.

Shivya sped like a pellet from a slingshot till he pulled up short before the animal, suddenly deflated. Etched against the black earth of the field stood a slim pure white, furry bitch, her head lowered and tail tucked between her legs. In her span-long snout, the mouth and nose alone were pitch black. She was panting, the tip of her soft, thin tongue hanging out. Her feet were almost completely covered in mud. Shivya saw that she was exhausted. He had longed for a playmate in that remote, solitary settlement and was filled with joy to see the delicate-bodied bitch. Wagging his tail in style, he walked up to her. He licked her long snout and mouth and rubbed his nose against

DOI: 10.4324/9781003159315-3

hers. Dancing and prancing, he sniffed every inch of her furry white body. Then, attempting to lower his loud, gruff voice to as gentle a pitch as possible, he said, "How tired you look. Where have you come from? Have you lost your way?"

Champi was nervous and confused. Even then, her heart, scorched by pain, felt soothed by Shivya's tender inquiries. "No, I haven't lost my way," she replied. "I have been walking since dusk yesterday, letting the way take me where it would."

"You've been walking since yesterday evening?"

Moved to greater tenderness, Shivya now licked her mud-covered feet sparkling clean. He begged and pleaded with her to accompany him back to the enclosure and danced all the way as he led her there. Telling her to relax for a while against the trunk of a palm tree, he bounded over the field to return with a large round *bhakri* between his teeth. He put it down before Champi with great humility and said, "Eat." Then added proudly, "I haven't stolen it. It's my very own. Yesterday, a flock of cranes swooped down on a heap of dehusked rice. One had a damaged leg and back. I dragged it down and made a meal of it. I had no appetite then for the *bhakri* that the *malkin* threw me. I picked it up and buried it in the field. I've just dug it out for you."

Champi cast a grateful glance at him, held the thick *bhakri* between her forepaws and, head bent sideways, started nibbling at it. Shivya sat before her, forelegs extended, watching her eat. The *bhakri* eaten, she lapped up water from the cattle trough with her long tongue. Her food and water bellies were both nicely full now. "Will you stay with me, here in our settlement? My *malak* will be happy to see you. When I take the sheep out to graze, there's nobody to guard the field. If you stay, everything will fall in place. You will stay back when I go with the sheep. I will stay back when you go with them. Once in a while, we will both hunt rabbits together." Even before Champi could say yes, Shivya was making plans and seeing visions of the future.

"No," Champi said with feeling. "I don't deserve to live with anybody. Look at this black face of mine. Black-faced dogs bring bad luck. Wherever they go, death follows. If you don't want your *malak*'s bliss-filled Gokul-like home to turn to ashes, stop pressing me to stay."

"My black face forced me to leave my *malak*'s prosperous home. Now I'm like a vaidu's dog, roaming the forest with him. I don't feel like living with anybody, anybody. I want to go far away where I will not meet even a dog from this world."

Shiva's eyes filled with tears to hear Champi's despairing words. He sat looking at nothing in particular, his heart heavy with disappointment.

For a while, neither spoke. Then Champi said in a tearful voice, "Come. I can't bear to hurt you. A dog is never unfaithful to the *bhakri* she has eaten. I have eaten yours. Let me stay with you for at least as long as I can."

THE BLACK-FACED ONE

Shivya was overcome with joy. He jumped up and down like a child. He crouched and pounced on Champi. He bit at her soft flesh playfully, making sure his sharp teeth did not nick her skin. The two leapt at each other, rolled in the dried leaves and clung together. Playing with the tip of her tail, Shivya flung himself on his back. Champi, sitting up straight, said, "Shiva, if you only knew my story, you wouldn't want me here for a moment longer."

"Why?" Shivya asked, unclamping his teeth from her tail and sitting up. "Whose cat have you killed? What's your big fault?"

"My black face. My body is as white as dough, but here's my face, black as the back of a *tava*. That is why I had to leave a home the kind of which doesn't come your way even if you've accumulated seven lifetimes of *punya*."

Champi began to narrate her story.

"Only a couple of mansions belonging to the great landlord Bidkar of Kauthuli still stand. I came to one of them as a pup. This mansion of some 75 rooms had turrets on all four corners. It was divided down the middle to make two households, one for my *malak*, Dadasaheb, and one for his cousin Bhausaheb. Dadasaheb had fallen on very bad times. The youngest of his five children, Anta, would share a scrap of his *bhakri* with me. It was enough to fill my small stomach. I spent my days running around in the large shared garden. I was three months old when my black face brought disaster to my *dhani*. His aged mother lost her mind. She began acting and speaking in a way that was quite unsuitable for her age. Already desperate because of his circumstances, Dadasaheb was driven to further despair. To prevent the family's reputation from being besmirched and to see if the old woman could be treated in a hospital, he went with bag and baggage to stay with his brother in Thane. Little Anta threw a tantrum, wanting to take me along. Dadasaheb scolded him, saying, 'We are fighting to find food for ourselves and you want to take a dog along like someone from the thieving Phase Pardhi tribe?' I saw their cart off to the edge of the village and returned to sit desolately on a bare veranda. I began to feel as though the house was pursuing me."

"A couple of days passed. Then Uma Ramoshi, the guard, said to Bapusaheb in a voice filled with emotion, 'Saheb, the dog is well-bred. She will be forced to sniff around village rubbish and turn into a stray. A winnow-pan is hardly any weight for a grain-laden cart to carry. Why don't you throw her a scrap now and then?'"

"That is how I became part of Bapusaheb's household. A new collar was put round my neck. I lived well. I was washed and fed on time. If I happened to run through the main room to the back door and somebody shouted at me, the old mother, who actually observed all the rules of pure and impure, would still plead, 'Why are you tormenting her, the poor dumb creature? Tie her up on the front veranda. She must be hungry. It's noon. Set this milk before her, go.'"

"Another two months went by. Taisaheb's little Lata learned to stand using me as support. I would sleep on Bapusaheb's bed. I'd run to greet whoever came to visit. Three-year-old Raja would pull my tail, pluck out my hair, take hold of my ears and push my head up and down and chant a nonsense verse: 'Jambayju you hukayjujuju.' And this Jambi would put up with it all, licking his whole body in return."

"Once, a heavily whiskered visitor turned up at the house. One look at me and pearls of wisdom began to drop from his mouth. 'Who gave you this dog, Bapusaheb? Black-faced creature of ill-omen. I have experienced the kind.' Then he recounted his experiences. When he kept a black-faced dog as a pet, his only son, Subhash, died. His strapping horse Moti turned stiff overnight and had to be thrown to the vultures. Two others, Shamrao Patil and a police havaldar, had similar experiences. They kept black-faced dogs. Shamrao's young bull, strong as an elephant, suddenly fell dead at his tethering post. The havaldar was caught accepting a bribe and thrown out of the service. After relating these stories, the man said, 'Finally, I shot down our dog. All was well after that. Don't keep this dog. Give her away to the itinerant medicine man, a vaidu.'"

"Bapusaheb ignored him. However, all my pampering ended after that. Everybody slighted and abused me as they went about. Days passed as they do, and one day, Putali the cow refused to touch food or water. Her stomach bloated. They fed her oil and lemon juice through a blow pipe, but she continued to writhe in pain. Putali died, leaving her two-month-old calf behind. My bad days had begun. Because of me, Dadasaheb's old mother had gone mad. The family started saying that it had not been two months since I had arrived when this calamity befell them. They began to starve me. Aaisaheb beat me on the back with a piece of burning firewood. A few days later, Raja fell in the backyard well and died. I was convinced my black face was responsible for all these events. I avoided returning home. I would sit by the gate, looking longingly at my leash."

"Finally, Fate did her worst. Bapusaheb himself suffered a stroke and took to his bed. The family sat around him. The entire village was immersed in grief. One day, I went into his dimly lit room and began licking the soles of his feet. Bapusaheb screamed. 'Shamya, Rangya, help. Where are you? Shoot this sorceress dead. I don't want to see her black face again.' He kicked me. I fell against a pillar. I ran out trembling. My stomach was empty, but I ran wherever the road would carry me, hiding my coal black face from the world. And I have ended up here, before you. None of them is to blame. I hope with God's grace Bapusaheb recovers soon from his illness. May his children and Aaisaheb live happily now. They were all god-like people. I am the ill-fated one. What can anybody do about that?"

Shivya, who had been listening to her story quietly, wiped his tears with his paws and said, "*Chche*! You are blaming yourself needlessly. If a branch breaks when a crow sits on it, is the crow to blame or is it coincidence? You mustn't take the blame. Bapusaheb's fate turned against him. Nobody could have helped that. Stay with me here and don't worry. Be happy. Your black face is a blessing. It has given me a companion."

Shivya was back then at his childish tricks.

The moon went down. A dense darkness spread. Stars twinkled bright. Shivya and Champi fell asleep in each other's arms on a bed of dried leaves. They woke up with a start when they heard a commotion and looked around fearfully with sleepy eyes. Shivya's heart filled with terror. An enormous haystack standing beside a hut had caught fire and was burning swiftly like a piece of camphor. Plumes of smoke swirled skywards like a whirlwind. The entire field glowed with the reddish light of the leaping flames. The smell of burning straw filled the air. Men, women and children from the settlement screamed in despair. Shivya sped towards the rick like an arrow.

Champi saw it all through glazed eyes. Flames, like those burning the rick, licked at her heart. Through all that commotion, she thought she heard shouts of "black-face", "inauspicious witch", "spirit from hell" tearing into her eardrums. The next moment, she had turned away and soon disappeared into the far reaches of the deep, dark field.

Source

Translated from the Marathi, *Kalya Tondachi*, from Vyankatesh Madgulkar, Yanchi Katha, Arvind Gokhale ed., 1964, Pune, Continental Publishing.

2
DEVA SATVA MAHAR

Translated by Sudhakar Marathe

It was lamp-lighting time. The farm labourers' women, having just returned from the grazing land, had quickly lit the cooking fires. They'd taken millet flour in platters and flopped on the ground cross-legged to pat the *bhakrya* into shape. The cowherds, sour in body after a day's work grazing their herds, had tied the cattle in the sheds. Bundles of fodder had been given to them. Then the cowherds squatted by the veranda wall, undid their turbans, put them on their knees and rested.

In front of the Maruti temple, children frolicked about. One could hear their noisy merry-making. On the big neem tree in front of the goldsmith's house, hundreds of crows were cawing, squabbling with each other for space. They were restless.

Devya Mahar and Topa Varhal had gone past the *chavadi*, the village office, and were waiting by the Patil's wada nearby. Devya switched the staff with bells on it from his right to his left hand. Then he pushed up his turban, put his hand on his ear and began to bellow, "The doctor of this district will come to prick the infants . . . tomorrow mor . . . . . ning. Everyone must bring their little wards . . . to the *chavadi* . . . . . . and have him prick them . . . o . . . !" Topya tuned his tambourine and, standing behind Devya, beat it.

"Has the whole village been informed?" Topya asked Devya.

"Ten times have I hollered, is enough. . . . Let's turn back now." Deva turned and began walking towards the Maharwada. And Topa started in the direction of the Mangwada.

After this, Deva was going to take a basket from his house and go to the barber's, washerman's, carpenter's, goldsmith's and other balutedars' houses to ask for food. "Give some *bhakri* to the Ta . . . r . . . a . . . l!" Yes, that was his right because the baton had passed on from the last Bendur to him, Taral. He was going to serve the village and the government without a murmur. Until the next Bendur took over from him.

If not a hundred per cent good, Deva was a decent Mahar. One would say decent because he lacked the arrogance and rottenness generally found in the Mahars of the village. The Mahars aren't born with these shortcomings, of course. But because of the treatment meted out to them, they turn out that way. The Kunbi, the Vani, the Brahman, all treat them like beasts, make them work very hard, chopping firewood, delivering and piling it up, sweeping courtyards, grazing cattle, numerous such jobs for very little in return. And they must keep everyone in good humour too. That's why they tend to become cheeky. But Deva wasn't like that. He was very civil.

He was big-boned, short and mild-natured. He didn't behave cunningly like other Mahars. One oughtn't to hurt anyone's feelings or wish anyone ill, one must work until one was dead tired, never mind whether one got fresh *bhakri* or stale in return, one must be satisfied with it. Such was his simple way. He didn't find fault like the other Mahars – "Oh, that skinny brahman? What does he have? Not a grain in his house to eat! Yet he hollers at the Mahars." If someone said, "Chop these four bits of timber, will you?" they made faces and said, "Oh, I surely would've done this for you, but I have hurt my left hand", or "The cow butted me with her head . . . O . . . I have been writhing in pain these last ten days, see?" But Deva wouldn't cook up excuses to avoid work. If someone said, "Deva, go bring some fodder," he wouldn't skive, saying, "Oh yes, I will be back shortly," and disappear. No, sir, Deva would never be able to manage that. From morning till evening he worked, and worked and worked. He would spit on his callused palms in the burning heat of the sun and, drenched in sweat, chop a babul trunk into slips and pile them up. Then he'd take whatever food was given, fresh or stale, and go to the next balutedar to do his bidding. There, he might pile up a hundred or even five hundred sheaves of fodder, take the grain given to him, whether a seer or a small measure, tie it up in a fold of his *dhoti*. He managed the difficult work and all the hardship without letting it interfere with his job as a government servant. To work and serve well was his motto.

From his house, Deva took a basket. He roamed about the village, begging for *bhakri*. Fresh and hot as well as stone-cold and dry, *bhakris* half-filled the basket. After he'd been to every balutedar house, he returned home banging his stick at every step.

The faint light from the bitter-oil lamp fell on the wall, freshly plastered with dung. His young son Ishwar was making hand-shadow shapes of deer on the wall. Hanging about close to him was Tani, the little one, on all fours like a cat. Wide-eyed, she was looking at her brother's wondrous antics. She had on a large and ill-fitting blouse that Nana, brahman's daughter-in-law, had handed down to them. She constantly pushed back the strands of hair that fell on her forehead. Ishwar, with just a patch of hair on the crown of the head, had on a dirty sleeveless jacket that seemed to suit him just fine.

Rani was nursing the infant Parlad. Although she was Deva's wife, she was larger than him. When she walked, her feet thumped the ground. When she talked, she thundered like an officer's wife! But like her husband, she too slaved away like a beast. She was prepared even to use an axe to chop wood if need arose. Deva loved his three offspring and his wife very much, indeed.

There were still some embers in the fire. A little smoke tarried about the hut. The dry sugarcane-stalk fire emitted a rubbery odour that mingled with the delicious aroma of the gourd cooking in the pot.

As soon as Deva came in, Rani laid the infant on the floor and stood up.

"The gourd is ready, you'd better eat."

Hearing her words, Ishwar stopped his shadow play. He rubbed his nose vigorously with his right wrist and said, "Mother, gi' us *bhakri* too." At this, little Tani got up hurriedly and, with both hands, patted her belly and whined, "Me too, Mother!"

Deva washed his hands and feet outside and went in. From the pot on the stove, Rani put some gourd stew on a pewter plate and pushed it towards him. Deva pulled the basket close to him and picked up a pile of *bhakri* quarters. He raised the front end of the plate so that he was able to crush the *bhakri* in the sauce of the gourd dish. Tani and Ishwar took their *bhakri* pieces in their hands and dipped them in the large dish of stew and began to eat. With Parlad on her lap, Rani too began to eat. As she ate, she asked,

"Which officer is coming, eh?"

"The smallpox doctor, who pricks babies."

"Oh, dear! Then must we get Parlad pricked?"

"Yes, we must."

"I won't allow it! Tomorrow I must go with the morning star to weed in Appa brahman's field."

"But then what will I do for my *bhakri*?"

Rani put down the morsel she had taken to her mouth, turned around and said, "You have forgotten, have you? It's Thursday tomorrow."

Deva was a good man and a bit sentimental too. He fasted every Thursday. He didn't partake of any food the livelong day. So, for his dinner, Rani made some fresh stuff to go with the stale; even made something sweet, and then he broke his fast. As soon as the wife spoke he said, "Yes, my dear, yes. Because of the doctor's visit, I reckon I just forgot."

At that, she smiled admiringly and pulled Parlad's cheek fondly.

Ishwar, who was gulping water from a tumbler with his mouth to it, swallowed and asked, "Then, Deva, will he prick me too?"

Ishwar addressed his father informally, in the way of Mahar children addressing all grownups. At that, Deva laughed and said, "Silly ass! Are you an infant now? You were pricked when you were Parlad's age."

Ishwar looked at the vaccination mark on his upper arm. Tani too looked at her arm. Then the two put their arms next to each other's and started arguing about whose mark was larger.

Soon they all finished their meal. Deva took his stick and went out towards the stone platform, a public edifice in the Maharwada. When he had leisure, every Mahar came to rest there. In every Maharwada, there is this small but well-built structure. So it was in the Maharwada at Tadavale too. The houses were built of mud brick, with mud or thatched roofs; occasionally, a rich Mahar's house would have a properly laid floor. Amidst twenty-five such houses, the stone platform stood out in the Maharwada. The inner walls were smooth, plastered and painted white. Some enthusiastic people had spent a few rupees and had the Taluka painter Rangnath Sonar paint a picture of Babasaheb Ambedkar.

When Deva came to the platform, seven or eight others were already sitting leaning against the pillars. A lamp in a corner lit up the dark. Light-skinned Maruti Mahar was speaking a few words of wisdom. He had learnt a few boxing tricks in his day. Besides, he had lived in Mumbai once in a while, doing a mason's job. That's why he knew a variety of things. All the Mahars of Tadavale looked up to Maruti. The Maharwada knew him as Maruti Engineer, to acknowledge his experience.

Deva leaned against the wall and began to listen to Maruti Mahar.

"Now we are no longer ruled by the Sahebs. The Congress has defeated them and taken over the government. Gandhi baba and Nehru manage everything. Gandhi baba is the reincarnation of Eknath Maharaj! He doesn't like the way people treat Mahars, Chambhars or Wadars. He doesn't approve of their language at all. No one is untouchable or a half-caste any more. All are equal!"

Deva found this most strange. On hearing about this great king, he felt great admiration and respect for him. In a pause, he asked, "Are you telling the truth, Maruti?"

"Why would I lie to you? For us Mahars, now the good days are coming. No one will now say, 'Careful, you will touch me!' No, no one. Baba Ambedkar from our own caste has become the Chief there in Delhi now. He sits right next to Gandhi and Nehru. Oh, yes, he is our 'ba', he is going to take great care of us like his own children. He ordered those *bhadavas*, pimps and procurers to allow the Mahars to visit the Vithoba temple!"

Someone else interrupted Maruti, "Now will our children be able to go to school, get educated and then get good jobs, Maruti? No one can come along and kick a Mahar around like a football, utter foul words to him? Will all this end now?"

"Why, surely it will, just let this awful day pass."

Deva's heart was full. A man of our own caste is the Chief, he sits, thigh touching thigh, with Gandhi baba! What a miracle! Bless Babasaheb.

Deva couldn't help bursting out, "Then we too have a kind of . . . father?"

Maruti again emphatically said, "So then, what? Tomorrow he will give our people government jobs. All these small village appointments of Taral and what not will disappear. Hey, Deva, now we Mahars will be the brahman's equal!"

But all this news confused Deva. With great emotion, he said, "Let sweet sugar fill your mouth, Maruti."

Then the topic changed, and the usual daily stories began.

The labour that Deva had done all day had wearied him. His eyes grew heavy. He got up and started walking home. Today he had experienced a new kind of joy. The realization that this Babasaheb Ambedkar sits close to Gandhi baba delighted Deva Satva Mahar in the little village of Tadavale. He was intoxicated with joy. Ishwar and Parlad had a golden future!

Rani had turned off the lamp. The children and she had gone to bed. Deva went into his hut and said softly, "Ishwar, Tani, are you asleep?"

Still only half asleep, Rani mumbled, turning over, "Hanh, look out. The children are in the middle. You might tread on them."

Deva went in gently feeling his way and lay down on a sack on the floor with his turban for a pillow. Rani put some sort of a cover on him. Feeling suffocated, still yawning, he said, "Wake me up betimes, my dear. I must clean the *chavadi* yard. The doctor's coming."

Rani woke up Deva with the morning star. He tied his turban, wrapped himself in a *ghongadi*, stepped out into the starlight and swept the yard. He dusted off his hands and went back home. He took his loin cloth and went to have a wash in the stream.

The morning brightened, filling everywhere with light. The sun climbed a rope's length. The district doctor's carriage entered Tadavale. The village Patil, Kulkarni and others who were there saluted the doctor, lifting the ends of their shawls. The doctor reclining against a cushion in the carriage accepted the salutation with childish arrogance. Still he didn't alight from the carriage. The Patil and others had all this time followed in the wake of the carriage attentively. It reached the *chavadi*. In a clean white shirt, shorts, shoes and stockings, hat in hand, the doctor finally descended from the carriage. The Mahar and Ramoshi folk standing around bowed respectfully to him. Deva also greeted him with great respect, performing a deep obeisance. In response, the doctor half raised his hand with the hat towards his chest.

In the *chavadi*, Martand Chowgule had laid out a mat mottled with ink stains, with cushions and bolsters for the guest's comfort. Beside it in a wooden block, there were two china inkwells filled with red and blue ink and some soft black sand in lieu of blotting paper. A variety of registers, a ruler, everything was placed just as it should be.

Raosaheb – the doctor – went in and sat down. He said to the Patil, "Yes, Patil, let's get it over with, then. I want all the work done by the afternoon."

The Patil got up urgently and yelled, "Hey, is the Taral in his place?"

Meanwhile, Akaram had asked Deva for a pinch of tobacco. Deva took out his tobacco pouch from the pocket of his tattered jacket. He shoved his hand up to his wrist into it and pulled out the tobacco and lime in a little old tin container. By the time he could put the tobacco in his mouth and respond, the Patil yelled again. Upon that, Akaram quipped, "Hey Deva, run, the Patil has started howling as usual."

Deva rushed to him and said, "Sir, it is Deva, I'm here, aren't I?"

"Where the deuce have you been?" the Patil barked. "Go and inform every household that they'd better bring their infants here. Now hop."

From the time the carriage entered the village, the women had been going from house to house, making frightened remarks to each other.

"Hey, Dwada, the vaccination doctor's come. What'll happen to my Sundari? Oh, dear." Whenever the doctor came for vaccination, the uneducated Kunbi women were unhappy. They didn't at all believe that vaccination was beneficial. In fact, a child fell ill for eight days after it was given, or even fifteen days. One had to fast and pray for a recovery. Occasionally a child died! So they tried to avoid vaccination as far as possible. The Taral went round the village four times to tell the women to bring their infants to the *chavadi*, but in vain. They made silly excuses to avoid going there.

The same happened today. He went to every house and said, "Take your infants and go to the *chavadi*." Even after an hour or hour and a half, hardly half a dozen women showed up with babies in their arms. This vaccination doctor was very young and had newly come to this rather old-fashioned place. Naturally, he was quite impatient. When he saw that no one was coming quickly, he roared at the Patil, "Patil, what ingrates the people of this village are! And you don't seem to have any control over them." At this remark, the Patil just smiled helplessly and stood on the veranda and shouted, "Hey, you, Taral . . . there you are sitting, like a king, you bum. Who will call these people, your father?"

"Sir, but I told everyone a long time ago."

"Don't tell me stories. Drive everyone before you and bring them here. Do you think you receive government largesse because it is your hereditary due? You skiver, get up."

Deva got up again with his stick and went to every house shouting, "Bring your tiny babes to the *chavadi*!"

Now the sun was overhead, scorching hot. Still on an empty stomach, Deva was making the rounds. Even as he did so, some cunning chap handed him an axe and had him chop wood, saying, "Come in the evening and take your *bhakri*." So Deva lost time as well as energy. After he had finished crying his message all around the village, he returned to the *chavadi* once again.

In the meanwhile, the doctor had dined on chicken at the Patil's house and was now sprawled, smoking a cigarette.

No food in Deva's belly yet! The heat had tired him, soured him all over. He sat in the shade of the *chavadi* wall with great relief. His black face had burnt even more in the sun, his torn vest was dripping with sweat.

"Devya!" the Patil yelled again.

"Sir?" He wrapped his turban about his head again and stood up.

"Now go to a couple of *vastis*, Dhaygude's colony up here, Babar's field down there, Santu Tukaram's, Ram Kamble's. Go to all of them. Run."

These four communities were scattered in all directions. To avoid having to trudge all the way to their fields every day, some villagers had made their homes in their fields. To go to those places meant a great nuisance, but Deva had to do it. With weary legs, he must plod everywhere. It was a government job, after all, and the Patil's order. Deva rinsed his mouth with the water in the river flowing outside the village. He gulped a lot of the cool water. That stopped the gnawing pangs of hunger in his belly and he was refreshed a little. Then he briskly stepped to all the *vastis*.

In the Dhaygudé settlement, Bala Dhaygude yelled at him. "Get lost, you doctor's lackey. There are no women here, tell him, 'they have all gone for the annual pilgrimage to Pandharpur.'"

Deva turned back and went to Babar's field. There Babar's wife said, venom dripping from her words, "Go tell that doctor . . . tell him no one's got time to bring tiny infants at his beck and call. Who will pick the chillies, then, the doctor's father or the Patil's woman?"

Quietly Deva went to Santu Tukaram's *vasti*. He was at the draw well on the wheel. The moment Deva told him why he'd come, he said, "All right. We'll see. But here, Deva, do a couple of turns with the bullocks at the well. I will go to Warli and be back shortly." At that, Deva told him mournfully, "Please don't do that. I have a job to do there. The officer will kill me if I don't."

"Pah, what officer? You can tell him what you like. Here, hold these reins and drive the bullocks." Deva began driving the bullocks. "I will be back in a jiffy," Tukaram said. But he didn't return until Deva had done twenty-five revolutions of the draw wheel. Only when Tukaram returned was Deva free at last!

Finally, after a futile run around, Deva returned to the village. Three-fourths of the day was over. His dark skin was burning and his toes were throbbing.

He came and reported to the doctor, "I've been to all the *vastis*. Dhaygude's and Babar's women have all gone out of the village . . ."

The doctor's temper had risen very high. He snapped at Deva like a rabid dog: "Stop your blabbering, you lousy half-caste. I'm sure you didn't go to those places. I know. Somewhere you must have stopped to chew tobacco and betel leaf and to gossip. You *haramzada*, good-for-nothing, are you trying to fool me? I have been hollering here since morning, and but for some ten babies, no one has turned up."

To this, Deva said, "*Annachyan*, I swear by my food! I did go to all the places, your honour."

"Shut your mouth! You have the cheek to answer me back! You rascal! You half-castes should be kicked all the time, nothing else will sort you out."

The doctor's voice had risen. He stood in the chavadi and yelled like a Kaikadi. He hurled foul abuses at the Mahars. When they heard his language, all the officers and the Patil and Kulkarni were greatly embarrassed. As onlookers began to gather to see what the matter was, the doctor's voice kept rising. Deva was intently listening to what the doctor was saying, chin on his hands at the end of his stick.

Suddenly his eyes widened and became blood red, his nostrils began to flare, he clenched his teeth, his arms started trembling. The doctor shouted at him, "Why are you standing there listening to this, you *bhenchod*, you . . ."

All of a sudden, Deva bent down, took off his dusty, broken chappal and shouted, "Hey, you, you *babalichya*, just step out of the *chavadi* . . . See if I don't batter your foul-mouthed face . . ."

Next evening, the villagers were sitting gossiping under the neem tree. The little hamlet had been churned up by Deva Mahar's astonishing behaviour. Deva Mahar had taken off his chappal, meaning to thrash the vaccination doctor. Unprecedented! Everyone was talking. Deva squatted in the dust, listening to the clamour.

Someone said to him, "Deva, my good man, you threatened the officer with your slipper in public! Had you come back from the village dead drunk? Boy, he will now go complaining to the State government, and you will surely cool your heels in jail for a year or two."

"Why just the State government, let him go to the Central government, that doesn't scare me. I will tell them plainly, You appoint an officer, what for? Did you order him to abuse us with foul words about our sisters and mothers? Any old *tickooji* comes along and kicks us about like a football . . . What does that mean?"

Then someone asked, "And when our Patil abuses you?"

"Our Patil's work is different. We have lived off his scraps, haven't we? He will hit us with his shoe, and then he will hug us. But who is this officer? He is like a crow that comes and goes. Let him go where he wants. We also have a guardian in the government now!"

Some days have passed since that incident. Meantime, the police have arrested Deva Satva Mahar of Mouje Tadavale. The government has heard the doctor's complaint against him. And Deva is in prison.

Here, Rani works for wages to feed her children and herself. The Tarali has gone as it would with the Bendur to another Mahar. Tadavale is prospering.

In a small southern principality is Tadavale, an insignificant little village with only eight or nine hundred souls. And Babasaheb Ambedkar has not a clue about what happened to a decent Mahar by the name of Deva Satva. In all likelihood, he will never know either.

Source

Translated from the Marathi, *Deva Satva Mahar*, from "Sweet Water and Other Country Stories", 2013, Delhi, Sahitya Akademi.

3

DHARMA RAMOSHI

Translated by Chinmay Dharurkar

The evening twilight spreads. Sunlight and shadows mingle and rest. Cattle return home from grazing. Sparrows, exhausted after chirping and twittering and wagging their tails all day rush into the eaves. Lamps are lit in every house. At this evening hour, to stroll in the front yard, one end of the *dhotar* flung over the shoulder, or perhaps lie on the wood and coir *khaatla*, looking at the slowly dimming sky, or rest on the *tulsi vrundavan* platform, or just stand still at the door with hands folded, and hear the tap-tap of a stick approaching, and a voice calling out, "Bring the grains for grinding, ji Akkaaa . . ."

I have been listening to this cry of Dharma's for more than a month and am greatly troubled by it. Dharma now looks aged and tired. His once strong and sinewy body is like a piece of frayed cloth. He needs a stick for support while walking, sitting or getting up. He doesn't hear very well nor does he see very well. This fair-complexioned, well-built Dharma is going to be a companion for only a few days more, dragging out the final days of his life. He knows it. Most of the people in the village know it. So do those who live and work in the city like me and return home only for a month or so in a year. I came to realize it only when I observed Dharma closely the other day.

I had come home for a couple of months after a very long time. Being habituated to city life, I would get restless in the house. Going out and socializing with the village folks didn't appeal to me. So I would stay home doing something or other.

One morning at *nyahari* time, I was keeping myself busy digging a pit around the hibiscus plant, basking in the mild golden sunshine. A fairly wide pit had been dug, so I plucked the dry, yellow, worm-eaten leaves and put them in the pit. Drew two buckets of water from the well and poured it into the pit. Just then, Aai came rushing out and said, "See if you can find some *aamb*. Your uncle has a stomach ache."

Aamb is a local remedy for stomach pain, a liquid collected from the dew on the leaves of the Bengal gram plant.

I washed my hands and went to the veranda where my uncle was lying on a *ghongadi* and groaning. "Just go to the Ramoshi wada. In fact, even Dharma may have it," Aai said.

I headed for the Ramoshi wada. In fact, I first went to Dharma's place.

Dharma was sitting right outside his hut, in the slanting rays of the sun, his body bare, and a *thali* in his hands. He had wrapped a loin cloth, barely an arm long, around his lower body. The shiny copper plate had a glob of some boiled leafy vegetable and three-quarter pieces of reddish-brown *bhakri*. Resting one palm on the vessel of water beside him, Dharma was eating every single morsel languidly.

"What Dharma, having your *nyahari*?"

Dharma looked up. Put the *bhakri* he had raised to his mouth back on to the *thali* and, with an apologetic expression, said, "ji Whai ji . . . yes, ji. . . ."

Moving away slightly from where he was seated, Dharma pulled a ragged piece of cloth from the corner and said, "Rest here. How did your feet turn my way at this early hour?"

I was also feeling embarrassed because I had interrupted his breakfast. I said, standing where I was, "Won't sit down now, Dharma. If you have some fresh *aamb*, will you give it to me? My kaka has a stomach ache. Will give him some *aamb* and sugar and see . . ."

"Why did you take the trouble to come, ji? You could have just sent word or shouted from your doorstep and I would have brought it myself." Having said that, Dharma turned to the door and said, "Baje, get that bottle of *aamb* for the *dhani*."

There was some movement within the hut, and then only a pale-brown arm came out of the door. It placed the bottle down and disappeared. I was in a hurry, so I took the bottle and started from there. But I kept wondering why Dharma was eating this kind of food – one glob of some vegetable and a quarter piece of *bhakri*. And why Bajaa didn't come out of the hut. She wasn't the daughter of a Patil or a Deshmukh of the village to be coy about coming out in front of a known person like me.

After that, one day, I went to meet Dharma more leisurely. I asked him everything, and he too gave candid answers. In a quivering voice, he told me, "The horse has grown old and tired, *dhani*. I can't do any work. As long as the hands were able, I got a fresh or stale piece of *bhakri*. But now? Now these days have come. Bad! Bad! Even the well-off are struggling for their meals, what do we poor people do!? Two years have passed, no rain, no water. There's drought in our region. Prices have gone up by five measures. What to buy and what to eat! If that wasn't enough, Baje's husband has left her, so she too is here now."

"Then how do you manage to live, Dharma?"

"I manage somehow, on bran and husks. Sometimes we father and daughter eat boiled sweet potatoes or carrots and survive. When you came yesterday morning, the girl had got a whole lot of *tandali* leaves from the forest. We boiled it with salt and chewed it with dry *bhakri*. It is our fate to eat leaves and roots to survive, like goats and sheep. Bad! Bad! Bad!"

Dharma was speaking straight from his gut. I felt terrible. That an old Ramoshi who had served my father well was stuffing himself with leaves to satiate his hunger, and I should be completely unaware of it?

"If this is so, why didn't you ever come to our house? Why didn't you speak to me? Okay, if not me, why didn't you talk to my mother?"

Dharma lowered his head.

"I didn't. How many people should they look out for? When the sky itself is ripped, where should one patch it?"

What was I to say to this reply of Dharma's!? We both remained silent for a while.

Finally I said, "Okay then, I'll see what can be done," and took leave of Dharma. I came home with a heavy heart.

That evening, I mentioned Dharma's plight to my mother when we were sitting and chatting. She too was deeply saddened by it.

"Times are bad, see. The poor are left with no option but to starve to death. Several young Mahars have already gone away, searching for livelihood to survive. The young and able can go, but where can old Dharma go!?"

"Yes, he is frail and worn out."

"A very honest man he is, see. Once I, Anna, your older brother and your father were returning from Sangola. We had a horse then. Father had brought Dharma with him to accompany us on the return journey. What with this and that it got very late. Anna was a small child. I sat with him on the horse while your father and Dharma walked alongside. Dharma was young and energetic then. He led the horse well, but it was past lamp-lighting time before we reached home. While seated on the horse, I noticed that the golden flower ornament I had put in my hair was not there. Must have fallen somewhere on the way. I felt very bad. Couldn't tell anyone about it. Dharma had just unharnessed the horse and was putting hay before it. I said to him, 'Dharma, the golden flower ornament has fallen somewhere on the way.'"

"Immediately, without having any food, he said to me, 'Akka, light a lantern for me.'"

"In the dark of the night, he set out to search for the tiny flower. The best part of the story was that before the morning star rose, my Dharma Naik was back with the ornament. Such is our man!"

"Indeed! But Aai, he is now dying of hunger. He is surviving on boiled leaves."

"How will I let him die of hunger, *re*? I didn't know. Where do I have the time to look around, with all these daily chores . . . But tell him to come and take four to eight *payli* measures of grain. And also tell that Bajaa not to sit idle. Tell her to come and collect the grain for grinding every day. I can't find anyone to do it. At least it will earn them some money every month for salt and chilli powder."

"Aai . . . you are all right with the grain she grinds?"

"We have such a big number of people to look after, the flour can be used to make *bhakris* for them." And from then on, Dharma started coming to our place every evening to collect the grains for grinding. He found it very difficult to walk over in the dusk, feeling his way to our house. At first our pet dog used to attack him, and Dharma would stumble as he tried to avoid her. He often fell against the neighbouring wall, trying to escape her. It made me very unhappy to see him in that state.

I even told him once, "Dharma, why do you drag your old, worn-out body like this every day? Bajaa is at home, why don't you send her? Don't take the trouble yourself."

"What trouble! I am not decrepit yet. I can go to Sangola and come back in no time at all. Baji refuses to come to your wada, she is afraid of your dog, she says."

I did not say any more. As dusk fell, Dharma would show up, tapping his stick, and take the grain. The next day, when the sun had climbed above the horizon, he would return with the flour. If he felt like it, he would sun himself in the yard or speak a few words to me or my mother and go away. Now things were better for him.

A month passed. The chill of the Paush month began to bite. The coarse woollen *ghongadi* pulled on in the evening would not be taken off even at *nyahiri* time the next morning. The fires, made from wood chips and shavings from the carpenter's yard, would continue to burn till noon. The children would collect twigs, straw, and sticks and make bonfires to keep themselves warm. Even in that extreme cold, Dharma would come twice a day, a tattered *ghongadi* wrapped around him. He would bask in the sun for a little while in the mornings. The cold must have affected him, and his old body shivered and trembled as he walked. It was heart-wrenching.

It was difficult for me to see this any longer, so I suggested to Dharma again, "It is getting too much for you, Dharma. Why don't you send Bajaa?"

Dharma looked at me, his eyes filled with sorrow. His loosely hanging lip quivered as if he wanted to say something. For a couple of moments, he just sat and stared at the ground. I have noticed that in times of hardship, the Mahars and Mangs come home and sit. Just sit. Only when they are asked repeatedly do they speak. "Nothing really, ji. Just came to ask Akka if there was something wet to go with the dry (*bhakri*)." How small were their needs! And yet, out of embarrassment or fear of being refused, they would not ask directly. Knowing this habit of theirs, I said, kindly, "Why are you silent, Dharma? Is something wrong? Do you need some *jowar*?"

Still staring at the ground, he replied, "No ji . . . not that. See if you have a piece of old *dhotar*. For many days, I've been thinking, I'll ask, but then I feel ashamed . . . I have nothing to cover myself with in this bitter cold."

"Oh! Why did you hesitate!? Wait! Let me see."

I went into my room and brought a *dhotar* of mine and put it around his shoulders. "Here, take this. You can easily use it for two-three months." Dharma stood up and slowly ambled out of sight.

The next day, I had to go out of town on work, I returned after three-four days and to my surprise, I saw Bajaa bringing the flour instead of Dharma. As soon as she saw me, she drew her sari across her face and turned away. I was about to say, "Why did you trouble the old man all these days?" Instead, I said, "You brought the flour today, Bajaa? Is Dharma all right?"

She nodded. "Yes, ji, he is fine."

Then I understood why Bajaa had not been coming to collect the grain. And why she had put the bottle of *aamb* outside the door and not come out herself.

Bajaa had wrapped the *dhotar* I had given Dharma the other day around herself like a sari.

Source

Translated from the Marathi, *Dharma Ramoshi*, from Mandeshi Manase, 1949, Bombay, Abhinav Prakashan.

4

VYAGHRI

Translated by Vikram Bhagwat

Evening was setting in fast, and yet not a single animal had showed up at the small pond in the heart of the forest so far. I'd been sitting atop a tree for long, and now I was fed up. Besides, I was desperate to urinate. For how long can one bear the discomfort? Somya Lamani was supposed to be somewhere around here. Should I whistle out to alert him and climb down? "Sit right here, Dada," he had assured me repeatedly. "Definitely you will get a hit." In spite of that, I went and checked out the edge of the pond myself. Fresh footprints of many animals were visible in the damp mud. Wild boar, sambar, chital, the spotted deer had to be coming to this watering hole, I thought. Yet not a single animal was seen so far. This was the reserved Kondankeri forest in Karwar. No hunter could enter unless he had a permit. Therefore it was unlikely that someone had frightened the animals away. Was this some kind of witchery, the work of ghosts?

I had been perched on the tree like a monkey since four-thirty. It was now forty-five minutes past six. In that time, all I had seen at the pond were two wild fowl, one peacock and six quails! Such birds can be seen even on the ponds of our Sinhagad in Pune!

Now this Somya Lamani fellow had said, "Dada, I am having cough, so I will sit at a distance. I will come as soon as you make a hit," and disappeared. As if he had fallen into the pond himself. If you have a companion, time passes quickly.

I was desperately uncomfortable. To hell with this shikar! What if I empty my bloated bladder from right here, the top of the tree?

There were lots of dry and dead leaves below. The urine stream would make a loud noise. Should an animal approach just then, it will dash away. Looks like it will be just *dal-bhath* for dinner tonight! While wandering around the camp with a torchlight, two rabbits had been hunted. Their skinned carcasses were hanging in the camp kitchen. But rabbit meat had become distasteful. Needed a change of flavour.

Should I climb down?

How slowly the second hand of my wristwatch was moving!

Should I climb down?

It was impossible to control any longer. I made up my mind. I would get down. Slinging my rifle on my back, I was about to uncross my legs when, on the path leading to the pond, something reddish yellow moved. With bated breath, I watched. From behind the bushes, the huge head of a *bibalya vagh*, a panther-tiger emerged.

I was stunned.

This couldn't happen even in a dream. A bibalya at the watering hole at this odd hour? There was no time to think. Fifteen-twenty yards away, the long yellow body was walking across the path. It was walking towards the water. I pressed the stock of the rifle tightly to my shoulder, clenched the right side of my jaw and pulled the trigger.

A sharp 'dhadam' sound followed. Storks roosting on the tree flew off squawking. The bibalya lay on the ground, motionless. The echo of the gunshot faded away. I waited for two minutes with my finger on the trigger. I looked hard.

Chche! No! There was absolutely no movement.

The right barrel was still loaded. I muttered to myself, "How can there possibly be any movement?"

I could see it clearly, lying there like a lump of flesh and bone.

No movement? Sure?

Then I pulled back the safety catch, hoisted the rifle over the shoulder and climbed down the tree with my back towards it.

Actually, does one need to observe etiquette in the forest? And yet, I automatically walked a few steps away and squatted down to pee. A huge puddle like Ravana's. I was still sitting with my back towards the animal when I heard a rustling sound. It was Somalya approaching. His body odour reached me before he did. As he came close, I whispered, "Somalya, *arrey* the tiger came to the pond."

He stared at me, open-mouthed.

"The animal is huge, we two cannot manage. Will you go get more people?"

"Where's it, the animal?"

"There . . . over there by the path . . ."

I had seen the animal flattened out on the ground from the top of the tree. How could I see it from the ground? There were shrubs and bushes, tall grass . . . so I walked hesitatingly, five-ten, fifteen-twenty steps, and I suddenly broke out in a deep sweat. My heart started pounding. My legs lost their strength.

At the exact spot where the bibalya had fallen, a middle-aged woman slowly raised herself and sat down, her back towards us.

With eyes widened and hands covering his mouth, Somalya spat out a curse in his language.

"Sayeba! You fired on a woman! I am dead, finished!"

But just then, the woman rose to her feet. She started looking around like a wild animal would.

I wonder even today, how I had not fainted! I grabbed Somalya's hand and stood there, trembling for a few moments. "Don't be afraid," I whispered, cocked my rifle, and started moving forward one step at a time.

The woman was not injured for sure. Because she was not groaning or moaning in pain. It was impossible for her to stand after taking a hit from two bullets.

Now I could see the entire stretch of the path clearly. There was not a trace of the tiger's body, the one I had shot.

Somalya jerked his hand away, and the terrified Lamani swung around and ran. Instinctively I ran after him. Both of us were out of breath. We stopped and leaned against the trunk of a tree to regain our breath. Somalya was panting like a dog, with his mouth open.

All kinds of thoughts flooded my head. That I saw the bibalya, shot it, was one hundred percent true. Then where did it go? Where did this woman come from? What extraordinary occurrence was this? From its shape and its gait, I knew it was a female. But how did a female tiger become a female human?

After catching his breath, Lamani said, "Dada, this bibalya caste is very *harami*, treacherous. It changes its appearance. One moment a deer, another moment a hyena!"

"That's foolish!"

"I swear by my mother!"

I had read in one of Jim Corbett's books that a tiger had made sounds like a human being, but I had never heard that a tiger changes appearance. Somalya, being a tribal, could have believed in ghosts and spirits. But I believe in them? So why did I run away then? I felt ashamed about that.

In the meanwhile, we noticed the woman walking towards us.

Immediately Somalya squeezed my arm and whispered, "Dada, hit her! Fire the round! She is a tigress, not a human being."

His voice was quivering, body trembling.

The very thought of shooting a human being, that too a woman, gave me the shivers.

The woman saw us. Like a wild animal, she stopped where she was.

She was looking at us without blinking.

She was wearing a dusty-red Lamani woman's outfit and silver jewellery around her neck and wrists. Her hair was dishevelled.

Dusk was setting in rapidly. We had to walk almost two miles to reach the camp. And what kind of a camp! Right next to the forest bungalow were the Lamanis' dwellings. Since I was not accompanied by friends, I had not booked the forest bungalow. I had erected my tent under a banyan tree, a short distance away from Somalya's hut. I had brought along essentials like a camp cot, chairs and stove. My old rundown jeep was with me. I hadn't brought any servants along because these Lamanis were known to me for years. For a few coins, they would do the work. Besides, my stay was for ten days only. I had to get to Hubli and resume duty.

There was no dearth of occasions when I had shrunk into a fist-sized ball out of fear, in this jungle. But today's instance was extraordinary. I must admit that I was very frightened. No point pretending to be brave. It was a fear quite different from that which you feel when facing death. But my mind would not accept Somalya's words. Anyway, I realized that it was important to get back to the camp first, so I turned around and started walking briskly without looking back. Somalya did not leave my side because he felt walking alone, without a weapon in hand, was dangerous. He kept muttering something, kept looking back, but nothing was visible now. Leaving the forest path behind, we reached the road and soon arrived at the camp.

Somalya lit the lantern. I changed my clothes, pulled out a camp chair, lit a cigarette and sat down.

It was a dark night. The sky was bright with stars. A cool breeze was blowing. A solemn silence prevailed.

I told myself that I must get rid of the confusion in my mind and put an end to the matter. But then a thought came to me. Why not get up early in the morning and go to the pond to look for blood or tiger hair? The bibalya must have left imprints on the grass along the route. If found, they would confirm that it was the bibalya who had come, not the woman. But to even think that was silly. It was the animal that had come, it had fallen, it had rolled around . . . I had seen it with my own eyes. Given, for just a moment, that I had missed my mark, then I should have seen the bibalya leap up and disappear. So who was this woman? When did she come to that exact same spot? Why did she sit up? Why did she follow me? This situation was certainly intriguing. Was it not my duty to investigate it?

No intelligent, sensible person will ever believe Somalya's statement. But are there not things beyond human intelligence and comprehension? While I was pondering over this, there was a movement by the banyan tree in front. I looked with wide-open eyes but could not see anything clearly. An animal, perhaps a hyena, I thought. On silent feet, I went inside, brought out the torch and flashed it.

The same woman was standing, looking straight into the beam of torch light. Her dark green eyes were shining.

I don't know where I got the guts from! I put the torch down and went up to the banyan tree. In a loud and menacing voice, I said, "Who are you? Why are you here? What do you want?"

The woman's face was expressionless. She was looking at me with cold eyes. She had found her way straight to the tent in the darkness.

I tried saying all the Lamani words I knew, tried speaking in Kannada, but there was no reaction on the woman's face. Was she dumb and deaf? My fear had abated considerably. I decided to be brave and look into the matter.

VYAGHRI

Somalya had lit the lantern and then gone off to his hut in the settlement. I called out to him. As soon as I heard his "O . . ." in reply, I shouted, "Come back early in the morning. I don't need anything now." I had two-three reasons for keeping Somalya away. The woman should not feel nervous. Somalya should not bungle, and if there was any real danger, I should take it on myself. It was not right to involve the trusty Somalya in it.

The woman must be hungry. Even an animal finds courage if food is in front of it. And she, after all, is a human being!

I went inside the tent and brought out a *thali* with slices of bread, pieces of mutton and curry in a bowl and held it in front of her.

She merely sniffed at it from distance, her eyes fixed on me. What do I do, I wondered. She did not want food, obviously. Then what did she want?

Was her coming here and staying here only animal curiosity?

Maybe I should sit quietly in the chair and wait to see what happens. She might go away just as she had come. Thinking thus, I put away the *thali*, switched off the torch and sat outside the tent in my chair. I kept my eyes and ears alert.

For a long time nothing happened. My eyelids were heavy, my body stiff due to the whole day's work. For how long was I going to sit like this?

It was very cold. The forest was quiet.

Suddenly there was the sound of a muntjac deer barking.

I did not know when I had dozed off. I woke up with a start and looked around with big eyes. The woman was still there by the banyan trunk, and there was the sound of munching. What?

Suddenly I remembered that Somalya had hung the two skinned rabbits on the banyan tree. As they were high up, no fox or dog could get at them. At night, no kites or crows would attack them. Also, when hung like this, meat does not get spoilt.

The woman must have taken those rabbits.

Once again my mind was gripped with fear. So, is what Somalya said true?

Chche! Impossible! Even the Katkaris eat raw meat at times. So do many other jungle tribes. Don't even the advanced Australians relish raw oysters with beer? What is non-human about that? But this woman was an extremely strange specimen. A subject for study! I will observe everything carefully and then write a book. Even if there is danger, I will face it. Besides, this kind of subject, this kind of experience, doesn't come to everyone, does it? At any cost, I will watch carefully, investigate the matter and make detailed notes of everything.

I wrapped a blanket around myself and settled down in my chair. It was only eleven in the night. I was not feeling sleepy. In between I got up, brought the rifle and torch and kept them handy. Who knows! I was sitting in the open, and this was a forest. Anything could happen. I was alert, as if waiting for a tiger.

After about an hour or so, I fell asleep again.

When I woke up, it was early morning. The birds of the forest were waking up. The moon had risen high. It was cold. I looked at the banyan tree. The woman was not there.

Had she disappeared into the forest? If I followed her tracks, I would know for sure. Where will she go? Let the day break, let there be sunlight. I will definitely find her, I thought.

I raised the tent flap and went in. In the corner, like a cat sleeping on a heap of clothes, the woman lay curled up, legs drawn into herself.

Instead of seeking protection from the cold amid the clumps of bushes and trees, she had taken refuge in the tent. At the sound of my footsteps, she opened her eyes, raised her neck and looked at me. Reassured that she knew me, she closed her eyes, folded up her body and went back to sleep.

A little later, a Lamani arrived from the village with news that during the night, Somalya had developed a high fever. He kept waking up screaming and blabbering, all night. He would not be able to accompany me on my shikar that day. I was sure that Somalya's fever was the result of his fear of the tigress.

I went to the settlement to visit him.

Somalya, eyes red and face flushed, was lying on the mattress. He got up as soon as he saw me and whimpered, "Dada, you may say it's all a lie, but it is a ghost, it is *bhutatki*! She's not a woman, a tigress only!"

"*Arrey* no *re*! You're not mad, are you? A courageous and experienced hunter . . . Your entire life has been spent in the jungle . . . Has anything like this happened before? I will go and check the tracks today. You get well first." I said something to that effect and gave him a Codopyrine tablet I had brought with me.

Somalya said, "If she was a real woman, would I not recognize her? I know all Lamanis in the neighbourhood. Some *bhutatki*, some witchery has happened."

"If it has, so be it. Strong and bold men are frightened of *bhutatkis*, or what?" I patted him on his back and went to the pond again, all by myself. On the way, I saw the pug marks of the bibalya. But no traces of blood. The footprints were up to where the woman had stood. No traces beyond that.

After much thought, I concluded:

1. That a tiger will change its form and become a woman is impossible.
2. That I saw the bibalya coming was an optical illusion. It was a Lamani woman who had come to the pond bending and crouching.
3. The shot from my rifle had missed the target completely.
4. Like Ramu, who was raised by the wolves, this Lamani woman had grown up among the animals.
5. The bibalya's pug marks must be from before or after.

I returned to the tent. The Lamani woman was there in the tent. I felt that she should not be seen by any Lamani. I was afraid that they would kill her.

I took the jeep and drove around the forest paths for a while. Got two big wild cocks. I prepared one of them. Before I ate, I tried to give some food to her in the *thali*. This time also, she did the same thing. She just sniffed the food and left it where it was. I plucked and skinned the second fowl and hung it in the tent. Then I went to fetch a bucket of water from a stream about forty yards away.

When I returned, the fowl was missing.

In the evening, before the day set, the woman left the tent for some time. I heard the birds in the banyan tree flapping away in fear. Especially the crows, they cawed loudly and for long.

I also noticed the water level in the bucket had gone down while I was not in the tent. This meant that she had lapped up the water as she would from the stream.

During the night, I slept on the cot in the tent after dimming the lantern. I kept the loaded rifle next to me. But I just could not sleep. There was too much pressure on my mind. Several times during the night, I could hear a male bibalya roaring in the distance. From the direction of the sound and the kind of sound, I could tell that he was wandering around the tent, and his growling and roaring were not normal. It was like the roar of a bibalya when its companion is killed.

I fell asleep at about three-thirty.

For the next two days, nothing happened. Each day went like the previous one. The woman did not understand any language. She was of no use to perform any household tasks. I had to do them all myself – sweeping-swabbing, filling water, washing clothes, cooking. The woman did not step out much during the day. On both nights, the male bibalya was stalking the area, roaring. I had spread thorny *babhli* branches at every point from where he could possibly enter.

I had noticed a few more things in these two days. The woman's ears were much sharper than a human being's. She would open her eyes and listen intently if she heard a deer barking far away. Her eyes too were different from a human's. She could see clearly even in the dark. Besides her feet did not make any noise when she moved around. Of course, the traits of the cat species can be found in a person who has lived their entire life in the forest among animals.

Three days after she had entered the tent, I went into the forest during the third quarter of the day and hunted down a muntjac deer. I threw the carcass in the jeep and drove back. It was seven-thirty. I went into the tent and lit the lantern, but the woman was not at her usual place. I looked around the tent but found no trace of her.

By eight-thirty, I started to worry.

She had never stayed out for so long. While I was wondering what could have happened, I remembered that the water bucket was empty. I had forgotten to refill it before going out. Could she have gone to the stream for a drink? But why was it taking her so long to return?

As soon as this thought entered my mind, I strapped the headlight onto my forehead, picked up the bucket and the rifle and set out. Somalya's and my frequent walks up and down had created a path to the stream. I walked along it, casting the torchlight on either side as I went.

About thirty yards from the tent, I found her *odhni*. Further down on the right, where the forest was dense and several small hillocks stood, I saw her silver bangles scattered about. A little distance ahead, I came across her *ghagra* and *kacholi*, the skirt and blouse, torn to shreds.

There was no need to guess what had happened. I was not aware that there was a man-eating tiger in the area. However, in a reserved forest spread over a hundred square miles, it was quite possible that the tiger had wandered into these parts that day, and the unfortunate woman had fallen prey to him.

Her remains could have been found in the vicinity, but it was late in the night, and it was not worth looking for them now. I felt very sad.

Cautiously I returned to the tent and lay down on the cot. I foolishly kept wishing that, by some miracle, the woman would come back. I felt an unexpectedly huge opportunity had come my way, but it had equally unexpectedly slipped out of my hands. I wanted to see a lot, study a lot more, and on this subject, write a valuable book. Some foreigner, a saheb, had kept Elsa, a lioness, as a pet in his home and, based on his experiences, had written a book that was world famous. I had got an even better opportunity but had lost it.

I was extremely dejected.

The next morning, I ventured out again on my search. I roamed and roamed a lot but did not find the remains of that Lamani woman. Soon I was convinced that I would never find them. At about nine in the morning, I saw a telling sight.

Many boulders lay scattered by the slope of the hillock in front of me. On one of them, basking in the sun, was a pair of *bibalya* tigers.

Source

Translated from the Marathi, *Vyaghri*, from Vaghacha Magavar, 1997, Pune, Mehta Publishing House.

5

WAY TO THE BAZAAR (*BAJARACHI VAAT*)

Translated by Keerti Ramachandra

When a cycle bell suddenly tinkled sharply behind her, Vancha, with an untidily tied bundle on her head and bottles of kerosene oil in her hand, quickly moved to the side of the road, her chest heaving. The day was coming to an end. Most of the marketers, buyers and sellers had gone back a long time ago, and the good-looking young Vancha, who'd stand out among a hundred women, was left to walk back all by herself. The chillies she had brought had taken a long time to get sold. Finally, as the bazaar was folding up, she got rid of the last measure, dusted the cloth the chillies were tied in and set about buying what she needed – oil, salt, copra, a broom . . . She chose every item carefully, so by the time she was done, the day was gone. Hoisting the clumsy *gathuda* onto her head, Vancha had looked around to see if she could find someone from her village to go with her. In the morning, the grocer's Gabaa, the goldsmith's Kishi, Pawar's Dhondibai had all walked with her, and they'd even said, "Going back also together . . . we say" . . . But why would anyone wait for so long? Maybe they are by the banyan tree beside the stream, Vancha thought and stopped looking around. She started walking towards the banyan tree on the outskirts of the village. But when she got there, no one was there. They must have stopped for some time, then carried on, Vancha thought. She started to feel a little nervous. Her legs began to move faster. She would take the road to Udanwadi. But first she had to cross the narrow path through the fields. When she reached the top of the slope, she looked up and down the cart track with great hope. But not a soul was to be seen, as far as the horizon. How was she to cover the deserted five-mile stretch with no one for company? By the time she'd walked the first mile, it would get dark. Night would fall. Should a handsome young woman trudge the distance all alone?

Vancha Pawar kept turning back as she walked. Under the bright green sari, her breasts were rising and falling. Her skin, like fresh golden turmeric, was shiny with sweat. This path was not unfamiliar to her. Nor was taking that path at night a new experience. She returned home late from the fields every day. Vancha knew all this, yet she was afraid. And was beginning to feel utterly miserable.

At that very moment, the cycle bell had tinkled sharply, startling her. It was Sukha Jadhav. Pedalling furiously past Vancha, he almost knocked her down. He turned to glance at her but did not stop. He was in a hurry to get home before darkness fell. The sack-load of grass he had tied onto the carrier and his own weight was making the bicycle creak.

As she walked along, Vancha thought to herself, if this fellow had been on foot, he would have been company for me. He may be a man, but so what, he is from our village. But he's gone and bought a cycle. What to do, a misfortune . . .

Sukha continued to pedal as fast as he could. But when he'd gone some eight-ten yards, he suddenly stopped. He got off the cycle and bent down to examine the tyre. Vancha saw him from a distance and said to herself, *Baya ga*! Breath gone out of wheel or what!

Sukha stood at one side of the road, holding the cycle with one hand. He kept looking down at the wheel and then at Vancha approaching him. Will it look good for me to stand and wait like this till the woman reaches here? Should I go on? If, when she covers the distance and says something, only then should I speak, give her company, Sukha wondered. There was a reason for this. Talking to the women from the village was one thing, but initiating a conversation with this Vancha was another matter. Every young man of the village had to think ten times before addressing her. Because Vancha was beautiful, like the princess Padmini. She had been married for eight years, but she looked more and more youthful over the years. She had so much beauty, yet she was a very respectable woman. She gave no reason for anyone to speak ill of her. That's how she was. It is to be noted that even in Udanwadi, no one dared to speak loosely about her. Udanwadi was actually a rather crude town. There were some seven or eight young men who had left no woman virtuous and unbesmirched. These good-for-nothing fellows went about in their gaudy clothes, poking holes in everything. Their behaviour was such that simple, ordinary women were made brazen. Why, even the most respectable women of Udanwadi had been enticed by them, and the whole town had changed. Too many affairs were taking place. It was becoming difficult to keep these happenings in check. Finding a solution to this problem was a very delicate task. To guard your reputation, you must lock your mouth up and silently bear the blows. Several families in the town did that. Husbands who never dreamt that their wives would behave in this manner went about with their heads bowed. Others kept a sharp eye on their women, and beat them up every now and then. Yet the affairs continued, clandestinely. A few women had remained unsullied in this filth. Vancha was one of them. This attractive young woman, who had not borne a child, managed to keep her home life respectable, decent. Nobody had tried to seduce her.

Sukha was standing where he was. Vancha was drawing closer. Day had given way to night. Very soon nothing would be visible in the dark. Stars would begin to shine. Crickets would start their kirrrrr . . . kirrrrr . . . A cool breeze had started blowing. Hundreds of flying foxes were emerging from the orange-red western sky and heading eastwards. The smaller *pakoli* bats were circling around. And a fair distance had still to be covered.

Vancha, wearing a nine-yard sari tucked between her legs, took courage in her hands and, as she neared Sukha, said to him, "You started after dark?" She stopped a little away from him, put the bottles she was carrying down against a stone and, with the pallu of her sari, wiped the back of her neck. In a sweet voice, she said, "Kept telling myself, must go now, leave now, still it got so late . . ."

Bas. That's all she said. She adjusted the bundle on her head, picked up the bottles and started walking. Past Sukha she went, when he said from behind her, "Just at this time a thorn got the tyre. Have to push the cycle all the way to the village. No choice."

And wheeling the cycle, he began to follow her.

Vancha could hear the sound of his male chappals behind her. It reassured her. It didn't matter now if it got late getting home. She had company. Sukha was from her own village. A known person. Good thing his cycle got punctured. Vancha's mind kept running towards home. Her husband must have waited for some time, then started making enquiries in the village. Maybe he will yoke his bullocks to the cart and set off towards the bazaar. Her thoughts flew as fast as her feet. Sukha was right behind her.

Neither of them spoke for some time.

Darkness fell. Stars twinkled. Crickets chirped. Vancha thought. Walking beside someone who is giving you company without uttering a word, does it look nice? This man is not a stranger. He is from the same village. A respectable family man . . . I am not an immature girl either. What's wrong in saying a few words? The path will seem shorter if we talk. What if I let him speak rather than say something myself? He should start. Should women talk first? As these thoughts entered Vancha's mind, her feet slowed down. The distance between her and Sukha began to reduce. Soon Sukha and she were walking side by side. The sound of two pairs of feet was heard. The cycle creaked. The bottles in Vancha's hands clinked against each other. And the distance to the village was gradually decreasing.

Vancha was now close to Sukha. He could hear the soft swish and rustle of her Irkal sari. The sweet smell of the sari wafted across to him. With it came the aroma of fried foodstuff. She must have bought some sweetmeats for the children, he thought. But she has no children. So for whom was it? Maybe her husband likes that spicy-savoury stuff from the bazaar and had asked her to bring it for him? Or maybe Vancha got it for him on her own. Whatever it was, the aroma emanating from Vancha's bundle made Sukha's mouth water. He had to keep swallowing his saliva every now and then.

Then Sukha said, "It's night already and not reached *Sonaracha mala*, the goldsmith's farm, yet. Will be late reaching home."

Vancha replied, "*Whai ki*, yes it will."

"Arjun Patil must be saying she stayed with relatives in the night . . ."

"How stay?"

"No, no. I say because it's late he must have thought so." Images of the *sopa*, Arjun Patil, sitting there leaning against a pillar, floated before her eyes. Arjun Patil, short in height and wide in body, stroking his moustache and saying to his brother feeding the bullocks tethered outside, "*Arra dyeva* . . . your *vaini* hasn't returned from the bazaar yet. Why do you think she has taken so long . . ."

Vancha addressed Sukha. "Just as well no small children to create a commotion in the house."

The words were uttered casually, but the wound was a festering one. Every now and then, it would leap out through her words. Arjun Patil had been talking of getting a second wife these days, and that made Vancha's pain more grievous. She suffered and pined in silence.

Sukha said, "What to say of god's will? Arjun Patil longs for a child, yet nothing happens. We have no estate to speak of, yet every year or two, a child is at our door. Four-five years after him, I got married."

In the silence that followed, Vancha conjured up the image of Sukha's wife and kept looking at it. Dusky complexioned, average looking, of slender build, and yet god has made her womb fertile. But for me, nothing. That's what she was thinking. By giving me these good looks and making me attractive, what did god get? No child in the womb. Even after eight years, no end to the barrenness. All remedies tried. Medicines swallowed, vows taken, visits to temples, sages and saints. To no avail. At this rate, the youthful looks will fade away. All these years went in hoping. The rest will go in despair and suffering.

"Why, you are not talking? Without conversation, the road is endless."

"*Whai ki*! Of course! So it is. . . . but can women talk?"

"Now is not that asking! If four women were with you, you would have walked in silence?"

"Of course not. But women's talking matters are different."

Stars were jostling about in the sky. The breeze was making soft *surr-surr* sounds. Now and then, the *pinglas*, the owlet pair, chattered. The pedal of Sukha's cycle kept grazing Vancha's leg. The smell of the savouries in Vancha's *gathuda* was spreading. "Give those bottles to me."

"No, let it be."

"Give, *na*. Will hang them on the cycle, I'm saying."

"They'll break."

"Then give me the *gathuda* on your head. It isn't heavy for me. Will hang it on the handlebar."

After Sukha insisted, Vancha lifted the bundle slightly. Sukha rested the cycle against his stomach, then picked up the *gathuda* with both hands. His hand brushed against Vancha's soft, smooth arm. And the damp smell of

Vancha's sweaty neck and brow came to him like the fragrance of a dew-drenched rose.

Sukha's hard, muscular arm touched Vancha, and she was stung as if it was a red hot ember. Her neck was stiff, her arm was sore. She straightened the pallu that had slipped aside and continued to walk. When Sukha came alongside her, the bundle dangling from the cycle's handlebar, Vancha said, "The village is near. I've come this far, would have carried on further, the *gathuda* was not very heavy . . ."

"Where's the village? We haven't reached the *sonaracha mala* yet. Pick up your feet."

"*Baya ga*! I must keep pace with you now?"

"Otherwise how will the village come?"

"Let it come, slowly . . ."

"Aanh? You are taking your time because you want Patil to bring his cart for you?"

"Not that concerned about his wife, he is."

The words slipped out, and immediately Vancha felt she shouldn't have spoken. Saying what is in your heart before strangers is not good. Say one thing and some other meaning can come out. It will cause big talk in the village. To correct what she had uttered, she hastily said, "It is so late . . . people at home must be worried."

"True, it is worrying. But Arjun Patil is not one to worry in a hurry. He must have come back tired from the field . . . He might have dozed off."

"*Whai ki*, that is so. He falls asleep quickly, see. He will be talking, and suddenly he will start snoring . . ."

"When man has no worries, sleep comes easily. Has he any worries or what!? Lands and cattle, money and wealth . . . god has given him everything . . ."

"Yes, *baya* . . . that's true, see . . . no sorrows because of that . . ."

"So then?"

"One thing only he is unhappy about, say . . ."

"You mean a child? You think so, but women are more troubled by it. Men don't take it so much to heart. And what to say, youth has not passed yet. Everything will be all right. *Ava*, when god is behind you, you lack nothing. Man's intentions should be good, that's all. And you cannot find fault with Patil for anything . . . the one straight man in our village."

As they were speaking, Sukha, who was on the right, had come to her left. The cycle which had been between them was now on the other side. As she swayed gracefully along, Vancha's body would brush against Sukha's. Quickly she would move away and stay a few paces behind. But the cart track was narrow. It was difficult to keep the distance in the darkness. Their bodies would bump into each other. Accidentally. Don't people bump into each other by mistake in the bazaar? But bodies bumping into each other is one thing, and cloth rubbing against cloth is another.

"You say that, it's true. Now the matter has come up, so I will tell you . . . who would talk about family matters to outsiders otherwise?"

"*Whai ki* . . . of course."

"How is it my fault, you tell me? Children are god-given. Are these things in man's hands? But this man, he doesn't agree. He blames me, yells at me. Mother-in-law's the same, father-in-law, brother-in-law too. I say, go, get married again, but government doesn't give permission it seems . . ."

Vancha suddenly realised that she had spoken too loudly, so she immediately lowered her voice. To hear her better, Sukha came closer.

"But I am saying people have had children even after twelve-twelve years . . ."

"You need patience for that. The *ishtayte* is going heirless here, no!"

"Foolish of Arjun Patil."

"Taunting, mocking all the time, how long can one bear it, tell me? I also retort in anger sometimes. That's it. Raises his arm, grabs whatever comes to hand, tethering ropes or whip, like an animal pouncing . . ."

"And Bajibaba allows it? Then why wear the holy Pandhari beads around his neck?"

"To show the world! Too much the old man is. Speech soft and measured, but see him in the house, like father like son."

And then many stories from inside the house came out. Vancha opened up her heart and talked and talked. About everything. Tremulous and soft sometimes, agitated and loud at others. The conversation went this way and that, and the moon appeared in the sky. Moonlight spread across the earth.

Shadows began to dance, and the air turned cold.

Drawing her sari closer around her, Vancha walked beside Sukha. She was no longer afraid when their bodies touched. The tall and hefty Sukha is walking next to me, he has opened up a little in my company . . . the thought made her happy. But it was not an obvious happiness. She was not sure of it herself. On the one hand, she felt good, but on the other, she felt it was not right. This is not the way to behave. Sukhdeo had become a little bolder. And he was amused at himself. Like a cat sunning itself contentedly, he was drinking in the moonlight. This good-looking woman who never spoke more than a few words to the best of men in the village had been so frank with him . . . It made him feel proud of himself. But still his apprehension did not leave him. He was making sure that he would not lose self-control even slightly. But does a man not sway when he is drunk? How could he avoid it?

He spoke as gravely as he could, "It's very late. Your cart will come soon now."

At this Vancha, who was right next to him, turned and looked at him. She did not say anything immediately. And when she did, her words were like the moonlight.

"You heard it all for so long, yet you speak like this?"

The look, the tone of voice appeared different to Sukha. He felt fear inside him.

"Not like that . . . I meant the moon has risen high . . ."

"Let it rise. Even if we weren't on the road, it would have risen, wouldn't it? All this walking-walking, my legs are paining *baya* . . ."

"You want to stop for a little, then?"

"*Hunh*. You warn me it's late, and then you ask me if I want to stop . . . What to say of this double talk?"

There were fields on either side. The standing crops were soaking in the moonlight. Suddenly Vancha said, "The crop is grown waist high."

Sukha looked around. "*Whai ki*, it has."

For no reason, Vancha's heart began to beat faster. She felt hot all over. She felt her feet were not touching the ground.

Sukha came close to her. "Say, no, something."

"I was saying only, no, all this time?"

"But the distance must become less . . ."

"It has . . . now the village will appear . . . The *sonaracha mala* is left far behind . . . The baman's banyan tree is near, is it not? From this mound, the village lights can be seen."

"*Whai ki*, yes . . ."

Then suddenly Vancha stood still. She started moving towards the bund beyond the road. "Come, let's sit for a while."

Sukha leaned the cycle against a tree. They cleared a space on the bund and sat touching each other. From the fold of her sari, Vancha took out a paper packet. She opened it and held it out.

"Will you eat some *mewa*?"

The aroma tormenting him all this while was suddenly in front of him. He had been hungry for a long time. The savoury mixture of *churmure*, *sev*, *gathi* made Sukha's mouth water. He picked up a fistful, then asked, "What about you?"

"Afterwards . . . You eat first."

The *churmure* mixture crackled and crunched in Sukha's mouth. Vancha sat there staring at it. She had drawn up her knees and, resting her face on her fist, was gazing at Sukha with big eyes. Sukha was starving.

The moon was growing bigger. The moonlight was shimmering brighter. The trees and bushes were drenched. The road from the bazaar had almost come to an end. And Udanwadi was very, very close.

Source

Translated from the Marathi, *Bajarachi Vaat*, from Vyankatesh Madgulkar, Yanchi Katha, Arvind Gokhale ed., 1964, Pune, Continental Prakashan.

Excerpts from the Novels

6

THE VILLAGE HAD NO WALLS (*BANGARWADI*)

Translated by Ram Deshmukh

Chapter 9 the school had no regular calendar. Everywhere else summer was vacation time, here the school closed for the harvest. The boys came to school whenever they felt like it. The schoolmaster's lot was not unlike that of a bus-driver in the country – he could not do a thing until a sufficient number of passengers turned up. Half the time the schoolmaster had little work to do and it was impossible for him to confine his sphere of operations to the four walls of the school. The most important of my subsidiary roles was, of course, to act as a scribe – to write letters, petitions, applications for the village. My week-end visits to my home town were invariably embarked upon with my pockets stuffed with letters I had undertaken to post. When it was discovered that I did these time-honoured jobs without a murmur, every conceivable problem and grievance began coming my way and I became an adviser and counsellor to all and sundry. Whenever a sheep was lost, or wife quarrelled with husband, the schoolmaster was consulted in the belief that schoolmasters are as well-versed in law and equipped with common sense as they are educated and wise.

This kept me busy even when there was no teaching to be done. Whenever the authorities complained about the poor enrolment I found myself making excuses: the school is at an experimental stage, this is the sowing season, and so on . . . but I kept the school going. As the school building was a court, village-hall, police station and municipal office in addition to being a school, the teacher's role was varied. He was a judge, policeman, revenue official and even stamp-vendor! However, this much could be said for the arrangement: it was unusual for disputes to cross the boundary of the village. Most of them were resolved at a *panchayat* meeting, that is before a council or assembly of about ten people. The dispensers of justice included the schoolmaster and such venerable villagers as the old Karbhari, Rama's father Kakuba, Shekuba and others. As a rule the judgment of these ten was accepted as final by the offender and he would pay the fine decided by them. If the *panchayat* failed to give satisfaction, he was at liberty to go in appeal. The appellate authority was a supernatural one, the oracle of a deity recognised by every shepherd. The goddess was consulted before a large gathering of shepherds from all over the district. This step was taken but rarely, for a communal banquet had to be given before the Supreme Being could be invoked and a banquet of the required size might cost as much as seven or eight hundred rupees.

Weddings were similarly solemnised on a communal basis on an auspicious day selected by common consent. Whatever feasting there was, took place on that day so that no one was ever required to feed the whole village single-handed. There might possibly be ten or twenty weddings in a year and each family was required to feed more or less an equal number of persons. If financial difficulties threatened to postpone a scheduled wedding, the village often helped to tide over the situation. All pitched in to share the burden so that the wedding could take place on the appointed day.

Far from allowing myself to be discouraged by Dadu's threats, I had thrown myself wholeheartedly into the life of the place. A stage had come when the village could not do without me.

There were very few farmers in the place, fewer than the fingers of one's hands, but the village was not devoid of them. *Mriga* rains had left the fields overgrown with thick, hardy grass. Before sowing could commence the farmers had to clear their fields of this unwanted weed. Another rainy fortnight and the soil became softly pliant. But there was too much mud in the fields as yet, too much water. The excess water must be absorbed, the surface must become firm enough for men and bullocks to walk on. So the farmers had to wait until a spell of dry weather had made the soil flaky on top while moisture remained underneath. Then the sowing commenced, *bajra*, gram and other pulses. Every morning the farmers were seen taking off for the fields with their teams and ploughs and their bags of seed.

One day, while the sowing operation was at its height, Sheku came to see me. He was not often seen in the village. He had two or three acres of land outside the village and its cultivation was his only interest in life. It was early morning and the man had covered himself with a *dhoti* as if it were a blanket. All I could see of him was his scraggy face and dusty feet – they looked leathery from constant trekking; the toes had coarse overgrown nails on them. His hands were hidden from view. Ayubu and I were by ourselves when Sheku came.

"Teacher," he said, without bothering to sit down, "do find me a bullock from somewhere. It's sowing time, you know!"

It was pointless to say that as schoolmaster I was not likely to own a bullock. He said, "You can easily borrow one for me. I have one. The other died, I can sow if I get another. Otherwise it means starving – the whole year through."

"Tell me first, who has a bullock to lend? Then I can ask him."

"Those that own bullocks have their own sowing to do. Who would put up with a delay in his own sowing? I have tried everywhere."

"Whom do you want me to ask in that case?"

"Do what you like but help me in my need. The whole village says the schoolmaster is always helpful, always there in times of difficulty! Why do you treat me different?"

Ayubu, who had listened to all this without a word, now intervened. He turned his face towards Sheku and said, "Are you mad, Sheku? Where would the teacher get a bullock? Is he a farmer? Is he a cattle dealer? Have you no sense that you come and beg for whatever stupid thing enters your head? Go away!"

Sheku was obviously shaken – perhaps it was wrong of him to have asked.

"I-I am on my way, to be sure. But do try and do something for me if possible!" he said in a wheedling tone.

Ayubu got to his feet resolutely. Seizing the man by his elbows he propelled him down the steps and on to the road. He said, "You are a fool, Sheku! As if the schoolmaster carries bullocks under his arms, in his clothes!"

Utterly crestfallen, Sheku went his way muttering something under his breath. Ayubu returned to his seat and said, "You just ignore what he said, teacher! He is a simpleton . . ."

But I was unable to brush aside the feeling that it did not take the village people very far to teach them to read and write. Their needs were of a different sort altogether. Ayubu was without a family; Ananda needed bread, Sheku a bullock.

Two days later Sheku was still without his bullock although he had tried everywhere. He went home and slumped, exhausted, to the floor.

"It was useless," he told his wife. Sheku's better half was a strapping woman, standing head and shoulders above all other women and half the men in the village. In the fields she did a man's work.

"Who did you ask?" she inquired of her husband. He was sitting there motionless, face buried in his hands, utterly dejected.

"All over the village, no one is prepared to give me a bullock."

"What is to be done now?"

"We shall starve to death, that's all – kick up our heels and starve!"

The woman listened to her husband, saw the look in his eye. It was like a lamp which has nearly run out of oil.

"We start sowing tomorrow!" she said bravely.

"What about the bullock?"

"I shall get one."

"Where from?"

"From wherever I please . . ."

"But . . ."

"What business is it of yours? I shall get the bullock. Just you go across to the field tomorrow morning. That's all."

Sheku racked his brain; where was his wife going to find the bullock? In the morning he hoisted the plough on his shoulder and set off in the direction of his field leading his solitary bullock with his free hand. Once there, he turned his face towards the village and sat down on the embankment to await the arrival of his wife.

After an hour or so he saw her, she was alone. Sheku's face fell. The woman took a wager, but she was not able to procure a bullock. There will be no sowing now. A bullock might become available after others have done their sowing. What good will that do? The crop will be backward in any case, not as usual, and if the crop does not yield enough grain for a full year we must starve; or roam from place to place in search of work ... Sheku had made himself utterly miserable by this brooding when his strapping spouse reached his side.

"Couldn't you get the bullock?"

"Why not? Get the plough ready."

"But where is the bullock?"

"It is all right. Yoke the bullock at one end, I shall push at the other!"

Sheku shuddered at the thought. He found his voice with great difficulty. "No, no, that can't be!" But the woman had made up her mind and she knew that she was strong enough for the job.

"This is no time for 'whys' and 'hows'. Yoke the bullock."

Seeing that her husband was incapable of movement, too dejected even to lift his head, she rose and herself put the bullock to the plough. Placing one end of the yoke across her own shoulder, she commanded, "Now, rope me tight."

At that the frail man hardened his heart, got up and signalled the bullock to move. The animal moved, so did the woman. The ploughshare pierced the earth, began furrowing a path through the damp soil. Sheku released a handful of millet seed into the hopper – the grain coursed down the bamboo tube, then leaped to the ground. Sheku's wife continued to pull by the side of the bullock through sheer determination.

The sowing went on all morning. At midday Sheku and his wife, breathless from the exertion, sat down to a quiet lunch. Sheku was tongue-tied. The woman spoke of this and that. Together they went to work with a rake until the seed was evenly covered by the upturned soil.

By evening they had sown the two-acre plot; then the exhausted trio made tracks for home.

Next day the incredible tale was all over the village. There was admiration, some astonishment, occasionally even a feeling of scornful amusement.

That night, on my way back from the school, I stood in front of Sheku's house for a moment. Inside, the lamp-light revealed the prostrate form of Sheku's wife by the side of a wall. Sheku stood on her back kneading her body with his feet. Supporting himself by placing both his hands on the wall he was massaging his wife's aching back with the slow movement of each foot.

Source

Excerpt translated from the Marathi novel, *Bangarwadi* (Chapter 9), December 2008, Mumbai, Popular Prakashan Ltd.

7
WHIRLWIND (*VAVTAL*)

Translated by Sachin Ketkar

We sauntered through the crowd without much thought, just standing around sometimes, or attending someone's talk. We ran into Tatya Daptardar who was dressed in a Nehru shirt and khadi cap. He was known as a loud-mouthed leader in the village. Once, during a public meeting, he had told the ruler of our princely state that he, the king, was merely "a king in a pack of cards"! He was like a tiger once, but now he was going around gesticulating like a raving lunatic. I greeted him politely. "*Namaskar*, Tatya Saheb." He responded with an offhand "*Namaskar*" and walked away.

After a little while, he ambled back and stood next to us. "Look, young man, just look what has happened!"

I only stared blankly.

Tatya Saheb now started speaking as if addressing a crowded meeting, wagging his finger in warning.

"Thousands of lumps of jaggery destroyed by fire! Thirty-five sacks of wheat, forty bags of *jowar* and groundnuts all burnt! An ancestral mansion with seventy-five rooms which can't be rebuilt even with lakhs of rupees – all reduced to ashes! Nothing is left of me now, I am just a stark naked fakir!" He was looking at me with head bowed and hands on chest. I did not know what to say. He probably did not expect me to say anything. He just turned around and walked away. A school boy next to me said, "He has lost a great deal and it seems to have affected his mind."

This boy in khaki shorts and cap was impatient to report everything he knew. As soon as he learnt that I had just arrived from another place, he pulled me aside and told me everything that had taken place. The people who came to raid and loot were unknown men, outsiders. After burning down houses in my village, they turned to Nandwadi. Nandwadi was a taluka town. As it had several government offices and a relatively larger proportion of Brahmins, they were hesitant to come to Nandwadi. Some people from the mob provoked the others by calling them cowards. The leaders of the mob deliberated over it for a while, then decided that four people would go in first, speak to the local activists and take their help.

Accordingly, the four men moved into the village and spoke to the activists. The activists welcomed them with great enthusiasm. Soon thereafter, the rest of the mob of around a hundred, hundred and fifty people waiting on the other side of the stream ran into the town. Some excited people from the town also joined them. They showed the mob the houses of the Brahmins. They started setting them ablaze. In the beginning, they attacked selected and bigger stone-wadas. They asked the man of the house and the women to get out. Then they would enter the wada, collect all inflammable items and place them in every room. They poured kerosene and lit bonfires. In no time, the houses caught fire and cries of "*Gandhiji ki Jai . . . Bharat Mata ki Jai*" resounded in the skies.

The Mamlatdar of the taluka town, who was a Brahmin, fled, and so did the judge. People could not find them anywhere. The police constables could not do anything without orders from the authorities. They kept looking at the arson helplessly. Within hours, thirty to thirty-five houses were gutted.

Some courageous boy named Panchwagh stopped another young man of his age from going on a rampage. Five or six other boys came along and dragged that young rioter into the government building. He was made to stand in front of Chief Constable Shinde.

Chief Constable Shinde was furious due to the pandemonium in the village and the Brahmins coming every now and then to complain and whine. He yelled at the young rioter, "Where are you from, you son of a bitch?"

The spirited young man, dressed in a farmer's clothes, was wearing a turban, and his moustache was just starting to sprout. He replied, "From Sonapur" in a rather arrogant way.

"Why the hell have you come here to die?"

"Well, other people from the village were coming, so I tagged along."

Though he was standing before the Chief Constable himself, there was no trace of fear on his face. He did not think he was doing anything wrong. "How much have you robbed? Out with those things!"

The young man did not budge an inch. When a constable tried to put his hand into the young man's pocket, the young man pushed him away, saying, "Don't you even think of touching me!" The angry constable kicked him in his stomach, and the young man collapsed in pain. The Chief Constable flung the young man's turban aside in rage. He was trembling with anger. All of a sudden, he took out the pistol from his pocket and fired several times. The young man crumpled in a pool of blood.

After the loud sound of bullets, there were screams of "Murder! Murder! They have killed the boy!" The men who were plundering and burning stopped in their tracks and looked around. "Why wake up people needlessly? Sleep quietly. All of you!"

The boy who was narrating all this whispered to me, "Actually, Eknath was the man who invited the arsonists from other places to our town and just see how he is pretending now . . ."

WHIRLWIND (*VAVTAL*)

There were just too many leaders in Nandwadi. The man who owned the liquor shop, Hashimbhai, was in fact a leader. He did not have to worry about making ends meet because he mixed water with the liquor. Leadership was his side-business. He would grab anyone who tried to protest and fight deafeningly with him. Even Hashimbhai went about warning people with his pot-belly exposed, "Don't take it lightly. They will definitely come back. Keep your weapons ready – sticks, stones and whatever else you have."

Another manly leader, Patil Baba, was going around with his double-barrelled gun in his hand and his chest thrust out. "I am so well prepared for defence that even if thousands of people attack us, I will repel them. I am a retired army-man after all."

Source

Excerpt translated from the Marathi novel, *Vavtal* (Chapter 9, pp. 51–55), 1964, Pune, Mauj Prakashan.

8
TENDER DAYS (*KOVALE DIVAS*)

Translated by Sachin Ketkar

A dark, slender-waisted, red-mouthed bitch emerged from the shadows. She looked at me, halted, pawed and started sniffing me. I made some noise. Unafraid, she started growling. When she turned around, she saw her master approaching. So she walked into the shade and sat there panting with her tongue hanging out.

Faujdar Saheb, the chief inspector, was astonished when he saw me. I got up and bowed down to him, saying, "Namaskar, sir! Could you find anything? I heard some shots being fired."

Saheb took off his hat and wiped the sweat on his forehead. "A couple of waterfowls. What else do you find here in these lands?"

"One can find moor-hens or storks also near the ponds."

"No such luck. Those birds are usually deep into the pond, beyond the range of the gun."

"You've come a long way."

"I came down for an investigation and halted in the bungalow near the pond. So I thought I would try my luck at the game as well."

Faujdar Saheb was standing while he was speaking to me. His assistants cleared the ground of pebbles and dirt. One person spread a *dhoti* he was carrying on his shoulders on the ground. Faujdar Saheb sat on it. His face told me that he knew about my activities.

His assistants stood around him respectfully, holding the fowls. Probably they were Ramoshis. One of them held his gun for him. "Go to the bungalow and clean the birds. Carry the gun carefully," Saheb ordered. "I will speak to this person for a moment and join you soon."

Both of his assistants bowed and departed. I was left with Saheb and his bitch lying in the shade.

I had been observing Faujdar Saheb for several days. When we were at a village named Kundal, he was stationed there. He stood at least six feet tall, was well-built, with a broad chest and rippling biceps. He never slouched; he was always ram-rod straight like a flagpole. One could make out from his gait that he would never bow down before anyone in this world. His severe face seemed all the more fierce, thanks to his bushy moustache. Even his everyday conversation reeked of haughtiness. His rose-coloured turban ever-starched and well-ironed. His everyday outfit was a chocolate-coloured woollen coat over a white shirt, stylishly worn *dhoti*, and well-polished brown shoes. It changed only when he had to be in government police uniform. He used to garnish his language with the choicest swear-words, the way one would spice up the hot and fiery *usal* with an extra helping of red chillies. At all times, he carried a wooden stick with a silver knob.

I saw him in hunter's clothing for the first time that day.

La Fontaine has said, "People salute the uniform, and not the coarse inspector wearing it."

Faujdar Saheb had gathered renown for brutally thrashing criminals and using numerous methods of torture involving the use of smoke fumes and red chilli paste to make them confess to their crimes instantly. Therefore, criminals would pee in their *dhotis* whenever they faced him.

Like a wild bull, he snorted and uttered rapidly, "Here you are going around openly in broad daylight, it seems." Not only his lips, even the muscles around his neck and face quivered as he spoke.

Though I had been mentally prepared for this, my heart trembled like a peepal leaf.

I tried to act as if I had absolutely no idea what he was talking about.

"We had a confidential inquiry at our office some days ago."

I pretended to be indifferent to his comment and stood firm.

"I sent them back saying we found no such person in the village."

I was taken aback. So, the police *were* on my track after all. Out of the eighteen people who had raided the temple, they had caught sixteen, and these men were being tried in the court. It did not mean that I was considered innocent or that I had managed to escape. I was being pursued and was bound to get caught and punished for my crime one day. Even if our intention behind the crime was noble and political, it was still considered a crime, and the government was not going to let us go.

"I know your entire family, your father, your elder brother and your mother, very well. Vitthalpanta is a decent gentleman, and your entire family is good. I thought I would not put the kid who was green behind his ears behind bars," Saheb added.

At this juncture, I thought one should open one's mouth.

"That is very kind of you, sir. But may I know what the inquiry was about?"

Saheb was obviously a seasoned policeman. "A letter that had gone to the offices of the Commissioner, C.I.D., Crime branch of Bombay Presidency, with your complete name, full description of your colour, height, and birthmarks, said that you were wanted for a grave crime. You had to be immediately arrested."

A shudder ran down my spine. Thank God I had been riding my bicycle that day and the police constable was wearing his special footwear. That's how I was saved. I had wandered around my village out of sheer obliviousness. It was because of god's grace that I was moving around, eating and sleeping and waking up safely.

"Just because our princely state is free, and the police from the British jurisdiction cannot enter and arrest anybody on their own, I could manage it," he explained, "otherwise, it was not in my hands either."

If I expressed my gratitude to Faujdar Bhosale Saheb in clear words, it would amount to confessing. The field marshal of our group of freedom fighters, in fact, had tried to inform me that this princely state would not openly support the freedom movement but would be sympathetic to it. But why was I so careless?

I could only be solemn and silent at the inspector's words.

When the person who had offered his *dhoti* for the Saheb to sit on was seen returning, Inspector Bhosale got up. I got up too, and as if giving me a message, he said. "Be careful, you will not be so lucky every time."

He turned around and started walking towards the road. The dog jumped up, stretched and started to follow him.

Before the person who had offered the *dhoti* to the inspector could collect the *dhoti* spread out on the ground, I left . . .

After Harni, my pet cow, disappeared, my life had turned dull and boring. Had she been around, I would have taken her to graze and spent the day walking around the pond, gazing at the reflection of the sky in the water. Only when one is away from one's human family does one realise that one has other family too and how spread out it is. Why should one limit one's relations to human beings only?

Many thoughts zig-zagged across my mind on my way back. I explored all the nooks and corners of my mind and took two clear decisions.

One: I will neither risk my life nor waste it in my village. I will leave. If I cannot reconnect to my group of freedom fighters, I will join the Prati Sarkar group and follow every single instruction and every programme of theirs wholeheartedly, even if I have to get into physical fights, go to jail or face bullets. If I can be useful in any way, I will consider my life a success.

Secondly, I will take the help of Kachru Patil once again before joining the Prati Sarkar. There was a warrant against my name and so there was no point in hiding.

Death is a poem till the age of twenty-five, it turns into sad prose after fifty.

Source

Excerpt translated from the Marathi, *Kovale Divas* (pp. 60–63), 1979, Pune, Utkarsh Publications.

9

TRANSFER OF POWER (*SATTANTAR*)

Translated by Sachin Ketkar

The sun had risen quite high by then. Long tails were seen dangling from the lush green foliage of the white-fig tree next to the pond. Pregnant Taruni and Lajri, along with the other females, Unadi, Bokandi, Thoti and Kani, and Landi, Bothari's sister, were feeding quietly. What had to happen, had happened, yet the entire troop seemed to be very tense. The baby langurs were not playful as mothers clutched their little ones to their chests. All the females were looking around apprehensively. From behind the branches, the younger females stood on their hind legs and raised their heads to survey the surrounding trees.

Nearby, on the hefty root of a jamun tree, Moga sat, fuming in silence. Just as one cannot go near a raging forest fire, no one could approach him because of his fury. After sitting by himself for a while, he climbed up the tree on which the female langurs were and sat on the branch where Kani was nibbling at the tender leaves and shoots, her infant clinging to her belly.

There was a fair amount of distance between them.

Kani looked at her baby with her sole functional eye, signalled him to hang on tightly and made a dash for the neighbouring tree. She did not cast a glance in Moga's direction as if to say she had not run away because of him.

At around four in the afternoon, Moga climbed up a tall cotton tree near the pond, grumbling to himself. Like a soldier surveying a battlefield from a high tower, he looked around. Abruptly, he gave up his watch, scrambled down and rushed towards Kani, who was relaxing under the jamun tree. He pounced on her from behind and tried to snatch her baby from her viciously.

Kani promptly turned around, pushed Moga away, bared her fangs and growled at him. At that moment, the cantankerous Bokandi, the unyielding Landi, and the aged sister of Bothari came running and formed a barricade between Kani, her baby and Moga. They screeched at him, showing their teeth. They attacked him and chased him away.

When he scampered back to the tree, they continued to growl at him.

Kani's baby was bleeding. It was trembling with fear. Kani too was petrified.

From the tree, Moga glared at the female monkeys below and let out a ferocious shriek that should have sent shudders down the spines of the female monkeys. But they were not frightened, and they continued to squat under the tree for some time. Then Kani carried her baby to a tree-top far away. Thoti, with her own babies, and Bokandi accompanied Kani. They continued to feed as they huddled close to each other.

Moga, who was silent for a while, began to grunt and bellow again. He climbed down, grinding his teeth, and approached the tree where the females were sitting with their brood. They immediately became alert and fled like dry leaves in a gust of wind.

Moga kept howling frenziedly. He was determined to catch Kani and her baby. He went up again to where poor Kani was perched on the outermost tree of the territory. He climbed onto the same branch where she was sitting. Kani slid to a lower branch.

He sprang upon her with all his might.

Kani dodged him, or maybe he missed his mark and landed slightly further away. The branch dipped low, almost touching the ground. Even after Kani loped off with her baby, the branch kept shuddering.

Afternoons were usually a time to relax, but the tension in the troop had not diminished.

Mother monkeys were trying to avoid Moga. They kept their distance and did not even cast a glance at him.

In the midst of all this, Taruni, the young female, was aroused. Though she was pregnant she felt a strong lust. She kept twitching her tail on the ground and presenting her rump to Moga to draw his attention. She nodded her head and signalled to him. Had Moga been enticed and copulated with her, perhaps Taruni's unborn child would have been saved. Moga would not have bitten its head off and killed it. But now he was entirely disinterested. He turned his back to her and kept glaring at Kani.

After an inadequate afternoon siesta, Moga woke up muttering to himself. The female monkeys sat bunched close to each other, far away from him.

Taruni spotted Moga muttering to himself in anger and moved closer to him. As she started to run her fingers through the hair on his back, Moga moved away from her. She tried repeatedly to be intimate with him, but he glared at her angrily. So she silently withdrew.

Moga began to grumble and gnash his teeth again. He paced to and fro, looking wildly in all directions. Finally he settled down and, fuming with rage, began to make loud 'hoo-oop . . . hoo-oop!' sounds. His organ was now erect, and with two leaps, he reached the females. He snatched the baby from Landi's grip and tucked it under his right arm. He sank his teeth into its left thigh. He then jumped down and ran away.

The mother, Landi, Bothari's sister and a young male went after him. They desperately tried to retrieve Landi's baby, but Moga's strong legs lashed at them and they fell down. Moga's eyes were murderous.

The baby kept crying 'chee . . . chee-chee' piteously. After dragging the baby for about two hundred feet, Moga stopped. He bit off a chunk of flesh from the baby's left arm pit. His powerful fangs made a six-finger wide gash that exposed the baby's entrails. Then he dropped the baby and sat near it. The baby was covered with blood. It convulsed. When Landi rushed towards her baby, Moga leapt at her violently. Seeing his bared teeth and fierce look, the wretched Landi was scared stiff.

If she could have lamented loudly and beaten her chest, she would have wrenched anyone's heart with her grief. She would have rolled on the ground and stuffed her mouth with dirt. But one could see all these emotions only in her eyes and on her face.

Moga sat near the writhing baby for a while. It had lost a lot of blood and looked like a dark little rag on the ground. It lay on the scorched earth with its little mouth agape, its open eyes staring at the blue sky. When it was completely still, Moga quietly got up and climbed onto a laburnum tree far away and sat in silence.

Seeing that Moga had gone, Landi approached the baby fearfully. When this little one was born, all the females of the troop had gathered around to touch it, but Landi had hidden it under herself.

She gently brought her belly closer to the baby and held both its arms. She wrapped its feet around her waist, took its tiny hands in hers and stood up. She could not understand why the baby kept falling down as soon as she loosened her grip. She tried to clasp it to her chest repeatedly, but the baby kept falling away.

She then sat near her baby and brushed it with her fingers and touched its eyes tenderly. She tried to turn its head this way and that. She could not figure out why the baby no longer made its usual sounds or latched onto her breast or grabbed her belly.

Holding the baby to her belly with one hand, Landi wandered about. As usual the young females came to play with the baby. Landi let them hold it. But when they sensed that the baby no longer responded, they went back to their grazing.

Landi continued to clutch her baby to herself as she roamed around and foraged.

It had been four days since the baby had died, but Landi did not let go of it. She carried it with her all the time. The baby was dead, but the mother in her refused to die.

In the meantime, Moga killed the three remaining babies. He had snatched them, chewed off the heads, ripped open their bellies. Bothari's sister, who was quite old, tried relentlessly to prevent him from doing all this. In the bargain, she was injured, losing one eye and the finger of her left hand.

When Moga chased Bokandi for her young one, she was so terrified that she dropped her whining baby and fled. Immediately after Moga killed it, a kite swooped down and flew off with the baby. In all this clamour, another young orphan was carried away by a fox.

Only Thoti had fled the troop with her child into the forest far away. Just because you run away from the peril, it doesn't mean the peril leaves you. The sense of danger brings ten individuals together, and they start living together. One needs this sense of danger, internal or external, real or imaginary, to live together.

Minds spawn fears, and this is how sprites and ghouls are born.

Source

Excerpt translated from the Marathi novel, *Sattantar* (Chapter 6, pp. 45–51), 1982, Pune, Mehta Publishing House.

Excerpts from the Plays

10

OH, YOU SILLY POTTER
(*TU VEDA KUMBHAR*)

Translated by Shanta Gokhale

Act Four

(*Almost ten years have elapsed. Ranjanwadi has changed. A sugar factory has come up here. The villagers now work for the factory. Ijappa's home too has changed. Mangalore tiles have replaced the thatched roof. An electric pole has been erected where the neem tree stood. A cylindrical letter box has come up in place of the Hanuman temple.*

The time is around four o'clock in the afternoon. A six-year-old boy is playing with a wooden bus in front of Ijappa's house. Only one window of the house is open. An exhausted Ijappa enters, carrying a bundle on his shoulder. The boy looks up from his game.)

Ijappa: . . . Arra child, my son.
Boy: Yes, old man?
Ijappa: (*Bends down, his hands on his knees*) What do they call this village? Can *you* at least tell me the truth?
Boy: They call it Sakharwadi, sir.
Ijappa: Sakharwadi? Not Ranjanwadi?
Boy: It was Ranjanwadi. But they changed the name. There's a big sugar factory here. So it's Sakharwadi. Didn't you know? Where are you from? Where's your village?
Ijappa: (*Dejected smile*) I had a village, son. I'm looking for it.
Boy: Have you lost your way, baba? Did you take a wrong turn?
Ijappa: Did I take a wrong turn? Or did my village? Who knows? Is this your village? Where's your house?
Boy: This is my village. That's my house.
Ijappa: That one? What's your name? What's your ba's name?
Boy: My name's Asaram Bhojaram Kumbhar.
Ijappa: (*Astonished*) Asaram Bhojaram? My Bhoja's son? (*Touching the boy all over*) My grandson? (*Choking with emotion, tearfully*) My child, I'm your ajja. (*Still in doubt*) Do you know your ajja's name?
Boy: (*Now confused*) Yes. He was called Ijappa. (*Ijappa pulls him close*) But he went to jail. He killed a driver. He got punished.

Ijappa: (*Choking*) So he did, my child. I was in jail. But I'm out now. I've come back to my village. This is my village. I'm seeing it after ten years. It's ten years since my feet touched this soil. (*He falls to his knees and sniffs at the earth. He holds the boy close and kisses him. He weeps. He laughs.*) I hadn't thought I would ever see your face, little one. I thought I'd die in jail. But Lord Panduranga had mercy on me. I'm back in my village to die. But tell me . . . is this my village? You are my grandson. But whose village is this? My village wasn't like this. The houses weren't like this. The people weren't like this. My village had no gate. If a stranger came to my village, nobody stopped him. There were no sentries. One stopped me today.

Where are you going, old man?

I'm going to my village.

What's your name?

My name is known in ten villages, dear man. I am Ijappa Kumbhar of Ranjanwadi.

How do we know that?

From my grey hair, my man. Would I tell lies? I'm on the road to death. Would I deceive you? This is my village. My grandfather, my great-grandfather, they all lived here. I grew up here. We worked here. My kith, my kin, they are all here. My roots go deep into this place.

Go then. Go.

He noted down my name and let me enter. I looked around. The houses didn't look like houses. No cattle. Nobody I knew. I felt I'd come to some other village. Had I lost my way? I was thirsty. Not well in sight. I saw a man. I said, 'Dada, I'm thirsty. Could you give me some water?' He pointed. That tap's got water. I went to the tap. It was dry. I kept stopping passers-by. 'Dada, I want some water please.' They said, 'Water comes to the tap after six o'clock.' I am thirsty now. I'll get water after six, he says.

I was hungry. 'Aai, I'm hungry. I'm not begging. I am a *balutedar* of this village. I have a right to food.'

'You did once, old man. But times have changed. We have ration now.'

What does that mean, my child?

Boy: Ration . . . it's a card. You get it from the office. You show it and get sugar, wheat, kerosene and all that.

Ijappa: I don't have one. If I go to someone's home and ask for a measure of grain?

Boy: You won't get it.

Ijappa: (*Dejectedly*) This isn't my village child. This wasn't how it was in my village. If I was dying of hunger, a neighbour would bring me

OH, YOU SILLY POTTER

some *bhaji* and *bhakri* from his home. If I needed water, people didn't point me to the stream. They got me water. And a piece of jaggery. Man knew Man. All that's gone. Where? How? (*The light on the electric pole suddenly comes on.*) It wasn't like this. You've made miracles happen. We didn't even dream of such things, my boy. And yet, I see them with my eyes. I've wandered all over the village. There are wonders everywhere. So much development. So many facilities. *Divya divya deepathkar, kani kundala motihar, divyala baghoon namaskar . . .* (*Ijappa folds his hands to the light above.*)

Boy: (*Laughing*) Why are you praying to the light?

Ijappa: Don't you? We used to. (*Looking around*) See, this is where a tree stood, planted by your aji. It cast a cool shade. I'd sit in the shade moulding my pots. Your ba would sit, naked, watching me. He'd be chewing on a piece of *bhakri* and plunge his hands in the clay. Your aji would call, 'Come on in. The *bhakris* are ready.' I'd say, 'Wait, let me finish this pot. Haven't done any work since morning. I'd be ashamed to eat.'

This letter-box. Never seen one in my life. Write a letter. Put it in here. Our people get it. That's how it is, right? (*He folds his hands before the letter-box.*) A Marutiraya shrine stood here. Your great-grandfather, Hari Panduranga Kumbhar, installed the idol. Every day, after bathing in the river, I'd wash down the idol. I was young then. I would do squats and press-ups here. '*Dhanya Anjani cha sooth, thyacha naav Hanumanta*' (*He folds his hands.*) The temple's gone before my eyes. (*Returns to the present*) And where's your ba, child?

Boy: Gone to the factory.

Ijappa: And your ma?

Boy: She too. After locking the door.

Ijappa: Leaving you alone? Don't you get hungry?

Boy: My food's there. Kept covered for me.

Ijappa: When do they go, your ma and ba?

Boy: They leave at eight-thirty in the morning. I play out here. Sleep, if I'm sleepy. They come back at four-thirty. They unlock the door. And we all go in.

(*A child wails.*)

Ijappa: (*Concerned*) Who's that?

Boy: My little brother.

Ijappa: Where is he?

Boy: Inside. Sleeping in his cradle.

Ijappa: All alone? *Aga aai*! He must be hungry, *ra*. How will he keep quiet now?

Boy: He'll cry and cry and fall asleep. Aai was here at two to feed him.

Ijappa: (*Frightened, his insides churning*) My little one, hush, hush baby, hush. (*Goes to the door and peeps in through a crack. Tries to open the door. The child cries even louder.*) What a state the poor thing's in. How can I reach him? How can I quieten him? Take a look, boy. Something could have bitten the poor child . . . Go take a look.

Boy: Will you lift me on your shoulder? I'll look in through the window.

Ijappa: Get up then. Go on, look. See anything?

Boy: Yes.

Ijappa: Is he in the cradle, or has he fallen down?

Boy: No, he's in the cradle, standing up, holding the rope. He has pissed and wet his bedclothes. Wait a while, little Rama. Aai will soon be back. Good boy, aren't you? Aai out at work. She'll come back and give you milk. (*The infant has quietened down.*) He's fallen asleep. Put me down now.

Ijappa: (*Sets the boy down. Wipes his tear-filled eyes*) What have you gained, my child? Cars, railway trains, electricity, water on tap, door keys. And what have you given in exchange? Your honour, trust, pride, love, the strength of your body, happiness . . . Haven't you? You gave a big *bhopla* and got a little *avala* didn't you? Dear folk, you are not my people. This is not my village. This is not my house. My home wasn't like this. I swear it wasn't. Man was big. His chest was broad. His legs were strong. The factory wasn't big. Man was big. The village was big. Home and hearth, ma and ba, children, they were all big. (*Bending down to the boy*) My child, should Man become small because the factory is big? Hunh?

Boy: I don't know.

Ijappa: You don't know. You didn't see how it was. Where is all this going to end? What's going to happen to this village?

Boy: I don't know.

Ijappa: You don't know. I don't know either. You don't have knowledge. I have knowledge. Yet I don't know. All these conveniences. Roads, houses . . . everything so clean. But at what cost, son? It's a heavy bargain. We took a blanket to cut the cold and set it on fire to get warm. You can warm yourselves, poor creatures. Not me. (*He is terribly tired. He sits down. His throat is choked, his voice filled with pathos.*) My world is destroyed. I'll lie in some dark corner like an old, broken tool. Nothing's left that was once mine. I came with such hopes to my village. My home. I was going to put my head on a loved one's knee, take a sip of water from my river and die. But I couldn't find my village. I found another. Not mine. A strange village belonging to strangers. I didn't meet any of my own. My days are done, my child. My days are over. But how can I die in a strange village? I must look for my village. My home.

	(*Struggles to stand up.*) I must go. Don't forget your ajja, child. Remember this old man if you can.
Boy:	(*Tearful*) Don't go ajoba. The shift will end soon. Aai and Baba will be home . . .
Ijappa:	Whose Aai? Whose Baba? I have nobody. I must go, my child. I've stayed too long. I must go.
Boy:	Where will you go?
Ijappa:	Where else? To my village.
Boy:	(*Crying*) Don't go. Please don't go.

(*The factory siren sounds. The boy's words are drowned. Ijappa walks away step by step. The boy continues to weep. The curtain comes down slowly.*)

Source

Excerpt translated from the Marathi play, *Tu Veda Kumbhar* (Act IV), 1962, Pune, Continental Prakashan.

11

SATI

Translated by Vrushali Deshpande

Scene – III

(*It is evening. The puja room in the wada. The women of the house, all wrapped up in shawls, are gathered together and chatting.*)

Bhama:	The procession must have reached the *sangam*, the confluence now, isn't it?
Aau Aatya:	Aga, it must have reached long ago. Why would they take so long? In fact the rituals must have begun by now.
Bhama:	You saw how Lakshumi was looking? So beautiful! So radiant! I felt she was not a human being at all, someone from heaven.
Aau Aatya:	Not only you, the whole of Pune must have thought so. We used to hear big names like Sawkarbaisaheb, Ramabaisaheb, Muktabai, this girl went and sat alongside them! Her name is made, turned to gold!
Bhama:	Bai, what are the rituals they do there? We don't know anything.
Naa Aai:	Aga, how would I know? You should be fortunate enough to even see such ceremony. Ramabaisaheb gave *vaan*, auspicious gifts to all married women. I am told that my mother-in-law was among them.
Aau Aatya:	Yes, I believe. She used to mention something about it . . . for many days . . . it was talked about at home. You are supposed to tie five precious stones and a small box of *kajal* in the *pallu* of the sari it seems . . . Has anyone given her the *kajal dabi*?
Naa Aai:	Everything has been given. I haven't held anything back, okay!
Bhama:	Giving auspicious gifts to married women, a small *kajal dabi* and five gems tied to the pallu, and then . . . ?
Naa Aai:	What 'and then,' *ga*, Bhama . . . eleven offerings are made to the fire, circumambulations are done, the stone is worshipped, the woman stands on it. Worship the fire with flowers

SATI

	and fruits, and then go lie down in a hut made of grass and straw . . .
Aau Aatya:	It is said that the brother-in-law or a close relative must request her to come back, take her hand and raise her . . .
Naa Aai:	Is that so? I don't know . . . I have never heard of anybody who has come back . . .
Bhama:	Blessed, *ga bai*, truly blessed. What determination. What daring. It happens only because of deep faith in religion.
	(*While the women are talking about this, Haripant rushes in, panting. His voice strident*)
Hari Kaka:	Ruination! The girl has ruined everything. She has disgraced herself; she has disgraced both the families and our ancestry. I always suspected that she would do something like this at the eleventh hour! We cannot show our faces in Pune now . . . The girl turned out to be really terrible.
Naa Aai:	What happened? What did she do?
Hari Kaka:	Oh, she was very serious till we reached the *sangam*. People showered her with flowers and cheered her. They prostrated before her. Then at the last minute, she said she wouldn't stand on the stone!
	'My intellect does not accept this,' she said, 'I won't follow this ritual.' She argued with the priest. 'Don't tell me what the scriptures say. The *Bruhaddevatakar* has said that Kshatriya women should perform *sati*. But whether the women of other castes should do it, needs to be considered. The *Padmapuran* says Brahmin women should not perform *sati*. Not only that, it also says that anyone who helps her perform the ritual of *sati* will be a sinner for killing a Brahmin.'
	(*A frightened Bhama leaves*)
Aau Aatya:	Then someone should have asked her, '*Aga*, then why did you go that far? Why all this drama now?'
Hari Kaka:	What are you saying Aau? She stunned the priests. 'I am the daughter of a learned scholar,' she said, 'and you are trying to teach me the alphabet?'
	Finally, the priests told her about the dire consequences that would follow. They told her what a woman who refuses to stand on the stone has to face, but . . . no effect . . . totally stone-hearted!
Aau Aatya:	Why did you listen to her? You should have grabbed her hand and made her sit on the pyre and told the musicians to play loudly.
Hari Kaka:	She had already thought of everything, Aaubai. Before we knew it, she swept towards the river like a wind and said, 'Ganga Maa, take me in your arms, give me the final refuge'

and threw herself into the flowing river. The whole crowd was watching still, like a picture.

Once she went underwater, we didn't see her again, not even a glimpse of her nail. I stood there for a long time, waiting to see if she comes up. In the end, all the Brahmin priests paid homage to Krishna and returned, Aau.

It was a terrible humiliation.

Naa Aai: She wanted to bring disgrace to us! (*Goes inside*)

Hari Kaka: It's going to be talked about all over Pune tomorrow. How to face anyone now! It's a very big, very bad omen. As it is, the state is facing misfortune and tragedy. Now this evil omen on top of it.

Oh God! What more are you going to make us see? (*He goes*)

Aau Aatya: If she wanted to take death by water only, why all the fuss and furore? What was wrong with fire?

Scene IV

(*On that same day, after a few hours, Captain Ford's tent near Khadki by the confluence. He is pacing up and down outside. Just then, Saru comes.*)

Saru: Huzoor, the woman has regained consciousness. She can talk now.

Captain: Is that so? God is great!

(*Lakshmi comes out, Saru makes her sit down. 'Why did you come out, bai?' she asks and goes inside.*)

Captain: Are you feeling better now?

Lakshmi: Where am I?

Captain: You are safe. Don't worry.

Lakshmi: Safe? Where am I?

Captain: In Pune only. You are in my tent. This is the camp of the English platoon.

Source

Excerpt translated from the Marathi play, *Sati* (Scene III and Scene IV), 1968, Pune, Continental Prakashan.

12

OH, THE HUSBAND HAS GONE TO KATHEWADI (*PATI GELE GA KATHEWADI*)

Translated by Chinmay Dharurkar

Act Three

Scene Three

(*Janaki has just finished her chores.*
Sarjerao Shinde enters Aine Mahal.
Aine Mahal. Sarjerao strides in. He is still in his travelling clothes. He looks around suspiciously. The servants flustered with the master's unexpected appearance.)

Sarjerao:	Where has she gone? How could she go out at the exact time of my arrival?
Servant:	To the temple, maharaj. Had you informed in advance, she wouldn't have gone, but *dhani*, you . . .
Sarjerao:	I didn't give prior notice. I didn't halt anywhere. I rode straight here. I saw the message sent to Kathewad, 'The three tasks you had assigned have been accomplished. The naming ceremony of the son has been performed. It had to be done in your absence. Come now at the earliest, to behold the face of the child. Your immediate arrival will be precious, more golden than gold.' I went straight to the wada but found a huge big lock there. Residing at Aine Mahal now, I was told. I come here and find everything is new. New building, new servants. What is going on?
	(*Janaki returns from the temple.*)
Janaki:	Aga bai! When did your highness arrive? How is it there was no prior message? How did the troops enter the city without drum rolls and cannon blasts? No rangolis in the yard, no welcoming torans on the doors, no Gudis erected . . . Where are all the servants? Your highness returns from a mission and there is no celebration? Not in the city and therefore not in the house too? How unfortunate and inauspicious is that!

Sarjerao:	Can there be celebrations when the *malkin*, the mistress herself, is not in the house? As for the servants, loyal only for the food and the clothing. Where's the question of affection or concern?
Janaki:	I erred, It's my fault! I shouldn't have gone out at this time. Do forgive me. Should bath water be arranged for you?
Sarjerao:	No!
Janaki:	Won't you take off these clothes?
Sarjerao:	No!
Janaki:	What is your command then?
Sarjerao:	First I want an explanation of all that has transpired.
Janaki:	That you will get eventually. Coming home after so long, why the anger as soon as you arrive?
Sarjerao:	Jealousy is a very strange emotion. The male ego is huge. When I wasn't here, and you didn't have any money or resources, how did this big palace get built? Who built it?
Janaki:	I got it constructed, at your behest. A huge price had to be paid for it.
Sarjerao:	What price? In what form? If there was no money, what exactly did you give?
Janaki:	My cleverness, our Mohana's loyalty and a foreigner's obsession with a woman – That was the cost of the palace.
Sarjerao:	Don't talk in riddles. Tell me everything clearly.
Janaki:	*Aga bai*! So, you throw riddles at us and go away to another country, but when we talk in riddles, you get angry . . . It's a Kathewadi custom, it seems! And what happened to the threat? You were going to bring your favourite woman from there? I don't see any Kathewadi rival here . . .
Sarjerao:	No unnecessary talk. And don't change the topic. Who built this mahal?
Janaki:	The name is familiar to you.
Sarjerao:	Who?
Janaki:	That Joravarsingh's Diwanji.
Sarjerao:	Unh? That fox? How did he reach this place? Why did he come here? To die?
Janaki:	You had parked yourself there to collect the Chauth tax. The Kathi people didn't pay any attention to you. And I, sitting in one place, collected the tax.
Sarjerao:	What was that clever plan of yours? He came all the way here to give you the money. Why?
Janaki:	So, to bring down the plume on your turban, he sent his horsemen from Kathewad all the way down south. He didn't get a glimpse of even my nail, mistook Mohana for me, and in the euphoria of a victory, he went back. But all that cannot be

OH, THE HUSBAND HAS GONE TO KATHEWADI

narrated in a hurry. It's a voluminous book. Will tell you at leisure. Also, this mahal is not the only task I completed. The other two are also done. You wanted the second wife, na . . . Kuvarbai . . . yes, I'm just coming! (*Janaki goes inside. A servant enters.*)

Servant: Baisaheb sent me here.
Sarjerao: What for?
Servant: To help take these clothes off. It must have been quite tiring for you. At least let me unfasten the sword from your waist. I myself had tied it when you set out on your campaign.
Sarjerao: So what?
Servant: It has returned with success. So let me take it off with my own hands.
Sarjerao: Very well then . . .
Servant: *Dhani sarkar*, your mission was successful?
Sarjerao: Has your *dhani* ever been unsuccessful?
Servant: No, never! For two years you've been away . . . the *wada* was so desolate.
Sarjerao: It was desolate?
Servant: Indeed! They say that without the *dhani* a *wada* has no glory. That is so true.
Sarjerao: But your very capable baisaheb was here, wasn't she?
Servant: Are you angry, *dhani*? My father used to say, as soon as you feel anger coming, start counting numbers in your head.
Sarjerao: Who should count?
Servant: You! No, no, I will count, you listen. One, two, three . . .
Sarjerao: I do not want to count and I don't want to listen . . .
Servant: Sarkar, shall I remove your footwear?
Sarjerao: I said no!
Servant: Give yourself some rest for a while!
Sarjerao: No need! Just come here, but . . . Tell me, when did you come to stay in this *wada*?
Servant: Here? Fifteen and five . . . five days after the Dasra festival.
Sarjerao: Five days after Dasra you came?
Servant: Yes.
Sarjerao: Didn't you feel like staying in the old *wada* until the *dhani* returned?
Servant: We did, *dhani* saheb, but baisaheb ordered us. We obeyed.
Sarjerao: When did the wedding take place?
Servant: My wedding? You don't know when? My father might know. I was very young.
Sarjerao: Arrey, not yours. Hers. When did the new baisaheb come to live here?
Servant: New baisaheb?

89

(Just then Janaki enters in Kathewadi attire. She is veiled, and like a new bride, is coy and bashful. She touches Sarjerao's feet.)

Sarjerao: My wife? How can you be my wife? I wasn't even here. How could you get married to me?

Janaki: Don't you remember the moonlit night at the Shiva temple by the river? Don't you remember the intoxicating fragrance of bodies and words? You forgot? How could you? Like a golden dream, it happened, but it was real. It was unforgettable. Whose broad chest did this colourful shawl cover? Whose waist did this sharp-edged dagger adorn? To whom do these valuable objects belong? Who gave them to whom on which auspicious occasion?

Sarjerao: Janaki, you? It was actually you there?

Janaki: Yes, it was me. Would you have so readily and lovingly embraced another woman? Or pleaded with her to not go? Do you remember you made me promise, and I foolishly agreed, that the next time we met, it would be to stay forever? I met again, didn't I? In the same form as then? Should it have been at the same place, the Shankara temple by the river, in the pleasant moonlit night of the Sharad season . . .

Sarjerao: Janaki!

(A child's cry is heard from within.)

Janaki: The fruit of that union is this baby of ours. You want to see him, don't you? They say one should bring a golden ornament when one sees one's son for the first time. You have diverted the flow of gold from Kathewad to the Marathi land. Come, see the baby. He resembles his mother, and he who looks like the mother is always happy, they say.

Sarjerao: Janaki, I have lost. You have won.

Janaki: No, no. Haven't I told you that winning over you is not a matter of pride, and losing to you is no humiliation? I just acted as per your orders.

Sarjerao: How should I reward this clever queen for all her wise deeds?

Janaki: Since you are so generous, I will ask for an answer to a question.

Sarjerao: Why do you ask for mere words when there is so much more? Ask for something that will last you a lifetime. I am so very pleased today.

Janaki: When are you not pleased with me? What more do I need to make my life meaningful? I am content. But allow me to ask a question that women are normally not supposed to ask.

Sarjerao: Granted. Ask.

Janaki: Maharaj, why is this test of fidelity only for women? Is it a virtue only for them?

OH, THE HUSBAND HAS GONE TO KATHEWADI

Sarjerao: Yes, yes, only you women must take the test. Fidelity is a virtue only for you. There is another set of values for men. If a man errs, it is simply a slip. If a woman slips, she falls. People talk. They say she tripped. She is fallen.

Janaki: Why? A woman can also encounter a slippery path, the same as a man. Then why this duplicity?

Sarjerao: Yes, why? (*Again the baby's cry is heard.*) Here is your answer. God has given women the gift of motherhood. We don't have the boon, so we don't have the curse of falling.

Janaki: (*Gets carried away, mutters*) Wah wah . . . this is very clever . . . you cunning one!

Sarjerao: (*Surprised*) What did you say?

Janaki: (*Trying to cover up*) The cunning little one is waiting. Shall we go see him?

Sarjerao: Yes, yes, let's go. (*All of them exit*)

Sutradhar: O King of the connoisseurs
  May your blessing be upon us
  You are the one who sustains and protects us
  We all bow before you! O Lord Shiva who has an eye on the forehead!

Shahir: Our salute to you as you take our leave
  (The folk singer) *An earnest request to all of you*
  May there be love, and may it multiply
  This is the sole prayer to connoisseurs like you
  (*All of the characters come on the stage.*)

–THE END–

Source

Excerpt translated from the Marathi play, *Pati Gele Ga Kathewadi* (Act III and Scene 3), 1970, Satara, Shabda Prakashan.

Section 2

WHEN THE BRUSH WAS NOT ENOUGH

13
PRESIDENTIAL ADDRESS AT THE 57TH AKHIL BHARATIYA MARATHI SAHITYA SAMMELAN, AMBEJOGAI ON 4 FEBRUARY 1983

Vyankatesh Madgulkar
Translated by Manali Sharma, Sachin Ketkar and Chinmay Ghaisas

Dear literature lovers,

Marathwada is the homeland of Marathi literature, a goldmine of great souls. I am profoundly grateful to you for having honoured me by choosing me as the president of this Festival of Words that begins in this holy land today.

I see before me litterateurs, teachers, researchers, students, literature lovers and ardent readers. You are all interested to hear about literature, the creative process and purpose of literature. The great responsibility of telling you all this has fallen on me. I am neither a teacher of literature nor a critic. I am purely a creative prose writer. I have always limited myself to describing things that have been an integral part of my experiences. The fact that you have heard this during the Solapur District Literary Meet and the Gomantak Literary Meet gives me immense strength.

Perhaps if I speak about my journey, it will throw some light on my creative writing. And possibly on literature in general.

The first thing that I would like to say is that one does not become a litterateur, one just is. And literature comes to him/her as naturally as fruit to a tree.

Today, when I look back at the places where I grew up, I realise the contexts of my writing afresh. I was born in a typical cottage in a tiny, sparsely-populated village in the arid expanse of Mandesh. I spent almost eighteen years there. My village in 1935 was similar to Surgeon Cotts's account of Loni near Pune in the 1820s. His observations of village life, the communities and tribes that inhabited it and the numerous agricultural activities are astonishingly accurate. Cotts also describes the temples like the one of Bahiroba in Loni village, explains why they are famous and talks about the ghosts that populate the village. He refers to the houses of slaves in the village and also mentions that the village grocer kept the fragrant musk in his shop. My village too had a range of castes and communities, a temple of the god who cured people of snake bites and its share of ghosts. But it did not have the hutments of slaves, nor did it have a grocer's shop. One had to go to the taluka place five miles away to buy a matchbox! Few people could afford a matchbox! The village Patil would light his chillum by rubbing firestones, and fire for lighting the clay stove in the kitchen would be brought from the neighbours, and the already lit lamps would be used to light up other lamps in the evening.

There were eight houses of Brahmins in the village, but there was no separate lane for them as in other villages. Three of the houses were next to the Mahar colony, three of our houses were next to the Ramoshi wada, and two Brahmin houses lay beyond the stream next to the Mulanis, the Momins, the Kumbhars (the potters) and the Kunbis (the agriculturalists). Our backdoor neighbour was a Sonar, a goldsmith who used to take a lamp from our house to light the fire used to melt gold in his shop. A Kunbi woman, Sundarabai, used to come to our house in the evening, light her lamp with ours and go back, protecting the flame with her sari. If a child suffered from a stiff neck, Sakha Ramoshi would come and, without stepping on the mattress, gently massage the child's neck and release it. He could also fix a broken bone if you fell from a tree. He knew how human anatomy worked!

The Kunbi, Ramoshi, Momin, Mahar, Nhavi (barber) and Sutar (carpenter) children were my playmates. I learnt how to catch small fish hiding under the moss in the stream from the Muslim boys Akbarya and Abdullya. From them, I also picked up *vanavidya*, 'Knowledge of the Forest'. I acquired skills like catching baby parrots from holes in the trees, trailing a wild animal, digging up the monitor lizards' holes, hunting pigeons with a sling and taking down honeycombs from the lush green trees without getting stung by the bees. From the Kunbi boys, I learnt how to take cattle, sheep and goats to graze and search for edible roots, tubers and carrots. The Mahar boys showed me how to gather jamuns, edible parts of plants, wild fruits, vegetables, nuts and berries and then eat them while grazing my sheep and goats. Sankarya, the barber's son, taught me how to wrestle in the sand, swim and climb trees. I learnt to love the festive village congregations like the Uroos, Jatra, wrestling competitions, acrobats, dervishes and snakecharmers, among others, because of my friends.

We have many festivals associated with agriculture. Ploughing and sowing, reaping and harvesting are rituals to celebrate. During Bendur we express our gratitude towards our cattle, goats and sheep, and on 'Navyachi Punav,' we bring in the new harvest by hanging garlands of the fresh yield in our doorways. During Dasara we stick fresh sprouts in our turbans. And of course, we had our own 'festivals of taste' when we and our friends savoured green seed-heads of jowar, ears of wheat, cobs of maize, green gram pods and fresh groundnuts.

Some of my friends were garrulous. They relished gossip about the goings-on in the village. These accounts were as exciting and strange as the tales of folk-performers like the Gondhalis and the Bhorpis. Some of the tales also had that rare quality of innocent humour.

I once ran into my friend Gonda. His *dhoti* was tucked in and he was holding a dirty bag and a fishing rod. He had probably gone fishing in the Belwadi river. "Gonda, you went fishing?" I asked him.

"Yes, ji."

"What did you catch?"

He smiled. "Nothing. Today the river observed the *Ekadashi* fast."

I owe a debt to all these friends, not only for the stories they told but also their style. Like the fresh sugarcane juice served in the sugarcane juice shop, they gave me the gifts of stylistic effortlessness, limpidness and liveliness.

These days people ask me whether I am drawn towards folk arts and since when. We people are not natural readers, but natural listeners. We use the term '*bahushrut*' (one who has listened to many things) for the English term 'well-read'. We have heard the tales of Aditya and Ranubai at home. We have heard the Harikatha in temples. In our courtyard, we have seen and heard folk-performances of the Gondhalis, Jagars, Tamashas and Lalits. Considering our love for listening, wandering folk-singers and performers like Vasudev, Balsantosh, Bharadi, Vaghe, Ramdasi and others would sing and perform the devotional and didactic compositions of the saints for us, and we would give them food grains and flour in return.

After the Second World War, there was a great upheaval in our social lives. When food, grain and flour were distributed through ration shops, these wandering minstrels and performers disappeared from the villages.

After passing the fourth standard from the village school, I went to the taluka to study in the English high school. It was the educational centre of the princely state of Aundh. That is why we had to chant the mantra 'Om Hram Rheem" and perform twenty-five *Surya Namaskars* every morning. There used to be a five-day fair in the month of Kartiki in Didhanch village, which was seven miles from there. It was a major attraction for us, but because of our strict head master, we couldn't go during school hours. So as soon as school got over, my friend and I would leave our books in school itself and walk all seven miles to the fair. My uncle Bittakaka was a police inspector in Didhanch village, and he was in charge of the fair. Thanks to his influence, we could watch any tamasha performance from a special bench close to the stage. When the cock crowed at day break, we would have tea and snacks in an eatery (again thanks to Bittakaka's influence) and start for school. We would bathe in the school well and stealthily join the students performing *surya namaskars*.

Our extremely strict headmaster used to wait at the school entrance every day with a cane in his hands and mercilessly flog anyone who came even five minutes late. We did this for five days but we were never caught.

On the sixth day, the headmaster started the school assembly with the announcement, "I am going to introduce you to two very great men today." The students looked around to see who he was referring to. Then he called out our names and made us stand in front of three hundred students. He told them of our tremendous feat and said, "Had these great men shown the same dedication and hard work in their studies, I would have felicitated them with bouquets and garlands."

Our headmaster is no longer with us today. Had he been alive, he would have felicitated me with verbal flowers at least. My Marathi teacher did so.

The other great man who accompanied me to the village fair recently retired from the Public Works Department.

Many people are born in similar circumstances and environments, but that environment is not favourable to all in the same manner. Literature is the product of the amalgamation of talent, sensitivity and experiences. If the field is not fertile, the seeds of experience go to waste and the sapling of creativity never sprouts.

I was also good at drawing and painting. I was fortunate to have good art teachers in school. But the atmosphere around me was not conducive for art. Had I been able to see good art and sculpture exhibitions, I would have stayed with lines and colours and not turned towards verbal art. But the Muses are sisters after all, as Greek mythology tells us.

I was reading voraciously during this period. The poetry of Ram Ganesh Gadkari and Keshavsut thrilled me. I also tried my hand at writing poetry, but I was not satisfied with what I wrote. I was also experimenting with water colours and oil painting, but I felt that wasn't working for me either. Clouds used to gather, but it wasn't raining for me. I was in a strange state. I was always drawn to animals and birds. I had tried to keep a parrot, a cow and even a white and featherless baby partridge as pets, but it never worked out well for me.

Then one day, I wrote a short story. It was titled *Kalya Tondachi* ("The Black-faced One"), and it was about an unfortunate dog. The story, *Kalya Tondachi*, was about a stray pup that I had picked up from the street. In the beginning, everyone was fond of it and pampered it. But one day, someone said that it had a black face, it was inauspicious and would bring misfortune to the family if we kept it at home. And troubles did start coming repeatedly – illness, death and disappointment. The family started ill-treating the puppy. They told me to abandon it far away. And one fine day, the puppy left our home.

I wrote the story and sent it to *Abhiruchi* – a periodical known for its high literary standards. The story was published, it was praised and I was applauded for it.

At that moment, I felt I got a glimpse of what I had been looking for all that time. I could see my path ahead of me.

I had already discovered the great pleasure of reading by then. When I was nine, my father was transferred to a place called Kinhai. We had rented the house of some well-read, cultured person who had gone away on business. It had an attic, and houses with attics are great for a child because he can fly high in the air and weave webs like a spider. There was a huge trunk which had a treasure in it. Only it was secured with iron strips. I was curious to see what was inside. One day I managed to prise open the strips and open the trunk. It was full of books and old issues of magazines. It had a Marathi translation of the *Panchatantra* and the novels of Hari Narayan Apte. It had Nath Madhav's adventure novels like *Veer Dhaval* and stories like *Inamdarancha Balu*. And the Marathi version of the "Arabian Nights". I vaguely remember that I had also read the stories of Hatim Tai, stories of the Princes of King Thaksen. For several days, I read whatever I could by the light of the attic window. And realised how much pleasure reading can provide you.

A baby rabbit and a baby deer learn which herbs and plants are edible and which are not from their mothers. I haven't seen human mothers enthusiastic about advising their children what to read and what not to. Carefully selected reading is always fruitful. Books are more generous than business men. They don't hold anything back when they give. Not everything that is printed and published between the covers is worth the name of the book. They are not concerned with '*akshara*' (simultaneously meaning 'letters' as well as 'indestructible'). There are very few books that we recall, even in our mellow and mature days. There are writers who claim they are growing cashews but are actually fermenting '*feni*' illicitly. Is it not better to sleep or laze away our time instead of reading merely for entertainment? One can easily recognise such cheap books because they are decked with many colourful snares so that they sell well. They are also advertised widely and loudly like a quack hawks his medicines.

In 1942 the Quit India Movement began. I was in school. Slogans of 'Do or Die' were raised everywhere. Young minds are attracted to martyrdom, and I had read biographies of revolutionaries. Honestly written biographies and autobiographies teach us much more than scholarly tomes. The stream of our lives, because of some of the books we have read in our youth, may have started flowing upwards. I entered the Movement at the age of sixteen. I was declared a criminal, and I wandered about hiding in various villages and houses. The things that I saw and experienced were far more scorching and much more different from what I had experienced till then. It was an agonizing period for my body and my mind.

The Movement ended and so did my school education. The library of life however remained ever open for me.

It is said that Wordsworth's maid once told a visitor that Wordsworth's library is inside his house, but his study is outside.

At the age of twenty or twenty-two, I went to the city of Bombay and came face to face with friends and editors whom I had interacted with only through letters. They provided me with shelter and reassurance. The eyes, which were habituated to seeing only the drought-stricken wilderness of Mandesh, were seeing the great blue sea for the first time.

Between 1948 and 1949, I wrote my pen portraits titled *Mandeshi Manasa* (The People of Mandesh) for the weekly *Mouj*. When I was aimlessly loitering in life, these folks of Mandesh were born. I wrote *Dharma Ramoshi* and *Nama Mastar*. I did not know I was writing well. I only hoped this writing would get published and fetch me five or ten rupees. The editors read these two pen-portraits and suggested that I write more on similar lines, and instead of publishing them separately, they should be serialised every week so they would be more effective. When I was not able to think of more such pieces, the editors published an advertisement for the series and brought out two of the stories I had written. I used to strain my memory and turn out a pen-portrait every week. They were widely appreciated, and I suddenly found myself in the limelight!

Valuable and important books are born and turn out to be great, with the writers very often having no clue of their greatness. It is a natural and spontaneous happening.

Henry David Thoreau once said, "Poems grow on people the way the pumpkin grows on the vine".

I wrote *Gavakadchya Goshti* in a similar fashion.

For a short period, I worked as a teacher in a primary school in a very small village. I met my character Zhelya there. There was a community of Dhangars, the sheep herders, in the village, and nearby there was an exclusively Dhangars colony. My elder brother was a teacher there. I often used to carry food for him from home when I was studying in high school, usually walking the seven miles. Sometimes I would stay over in his tiny room.

After I moved to Pune, ten years later, I began writing *Bangarwadi*. However, I stopped half-way through it, worried whether it was headed in the right direction. I showed it to my editor friend, who said, "This is what they call a novel. Keep writing."

"But I can't think of anything," I said.

"It will all come to you. It is there in your mind. It will all come back once you start writing." This is how I wrote my first novel, and it immediately became famous. The English translation was later prescribed as recommended reading for students of Sociology.

In one's everyday life, social issues and conflicts are inevitable. An artist is a witness to them and cannot distance himself from them. But he does not need to be a flag-bearer for some ideology.

I could see my path laid out before me clearly after *Bangarwadi*. There were some mirages and traps on the way, and I have often wondered whether

I would land in some strange destination. But not trusting my eyes, I never let my feet forget the path I was walking on.

When I moved to Bombay, I met several excellent writer-friends, editors as well as knowledgeable writers. They advised me to read widely in English. You will find writers close to your sensibility like Liam O Flaherty, John Steinbeck, Gorky and Caldwell, I was told. I read determinedly. I had figured out that literature is a huge stream, but only when I started reading in English did I realise that it was, in fact, a huge ocean.

Reading is a nutrient for a writer. However, if one does not have talent, the nutrient cannot breathe life into a statue. A writer has to read beyond the written word, he has to read human society. I am a writer, and whatever is human is not foreign to me. Not only that, whatever is living cannot be alien to me. If the writer is able to read these things and convey it to the literature aficionados, he goes beyond small and insignificant differences. He can make what the great revolutionary poet Keshavsut has termed '*Pradesh sakalyacha*' (the Province of Totality) his own.

Why is it that I've been drawn to the world of nature and wildlife recently? Frankly, this fascination is not a new one. I've never really been able to look at people as distinct from Nature. During the rather frisky age, I used to hunt. Today that sport is outdated. However, people of the earliest civilizations were all powerful hunters. The education of any youngster whose hands have never held either a stick or a gun and who has never scouted through rivers, mountains or forests always remains incomplete. A boy-hunter, upon attaining physical and intellectual maturity, drops the stick and the gun and starts going to the river and the forest for altogether different reasons. He seeks relatives other than the usual ones there.

We can fortunately witness such magnificent Nature, forests, wildlife and birds in our country. The literati have still not turned their heads towards it. Their ears are yet to hear the cacophony of the storks and the shrill calls of the cranes. Their hearts have never skipped a beat seeing the flight of a royal blue peacock.

An obligation towards 'society' is expected from a writer. But which 'society' is being referred to? One that can be measured against the parameters of all the basic human needs – freedom, hunger, education, livelihood, security and love. Man-made differences arise due to differences in language, region, religion, caste and creed. If we refuse to accept these differences, then the 'society' seems as unified as Nature with no beginning or end. When Anatole France says, "Art is one man's gift to humanity," which society is he implying here?

Many expectations are expressed regarding what literature is supposed to accomplish. But why do we expect to get music out of a music-box and then feel like using the same box to keep valuables?

Language is the medium of literature and also the means of social exchange, which is why the burden of social obligations falls on its shoulders. When

I make a drawing of a monkey, it is not the drawing of a Marathi monkey. But the moment I write or speak the word 'makad,' it becomes a Marathi monkey. We do not expect such fulfilment of social obligations from art forms which do not have language as their medium of expression, like say painting or sculpture or music. But we have these expectations from writers because they do. When we regard Literature as an art form created for all humanity, we will not have such social expectations from it. We will then not put these restrictions on the writer. We will then accept that freedom, for it is the birth right of every writer.

Doing purposeful social work, bringing to the fore the issues of certain communities, igniting movements and protests – this is what activists do. Social obligations lie with them, not writers. In order to further clarify this idea, let's chalk out two triangles.

The first triangle has:

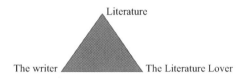

The second triangle has:

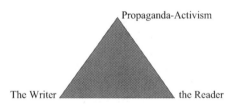

Both these triangles are perennial, and from them, we may infer that:

All writing is not Literature.
All readers are not connoisseurs.
All writers are not litterateurs.

What then is Literature?
  Well, that cannot be defined. Only its form can be specified.
  Emerson has said that "All good literature which exists in the English language till date could have been written by a single person."
  What we can conclude from this is that the creation of good literature happens very rarely.
  But if not social obligations, then what is the purpose of Literature?
  It is the same as that of a flower blooming. A rose doesn't bloom so that we may make *gulkand* out of it. A purpose is a social need. We can view literature from the viewpoint of utility too and thus synergise them. The day

before yesterday, as I was wandering around the Thar Desert in Rajasthan, I saw a beautiful yellow flower blooming through the sand at the base of a *karira* plant. It seemed like an ornament to that barren landscape. I was overjoyed to see this glimpse of spring in the month of January!

I did not ask myself, What is the purpose of this? If a botanist gave me the botanical name, its classification, its usefulness, it would not necessarily multiply my joy.

Every story has a moral, but a naïve man is happy just listening to the story. He does not immediately go in search of its moral.

What is the harm in such rare, organically-written literature not being produced?

Literature too, after all, is like a habit, and good habits are like clothes covering the human body. If they are not there, a man is naked.

And, once upon a time, humans were roaming around unclothed!

When a hardworking woman in a village sings an *Ovi* while grinding grain, fine poetry like Bahinabai Chaudhary's spills out with the flour.

It is white and wholesome.

That's why we must not insist upon a purpose or a utility. A tradition of slavery and bonded labour seeps into literature when there is an excessive dominance of politics and sociology on it. There is a compulsion then to write only that poetry where all arts bow down to one, to sketch only a particular kind of protagonist for a novel, to make only certain kinds of sculptures and paintings.

Then can literature not be used even at the judgement hour?

It can.

Even such writing has a place in the world of literature. However, Kusumagraj's poem *Garja Jayajayakar* and a publicity song in a fair are not the same.

The struggles and problems of the present wither away after some time. The tools used to sharpen them are cast aside and forgotten.

Our systems of categorising literature is very much like the way we practice social segregation. Rural, Dalit, Middle Class, etc. But literature can also be categorised from the perspective of innovation. The classification is in accordance with the evolution of literature.

1. Conventional
2. Fantastic
3. Realistic
4. Existentialist
5. Psychological
6. Surreal

Such classification happens elsewhere too. It is sworn by history. It is done in the belief that all literature is one. It is not restricted by the boundaries of nation, region or language. One can enjoy the stories by a Lopez from Spain or an O'Flaherty from Ireland. Here, there is nothing such as me, my fellows or my region, and that is why one never feels like one has nothing to do with it.

On the one hand, we dream of an ideal society which is casteless and secular, and then we find ways to aggravate caste bias within literature. Is this right?

We have seen the evolution of the didactic, the fantastic and the realistic in our language. In the past, there has been a long elaboration of Realism. We've given it names like Rural literature and Dalit literature, and it's actually a capacious and sincere invention of Realism. A structure which has certain inherent virtues avails an apt backdrop which is a bright, bold sight. All good literature too, is visible as clearly as a hillock against the vast horizon or a gigantic tree in a wide grassy plain. It does not need to be highlighted.

As I love my life, I also love literature. I like to write as much as I like to live. These are the only sublime qualities I possess, worthy of presenting to the world. Creating literature doesn't make me as tense as discussing literature does. There are, indeed, some talented writers who can knit with needles in both hands effortlessly. I'm really awed by them.

Based on all that I have said, about myself, my contemplations and my journey as a writer until now, you must have understood my outlook towards literature. And now, I would like to have a tête-à-tête with you, my true audience – a brotherhood of literature lovers listening devotedly. You have made a great effort to come here to avail of the joy from this festival of words. If you're not content with the experience, then the guilt of not having fulfilled my duties well will remain with me.

A friend of mine who loves literature told me that the generation of mediocre books has become rampant these days. It is a matter of great concern and should be restricted. It is true. However, placing restrictions is dependent on the readers. You may provide an ostrich with its daily dietary requirement, but even after that, it will ravish whatever comes in front of it and digest it too. Our reading should not be like that.

It should resemble the tweeting birds as they crowd around the bright yellow flowers of the *shalmali* tree in the early dawn to sip the nectar. Our daily reading should go beyond the columns in newspapers. Deep purport exists beneath words, just as constellations hide behind clouds. If you, thus, choose and aim to read only meritorious books, then the mediocre ones will be used only to wrap groceries, and their production will automatically suffer a setback.

I know that barring the few big cities, the stocks of good books do not travel far. Book shops don't always exist in villages in taluka towns. If books do get there, they are available only in the tiny libraries. Libraries are expanding due to the Government's schemes, and that is good news, but it needs to happen at a faster pace. Just as we need to provide water to quench the thirst of people in villages, should we not provide them books too? Maharaja Sayajirao of Baroda had started mobile libraries almost seventy-five years ago. If a patient in a hospital sent a letter to the library asking for books to read, then he would be sent eight to ten books in a sealed box by post. There was a system in place for him to lock the books in the box and send them back to the library at the government's expense. If an institution can run such a campaign, then a government should surely be able to do it with ease.

Also, we have no means of knowing which books are worth reading and what is popular across Maharashtra. Can the *Sahitya Sanskruti Mandal* have a monthly periodical like the *Times Literary Supplement* for this? It can also feature advertisements regarding where Marathi or even rare English books can be found. During the exhibition held in Pune on behalf of the National Book Trust, the biggest crowd was at the stalls selling rare old books. Whenever I write about writers like Ralph Thompson, La Fontaine, La Rochefoucauld and Burton, my readers have always asked me, "Where can we read their books?" These frequent queries keep coming regarding books about wildlife. I think these readers too require a periodical.

Compelling translations of the best books in Indian and foreign languages are not available to us easily. I'm very eager to read the fresh literature coming out in languages like Kannada, Telugu, Assamese, Bengali, etc., but I don't remember spotting good translations of these even in the big bookstores. We, in fact, must measure our literary prowess based on how much of our literature is accessible in foreign languages and how much of theirs we make available in our own.

The gushing streams of cultural dissemination which bring the best literature to our doorstep are Akashvani and Doordarshan. Because of them, writers, orators, actors and singers come to your home to meet you. I have experienced the tremendous response which a five-minute-long show like "Chintan" received from the audiences.

Once, a listener asked me, "Why do you do this show for only five minutes? Why don't you increase the duration to fifteen minutes?"

I said, "This is like demanding homeopathic pills the size of *besan laddoos.*"

I heard loud laughter of agreement in response.

We have seen an extremely good adaptation of Dickens's novel Nicholas Nickleby on BBC. Can we not adapt the best of our own novels thus and reach out to our audiences?

I'd gone to Australia and observed the working of small radio stations in little villages. It's been twenty-five years since that experience, and something like that is yet to start in our country. Just like local newspapers, those little radio stations echo the culture of that region. The Australians are extremely fond of these local radio broadcasts. Just as we feel ignorant if we don't read a newspaper, they feel the same when they do not listen to their morning radio broadcast. They get to know the daily weather report, market prices, water levels in the river, information important for agriculturists and the important headlines. They even come to know if someone has caught a big fish in town! They get to hear talks by visitors from outside. These radio stations are committed to be of use to every single person working in the area.

There is a three-minute-long program called "Market to market." A colourful program showing shelves full of fruits and vegetables in the background and an anchor giving information about what is available in the market, their prices, etc. Women sit with a notebook and a pencil handy and have absolute faith in what the American presenter Bob Logan says.

Doordarshan does make an effort to be useful to people. Can it and Akashvani also show similar excitement about our own culture and literature? We have ushered in a new age of cassettes, and soon it shall move to videotaping. These platforms will at least help to publicise good literature among people.

I know very well that the prices of books have gone beyond our reach. Government regulation is the solution to that. They did it in Kerala. *Sahitya Sanskruti Mandal* can also chart out some strategies in this regard. Today, the *Mandal* gives grants to budding writers and helps them to get their books popularised. That has surely led to a rise in the number of popular books. However, the same cannot be said about the rise in the standard of writing.

I'm friends with a couple who both have jobs. They are employed in what can be called the 'cultural' sector. Yet they watch all the movies and plays which are released.

When asked, "How do you manage to do all of this?" they replied, "We set aside a fixed amount for this in our monthly budget so that we never miss a good play or a brilliant film."

"Do you also have a fixed budget to buy popular books?"

They were silent for a while. Then they said, "Buying books is not really affordable. So we either get them from the library or borrow them from readers like you."

I had once stayed in a small town named Grenoble in France for a few weeks. I'd visited over ten to twelve homes there, and each one of them had their own small libraries containing entire sets of books of some great writer. Some had Anatole France, some had Balzac, while some had Zola. They had entire volumes of Larousse and full-scape portraits by some fine painters like Renault, Lautrec and Rembrandt.

The children would gather around and ask inquisitively, "Which is your country?"

"India."

"City?"

"Pune, near Mumbai."

They would immediately look for an atlas and try to locate a city near Mumbai named Pune.

Now you tell me, where can we find the entire collected works of any Indian or Marathi writer, even in the most well-to-do homes? How many of our homes have cultural dictionaries or volumes of the Marathi *Shabd Ratnakar* glossary? Do we ever have paintings of famous painters in our homes? And if ever a foreign guest graces our homes, do our children ever seek out the atlas?

How, then, can we expect great writers, painters or sculptors to emerge from Maharashtra?

Is this too not a shameful sign of our destitution?

Just food, clothing, shelter is not enough to sustain a person. Even as cave dwellers, had we not painted all over the walls of those caves? Look at the Adivasis, who live in far greater poverty than us. They decorate the mud-plastered walls of their huts with beautiful drawings of plants and animals and dance with abandon to the beats of the drums.

When has anybody heard of money being able to quench the thirst of the soul?

We may be poor in wealth, but we shall remain rich in culture!

I saw a cultural centre named *Maison de la culture de Grenoble* in Grenoble. It was a memorial built in honour of Stendhal, the great novelist. The entire construction was done in black and copper colours only. Stendhal's most famous novel is called "The Red and the Black." Anybody could pay a sum of ten to twelve francs and become a member of the organisation. This humongous centre housed a well-equipped experimental theatre, a cinema theatre to screen art films, an art gallery for new artists to showcase their works, special booths for anybody who wanted to listen to recorded music in peace. It had a beautiful children's library where little pieces of soft foam of varied colours and shapes were embedded in the floor so that the kids could loll around as they read under the light of colourful circular lamps. There was also a designated space for exhibitions. Anybody could exhibit anything as per their imagination. If someone liked an artwork from the exhibition, they could rent it for a month, keep it in their home and then return it to take another one.

If we are to create castles in the air, then why should our castles not be like that Cultural Centre? And why should we not start fashioning stones to give it a form immediately?

I'm sure that there must be many readers in the audience today who can also become future writers – saplings with immense potential to grow into gigantic trees. I'd like to tell them always stay true to your own experiences and swear by your own penchant. Do not tread the trodden paths. Make your own path with your own journey. This earth is so huge that it has enough space for new roads. Do not strive to be like someone else, strive to know your own self. Nature casts only one mould to create luminaries, then breaks it upon their creation. No two trees are ever alike. Similarly, no two artists are alike. Do not chase success with haste. Do not play on the extremes. A vine bears fruit as soon as the season arrives. The same season can be closer or farther from you. Do not give too much importance to awards given either by the Government or private organisations. The praise accorded by your audiences is the greatest award. Don't get disheartened by the opinions of the critics. They too are readers, and that is only their view.

Are you all aware of the story "The Sculptor and his Sculpture"?

Once, a novice sculptor, after putting in years of hard work, created a sculpture – a beautiful sculpture – and he exhibited it for all the critics to see in a gallery. He wrote on the notice board – "Wherever you see a fault, please mark it with a pencil."

He even kept a few pencils nearby.

There was a long queue throughout the day.

Before closing the gallery, the sculptor excitedly looked at the sculpture. What did he see? The entire sculpture covered from head to toe in pencil marks.

The sculptor, thoroughly dejected, said to his friend, "I will never become a great sculptor. I don't know anything!"

His friend replied, "Let's have the exhibition again tomorrow. Only this time, we will write – please mark whatever you like about this sculpture."

The next day, the sculptor cleaned the statue and kept it for display in the gallery. Again, many critics came, and this time marked all that they liked about the statue.

Again the statue was covered in pencil marks.

The sculptor was finally convinced that he'd made a good statue.

After all, validation is like ink on water, not stone.

Whatever you want to write, write it in simple Marathi. Writing simply is the most difficult thing. Let the words come to you. There is a line in one of Tukaram's Marathi *abhang* –

Kai dinkara kelya kombdyane khara (Is the place of the Sun fixed by the rooster?)

The word 'khara' here does not mean true in the sense of *khara* and *khota*, true or false.

Khara karne means to fix and finalise something firmly. The sun has not been fixed in the sky by the crowing of the rooster. I think that Tukaram used the word '*khara*' in that sense.

Always keep your curiosity alive. Do not ever build any fences. Rousseau says, "When Man first built fences, he laid the foundation of his misery."

If you hold onto your dreams firmly, go ahead with confidence and display the courage to live the life you imagined, then you will not pass by even the ordinary instances of life without being credited by the masses.

PRESIDENTIAL ADDRESS AT THE 57TH ABMSS

Let me recite a few lines by the foremost revolutionary poet Keshavsut, who had, in a bold voice, made a declaration for every litterateur, on behalf of you and me –

Anywhere I go,
I only find my own brothers
everywhere I go
I find signs of my own home
go wherever you want
you find the same Earth full of grass beneath your feet
the same blue skies over your head
the same cute children wherever you go
And the same sweet flowers lounging in the sun
My mind dances with delight
They are all mine and I am theirs
It is the same brook that flows through us

Source

Translated from the Marathi, *Pravas Ek Lekhakacha*, 4th ed., 2012, Pune, Mehta Publishing.

14

A CONVERSATION WITH VYANKATESH MADGULKAR

Vidyadhar Pundalik
Translated by Meera Marathe

VP: Vyankatesh, at the outset, heartfelt congratulations.
VM: Thank you.
VP: Who was the first person you thought of when you learnt that you were elected President of the Marathi Sahitya Sammelan at Ambejogai?
VM: Naturally, I thought of Anna, my older brother, and also my mother. I would have been very happy had they been present to hear and see this honour bestowed on me.
VP: No doubt their *shabaaski*, the pat on the back, would have pleased you. But one doesn't get everything one wants, isn't it? You just mentioned your mother. After reading your books, especially *Karunashtak*, one realizes that the deepest and most significant influence on you was your mother.
VM: You are absolutely right! Whatever impressions were formed on my mind in childhood were due to my mother. She gave me my first glimpse of the world so I might learn everything I know. Later on I became an artist. You know that. The foundation of my art lessons were, in a way, were laid by her.
VP: The impression one gets of your father from *Karunashtak* is that of a God-fearing, principled and honest man. On the other hand, your mother suffered the harsh realities of life, she recognized and acknowledged them. It seems today that, unwittingly, she made you vicariously experience those truths, that reality.
VM: You are right.
VP: You are here in the highly respected chair of the President of the Marathi Sahitya Sammelan. It seems as if you have trudged over the vast arid plains of Madgul, trod across the concrete jungles of Pune-Mumbai to finally reach here! Behind all this is a roaring furnace of experience. That furnace was ignited in Madgul, can we say? From reading your literary works, one realises that you didn't live in an exclusively Brahmin locality. There was a Ramoshi wada next to

your house. There were other castes in the neighbourhood. Did their proximity influence your writing in any way?

VM: Madgul is a small village. You will have to search for it on a map or in the Gazette. In a population of about twelve hundred people, there were a handful of Brahmin homes. Those too were scattered. By Madgul's standards, our house was a wada, a mansion! Behind ours was Patil's wada. To our right lived a gentleman called Karande. He was a Kunbi, of the trader caste. In front was a kasar, glass bangle maker. To the left was a Ramoshi's house. It was just four or five yards away from ours. His children were my playmates.

VP: Were you proud of being a Brahmin from the Kulkarni, the town clerk's family? Can one say that the picture you painted of the life that you saw was from an upper-caste perspective?

VM: There was no reason for that to happen because it was with those children that I went to graze goats and cattle in the forest. I went to the fields with them. Went hunting with them! I remember an incident from my childhood.

One day I rushed into our house, took a *bhakri* from the covered basket, put some chutney on it, poured a little oil into the chutney, then holding the *bhakri* in my hand, I squatted like a bird and started eating. Bitta kaka, my father's brother, saw me and yelled at me. He then said to my mother, "Vahini, this rascal goes to the Rāmoshis' houses and has learnt to eat like them." Meaning that *we* (Brahmins) ate off a plate, which apparently I had forgotten!

VP: I find this anecdote very telling. One can see that the arrogance of the upper caste had not even touched you in your childhood.

VM: It probably hadn't. Do you see any sign of it in my speech or behaviour, Pundalik?

VP: Not at all! A noticeable feature of all your writing is the variety of your characters. They come from different castes and diverse professions – Mussalmans, *teli-tambolis* (oil sellers and betel-leaf vendors), *nhavis* (barbers), *sutars* and *chamars* (carpenters and cobblers), Mahars, Mangs . . . !

VM: I have seen all these people. They are an integral part of village life and society. Hamid Dalwai once said to me, "Madgulkar, I read Marathi literature very closely and I have observed that there are far more Muslim characters in your writing than in anyone else's." Characters like Hamza and Eibu from *Bangarwadi*, and Babajan Darveshi from *Mandeshi Manasa*, they are all ordinary people, very much a part of rural society.

VP: Were you motivated to write from a very young age? Were you fond of reading when you were young?

VM: Yes, from a very young age! I was about eight or nine when we moved to Kinhai. We lived in a rented house that belonged to a man called

Havaldar. You know how curious children are . . . they want to find out what the previous occupants of the house have left behind. So they search all nooks, lofts and attics.

Now Father had sternly warned us not to go upstairs. But I was exploring the house, and I chanced upon a huge trunk. It had been sealed tight with metal strips across it. Slowly but painstakingly I prised open the strips and peeked inside. It was filled with books! Old books exude a peculiar odour which I smelt there. I said to myself, I must take the books out and look at them. What was in the trunk, you think? Novels of Hari Narayan Apte, Nath Madhav, Hatim Tai, books about the secret lives of the London elite, *Hitopadesa*, *Panchatantra*, among others. What a treasure I had found! For the first time I discovered the pleasures of that activity called reading.

VP: How old were you then?

VM: About eight or nine, I think. You know Pundalik, I believe that every young reader is a potential writer and every young mimic a potential actor.

VP: You're so right. Now tell me Vyankatesh, when did you come across S. M. Mate's work?

VM: When I went to the English school. We started learning English in the 7th class, I read his *Manuski cha Gahivar* and *Upekshitanche Antarang*. And I thought, "How beautifully he writes. I know this life. I know these people. I have seen them." These books made a lasting impression on me.

And then Bansidhar! Sitting by himself beside a stream. A dog lying at his feet. His natural parents have abandoned him and his foster parents have been nabbed by the police. That's how Bansidhar came to sit all alone by the stream.

Mate asks him, "Arrey Bansidhara, where will you go now, child?"

That's when it occurred to me that I could also write about an orphan like Bansidhar. Mate showed me the way, I think. I felt he was saying, "Look people, these are also paths. They also take you forward!"

VP: At this point, I remember Gogol's story *Overcoat*. It is considered a path-breaking story in Russian.

VM: Yes, he was the first one to write about the middle classes. Until then Russian literature was all about the affluent and the aristocrats. I recall Turgenev's remark, We all have come out of Gogol's *Overcoat*. Similarly, I feel we have all sprung from Bansidhar's Kathkari camp.

VP: I am reminded of a sentence from your novel *Bangarwadi* – "Those persons stepped out to find a life." I feel you also stepped out of the Ramoshi base in order to write.

VM: Yes.

A CONVERSATION WITH VYANKATESH MADGULKAR

VP: And that's how your travels began! When I think of Mate, I feel he was deeply concerned about the upliftment of the people of the oppressed castes. He felt a moral obligation to help in their advancement. You know that. Mate wished to see Tarkholkar's Pirya, Satya Rāmoshi and all grow up and do well. When the street-sweepers in Mumbai were given long-handled brooms, Mate was thrilled. They could now sweep with their backs erect. You think you also have a similar impulse?

VM: This thought does come to mind.

VP: So you turned to what we call ordinary humanity and chose them as your protagonists rather than well-placed or important people? You always had ordinary people in your sight. Could we say you tried to capture their alienation in your narratives?

VM: You are absolutely right, Pundalik. I have always felt that a huge, undivided, homogenous society offers an invitation to a novelist, and a novel is born. The realm of a novel is vast. Like a full orchestra. A short story is like a solo instrumentalist. It projects the plight of a single individual, his predicament, his world view. Where in India do we have what we call a '*samaj*', or 'society'?

A society split into castes and sub-castes, sects and divisions with innumerable differences, where the common man is left with feelings of isolation. "If I am in trouble, no one comes forward to help. Then what is to become of me?" he thinks. When this kind of loneliness is woven into its fabric, the short story flourishes and tells us the sad predicament of the lonely man.

You are a professor of Sociology. I am an observer. Do look at what I see and think about it. In Ireland the excellent short story was born. England and Russia gave birth to major novels. It seems that the short story form has caught on strongly in India. We can perhaps call it our National Literary Form. I read an excellent Italian short story translated by Mardhekar. It was called *Abhivachane* by Grazia Deledda. It is the story of a washerwoman. Whenever her children asked for food, she made them suck on the twists of the washed and wrung-out clothes! Her employers had a talking parrot. The children always asked her, "When will *we* get a parrot like that?" And she would reply, "We will, little ones, we will." But they never did.

I said to Mardhekar, "I want to read this writer. Where can I find him?"

He answered after a while, "Vyankatesh! How will you read him? I have adapted the story from the original Italian. There is no English translation."

VP: The poverty among the Italian and Jewish societies is the common thread that links our society to theirs. That's why their literature touches us.

VM: Even if their circumstances are straitened, they are rich in experience. That richness of experience is very useful for a writer.

VP: A question comes to mind. You too have written stories of immense suffering. Not that you haven't. Stories like *Aadit, Deva Satva Mahar, Gode Pani,* for example. All individual suffering cannot be linked to society's suffering. Man's life is so strangely twisted and tangled that everything isn't attributable to or dependent on society. Not all men's roots reach there. Some griefs do remain very personal. For instance, your story, *Bitta Kaka.* When this character sketch was published, you quoted a sentence from Dostoevsky as the epigraph . . .

VM: I am not bowing before you, I am bowing before the entire suffering humanity, or something to that effect.

VP: Actually, even when you write about persons close to you, you remain unbiased. Writing about people close to you poses a real challenge for a writer. But that is another subject.

So Vyankatesh, when did you become so obsessed with English and European literature?

VM: In 1947 or 1948, I went to Bombay. I was writing *Mandeshi Manasa.* I met some excellent editors and good publishers there. I also made many writer friends. Gangadhar Gadgil was one of them. He told me, "Madgulkar, you must read English literature because there are many writers there who write like you." I did that. From him I got books by the American authors, Steinbeck and Caldwell, also books by Gorky, especially his *My Childhood.* I read them painstakingly, and I felt, Oho, this is so *good*! And I continued reading voraciously. From then on, I read many English books. I feel that reading English is essential for a writer.

VP: It is noteworthy that you have written stories about extremely sly and deceitful characters. Is it because you are essentially a writer from the oral tradition? Did these stories arise from that? Were they born out of the chatter you heard at the village *chavdi*, or the *pars*, under the tree where the conversation revolved around the community and its experiences?

VM: Pundalik, if you look at the Marathi word we use for the English phrase 'well-read,' we say '*bahushrut*,' meaning well-heard. We all have learnt by hearing and listening. It's an ancient practice.

VP: We city dwellers too had something like an oral tradition of our own. That you turned to the literary tradition, meaning the written form, and yet maintained a balance between the written and the oral is commendable.

Very well . . . So far we have talked about your short stories. Now do tell us about your '*chitrakatha*,' the picture story.

VM: The *Chitrakatha* has a kinship with film. It is about an impressionable youth who is crazy about films but changes his path and becomes a writer. Why he gives up that path and how he turns to writing is its theme. The subject of the novel *Kovale Divas* is similar. A young, innocent lad who is obsessed with drawing and painting comes across many heart-rending experiences – birth, death, hunger, starvation and many more – that he feels he will not be able to describe in lines and colours. For that I must turn to words. I must write, he thinks. Pundalik, one very suggestive sentence appears towards the end of the novel, "Did you understand why I didn't become an artist, why I became a writer?" That question was on my mind too.

VP: Do you sometimes feel regretful that you took the path of words instead of the path of line and colour?

VM: No, not at all. Both give me great pleasure. I just feel that people who use colour and lines *own* their medium. Whereas I must use the same words when I speak to the vegetable seller, "What is the price?" "How much money totally?" as I would use in all social interaction. Language is the only medium for polite give and take and all social communication.

Art is not like that. An artist can choose his colours and decide how to use them to establish his individuality, and he does it with ease. But a writer has to work very hard to achieve it. He must choose his words and sentence structures very carefully. And that is difficult, I think.

VP: Do you think the descriptive power of your words, their precise quality, are influenced, knowingly or unknowingly, by your lines and colours?

VM: 'Descriptive words' means those that are required to present before you the subject in hand, isn't it? Yes, that's right. Because I kept hearing folk songs, folk music and other folk art forms, I became fond of words. From a very young age, I became aware of sound patterns and rhythms. I felt I ought to use that awareness, and it must have influenced my language. I learnt language from those people just as I learnt it from my mother. Our father was an excellent storyteller. I learnt how to tell a good story from him. But I also learnt from folk literature.

VP: Now I'll ask you a little about drama. I liked your play *Sati* very much. It felt as though, instead of just presenting reality here, you have created something new. Giving a form to reality is very much part of art. But it can become a wholly imaginative reconstruction. From that point of view, I felt *Sati* was a very moving play. But how deeply engaged were you with drama?

VM: Not much. The reason being that a play is not yours alone. It is dependent on many persons.

VP: It is indeed a collective, cooperative art form.

VM: That's why if it fails, one feels bad. If a novel fails, I say to myself, "*You* erred, so what can you do about it?" With a play, one can say, "This person made a mistake, that one failed, that's why it was ruined. It wasn't my fault." I felt that as a medium, it was too dependent on others, so I didn't get much involved. I did write four or five plays, then said to myself, Let's see what happens. If it works, fine; I'll go ahead, if not . . .

VP: What about films?

VM: It's the same with films. In fact, a film is even more dependent on other people. The cameraman alone can make a mess of everything. One's ideas can get totally distorted on the screen. Besides, it is far more commercial than a play. Where everything is commercial, one has to say everything in one thousand words to make a point. It has to sell after all!

VP: So do you say that literature is your "retreating corner" then!? Nothing more wonderful than writing?

VM: There is no alternative to writing.

VP: Here we must talk of *Bangarwadi*. Many people liked the novel very much. It made waves everywhere. In fact, Baba Pathak, one of your friends, says, "If in Ambejogai there is a procession with a palanquin for Madgulkar, there must be a few sheep in it too!" Yet your effort to depict this picture of a small village against a large backdrop was criticised by Gangadhar Gadgil sometime ago. Comparing Steinbeck's *Grapes of Wrath* to *Bangarwadi*, he had declared that the kind of large-scale devastation of life that took place in *Grapes of Wrath* didn't happen in *Bangarwadi*. What was your reaction to the criticism then, and how do you feel about it now?

VM: The devastation wasn't on the same scale, that is true. But I wonder if everything depends on whether the background is vast or limited! The real importance lies in its depiction of life – how authentic it is and how intense.

VP: I think that this kind of devastated village comes to us in a different form. For centuries the practice has been going on. Whenever there is a drought, the villagers temporarily migrate. But then they come back to re-settle. The bonds with the village remain ever strong. So do our villages ever get destroyed from their roots, are they uprooted?

VM: More thought must be given to this. American culture is not as old as ours. Thousands of years of tradition does not flow through their blood. Therefore, when they leave one place for another, they feel the same sadness that we feel when we move from one flat to another. But when we leave our villages, our links with our past, our traditions are broken.

VP: Some people say that it is the present we are bound to. With all the current developments around us, village life is changing. "We do not see this change reflected in Madgulkar's writing," they complain. What do you say to them?

VM: I'll say, "So what?" You don't see the changing life . . . that's okay. But what is the purpose of literature? Does my writing give you pleasure or not? Do you think it is excellent writing or not? When you look at literature like that, do you feel that you don't get a picture of 'yesterday' in it? Is it a page of a newspaper that it must carry today that which happened yesterday?

VP: Another thing that occurs to me is that what is understood as changing becomes static after a while. Change is the only constant. If reality, like life, flows, has movement, as time passes, it too becomes frozen.

VM: Exactly. It is inevitable. Whatever there is must be seen as an independent consequence of itself.

VP: There is another point here. You don't look at rural life as nostalgia, a convenient escape into the past. Anyway, Vyankatesh, let's turn to Nature. The Nature that peeps out of all your writing. It seems to me that there are two stages in your writing. After a particular period, you turned to Nature. Was it a subtle desire to get away from the barren, infertile land around your native Madgul that prompted you to seek refuge in the dense jungle?

VM: No. Nature doesn't necessarily have to be green. Nor does nature mean leaves and flowers and nothing more. The sparse grass in the barren land is nature too. The insects, the *tuntune*, the ants and grasshoppers, the creatures that crawl, they are nature too. Nature has been a part of my consciousness right from the beginning. If you look at a story from my early work, it's about a dog with a black face (*Kalya Tondachi*). It narrates the sadness in a dog's life. *Ekta is* also about a dog. I have written about two donkeys in *Hastacha Paus*. You will find many stories concerning animal life. You will notice that I deal with animal life and human life in the context of their relationship to each other. There is so much of what we call flora and fauna in *Bangarwadi*. It could be the subject of an independent study, "Plant life, animal life and birds of *Bangarwadi*" . . . From the beginning I have focussed on nature. Today perhaps there is greater description of scenery, more effectively embodied. But nature has always been there.

VP: I want to understand this bond that you have forged with nature.

VM: We think of Man as part of society. But I think he is one of the inhabitants of nature. Like a tree or a deer. I too am an inseparable part of this system. I emphasise that. Because I believe that I am not different from nature, the bond is easily established.

VP: Let me ask you then, doesn't the cruel, blind aspect of nature sometimes disturb you?

VM: No! If we look at it from a sensible perspective, nature to me appears as pure innocence. I don't see cruelty and all that in her. A tree that sprouted so easily today dies after a few years, making place for new grass and more trees. The earth doesn't keep mourning its loss. This is a pattern, a cycle. The old must go, and the new must come. I don't

	think we should label nature as cruel. What there is, we must accept with fortitude.
VP:	Finally, human society and nature are all classes of the one reality, and we must be aware of that.
VM:	Right. Nature is an inseparable part of ourselves.
VP:	Do you want to say that we must learn how to enjoy our physical existence?
VM:	Of course. Whatever be our life, we must not have contempt for it.
VP:	I am puzzled by something: you were known as a *shikari*, a hunter. Is there any difference between the attitude of a *shikari* and a *sant*, a hunter and a saint, towards nature?
VM:	All the men from our great culture were hunters in the beginning. Hunters and gatherers. So naturally, some of that hunting instinct flows in our blood! Of course, I gave up hunting quite early when I realised that hunting hurts what I call the innocence of nature. Now I go into the jungle with a black ink fountain pen and a white sketch pad and draw pictures. I don't even carry a weapon for protection.
VP:	There is no nature in the great writer Dostoevsky's novels at all. I always wondered why. In one place, he says, "Well! When I look at Nature I feel Man is solitary." You never felt that way?
VM:	No, never!
VP:	Now, the final but mandatory question: What are your plans for the future? After this Sammelan, what?
VM:	The *sammelan* is a festival of language. It is for the lovers and followers of literature. New and fresh creations take birth in literature. And a celebratory toran of these creations is strung here. It is a joyous occasion. We should forget all differences and prejudices and come together to give joy and pleasure to the devotees and lovers of literature. If we don't do that, I think we writers and litterateurs have failed in our duty.

You asked about my future plans. Even when I am at home, I always have one foot out of the door! Whenever I feel like going out, I go. I've recently returned from Rajasthan after roaming extensively in the desert. I have been thinking about it. I have drawn many pictures, made many notes. An English title also came to mind – "The Portrait of a Desert." Once I am free after the *Sammelan*, I will get down to writing it.

Courtesy of All India Radio, Pune

Source

Translated from the Marathi, *Sammelan Adhyaksha Vyankatesh Madgulkar Yanchi Mulakaat*, Vyankatesh Madgulkar, Lekhak Ani Manus, Dnyanada Naik ed., 2010, Pune, Anubandh Prakashan.

15

MY LIFE AS A HUNTER

Vyankatesh Madgulkar
Translated by Sachin Ketkar and Punit Pathak

I am a man given to whimsical diversions. I love to pick up and pursue uncommon hobbies. Where on the earth did I pick up such a trait? No one in my family – I have seven siblings – seems to have it. It doesn't seem to be hereditary at all.

Hunting as a hobby is considered to be a fairly expensive affair, and rightly so. It is meant for rich people, nobles and royals. Or it is considered appropriate for nomadic communities like the Vaidus, Phashe Pardhis, Ramoshis and others like them. There is a saying in Marathi – "*'Shikar'* Ani *'Bhikaar'*" – Hunting and begging go together. I was not born in any of these communities. I am not a hunter by birth, but by my acts, my *karma*. Out of curiosity, I once had a look at the page allotted to my fate in the *Brighu Samhita*. It read, "Though this child is born in a Brahmin family, he will eat meat and drink alcohol. He was a Kshatriya in the previous birth. He ended up killing a deer that belonged to a Rishi and was cursed that even if he is born in a Brahmin's family he won't be able to perform a Brahmin's duties. He will carry out violent deeds" (The *Brugu Samhita*: p. 154 and 92). So *satvai*, the local goddess who decides a child's fate, has spelled out that I will be a hunter.

Now, apart from this, what were the external influences responsible for such a quirky habit?

Though I was born in a middle class family, our financial condition was such that we could be considered as belonging to 'an economically backward class'. Our small village, with a population of around eighteen hundred inhabitants, was under a princely state. There was a Ramoshi settlement near our village. The Ramoshis are basically Adivasis, but instead of living in the forests or hills, they live in villages. They love to hunt using small axes, bows and arrows and slings. One such Ramoshi, who wrapped a *dhoti* around his waist but wore nothing on his upper body, hunted pigeons, small birds and animals with his slings and arrows, was my hero. He also had a rather old gun which he would use to kill deer in the jungle. He would use all sorts of clever tricks to get the deer within firing range, like tie palm fronds around his head and crawl on the ground for several yards!

DOI: 10.4324/9781003159315-18

My childhood companions were the Ramoshi kids Ishwara, Gonda and Bapu, the Muslim boys Akbarya and Abdullya, Lakhu the Mahar and Martandya, a Mang. Their daily occupation was taking cattle and sheep to graze in the wilderness and roam around. I used to follow them. Once the cattle and sheep were busy grazing, they would go off to do all sorts of things like hunting pheasants and other birds in the thorny shrubs, shoving their hands into holes in the trees looking for baby parrots, bringing down honeycombs, trapping monitor lizards or simply catching fish using their *dhotis* as a net. I used to happily join them in their activities. In the arid parts of Mandesh, there were no jungles or hills but only long wild, open stretches. The grazing land of Dabai was nearby. Some distance from there, in a place called Lotewadi, there was a grassland that belonged to the Maharaja of Satara. Wolves, land crabs and iguanas were found in the wilderness, and rabbits and deer lived in the grassland. There used to be all kinds of pheasants, doves and pigeons there those days.

There was also a tradition of the entire village going on a hunt on some special days. It would take place in the early monsoon, the day after the Bendur festival, which was to honour bullocks, and also on the day after Naag Panchami, the snake festival. Taking stale *bhakris*, leftovers from the previous day, the villagers would go to the grasslands of Dabai or Lotewadi, and we kids would tag along behind them. The grown-ups, accompanied by their hunting dogs, usually carried sticks, axes and spears with them. For us children, it was more of a picnic than a hunting expedition. It was a commotion of dogs and village folk for the whole day in the grasslands. They would be yelling and flinging stones in the grass. The uproar would wake up a deer or a rabbit, and people would be shouting, "there it goes, here it comes" and chase them with spears, sticks and hunting dogs. There would be people from other villages too in the same part of the grassland. Invariably, there would be quarrels and complaints, wrangles and grievances.

Continuous walking and hot blowing winds would burn us, and our faces would turn dark, and our legs would hurt. Thorns would prick our bare feet. We would sit down on a mound or elevated place and watch the game because the adults would have warned us against interfering in the hunt. When we got bored of sitting around, we would go off looking for forest fruit like wild berries and jamuns, or go looking for a rivulet, or eat the food we had brought from our homes and then lie down in the shade of the trees.

The villagers would occasionally get a deer or a couple of rabbits or, at times, a wolf or a fox. They would tie their spoils to a stick, and by the time they returned hungry and exhausted to their village, it would be late evening. When the procession reached the outskirts of the village, a message would go out to cattle-herders and music players. They would come and play traditional drums and instruments, and the procession would enter the village in pomp and festivity.

Portions of the hunt would be sent to the landlords, and the message would be conveyed to the village *kulkarnis* (accountants) and *joshis* (astrologers). Anna, my father, would hastily put his turban on and ask the messenger, "What did you get this time?"

"We got a deer this time."

"Great job! *Shabbas*!"

Of course, the portion meant for the eight Brahmin families, like the Kulkarnis and the Joshis, would go to the Ramoshis.

The tail of the hunted animal would be hung on the *neem* tree in the village assembly for people to see, and it would swing around in the wind and get wet in the monsoon showers. After some time, it would get frayed, and only the thread would be hanging there. The chatter around the hunting event would die down soon, and the villagers would get back to their routine drudgery in the fields.

My love for hunting began with such annual festivals. The nearby wilderness, rivulets and wooded areas would be wide open for us kids all the time anyway, and even if the hunting festivals were over and forgotten, we would be doing it for the whole year.

Apart from the annual hunting festivals, there would be many such celebrations in the year. Nomadic tribal communities like Phase Pardhis, Nandiwales, Beldars, Tattes, Gadhves and their families would come down to our village during the harvest season and settle down on the plains near the wilds and streams.

The Vaidus owned dogs which were branded and had no tails. They would let them loose to hunt for wild cats in the cacti, or the mongoose, creating a hullaballoo.

The Phase Pardhis would beg in the village and set up *fase* (snares) for catching birds in the nearby wilds. When Medvarya, a Phase Pardhi, set out with his snares, I would follow him. I thus got first-hand experience of how a Phase Pardhi sets a trap for partridges and then blows the whistle hanging round his neck in a particular manner so that the bird would feel someone was challenging it. It would get curious and start approaching the snare. Medarya would hide behind his cow that would be grazing nearby and cleverly close in. He would also throw small pebbles at it to bring it close to the bird-trap.

The Beldars would find a proper tree near the rivulet and tie their net underneath it to trap squirrels. They would summon the squirrels by making squirrel-like sounds with their mouths. The poor squirrels would be trapped in the net and, in the evening, find themselves being roasted on the three-stone-stoves out in the open.

By accompanying the Ramoshis and the nomadic tribes, I learnt how to hunt for the squirrels in the trees, wildcats and mongoose in the cacti, foxes near the grasslands, partridges near the rivulets, monitor lizards and bustards near the wet regions, herons and other birds during the harvest seasons and gained practical knowledge of the forest.

I clearly recall, it was my dream to own a gun, binoculars and a camera right from my childhood. I used to fantasize about what all I could do if I had them.

Later, when I grew up a bit and started earning a little, I bought a very good gun for myself. I was in my early twenties. I distinctly remember handing over a book to R. R. Kothawale, the editor of Lalit magazine, for publication and raising one-fourth of the price of the gun from it. I did not have to wait for long to own a camera. However, I had to cross the fiftieth year of my life to buy a pair of binoculars.

I used the gun from 1952 to 1970. I did not become an expert hunter or even undertake great hunting expeditions. But I had as much of a good time with my hobby as was possible for a lowly paid government servant and enjoyed wandering in the forest and in the wilderness. I have written about these experiences several times. You can find them in my book *Waghachya Magavar* as well as in my other short story collections.

One evening I was returning from Budhyaal Lake in a bullock cart. As soon as we left Chopadi village, I saw two dark cranes in the groundnut field. They had long curved beaks, red feet, white spots on their shoulders and a red triangular spot on their heads. The crane couple was busy pecking the groundnuts. We were travelling on the red lane surrounded by fields.

Two Ramoshi boys who were accompanying me in the cart said, "Tatya, two cranes are within our range, would you like to shoot them?" I fired a shot from where I was sitting in the cart, and the male crane fell down, fluttered for a while and turned still. The gunshot had scared the female away, but she kept circling the place and crying out loud as if asking, "Why did he fall down, and why doesn't he get up? Why doesn't he respond to me?"

She came down very close to her mate's body and kept screaming and going round in circles.

As soon as the Ramoshi boys saw that the male was no longer moving, they ran and dragged the dead bird into the cart by its feet. The female kept crying out and circling in the blue sky, then perched on top of a tamarind tree and became quiet and lonely.

I felt miserable.

One evening I had gone out towards the Mulshi Dam in a Jeep because I had learnt about rabbits coming out at night. As I was driving, a barking deer crossed my path, climbed up the nearby hill, halted and turned around to look at me.

Within seconds I fired a shot. My friend Nimbalkar, who owned orchards and gardens, was accompanying me in the Jeep. He stepped out and brought the deer with him and said, "What a pity, this deer is pregnant!"

When we were skinning the deer at two in the night in Nimbalkar's garden, a fully grown baby came out of it. Nimbalkar's old mother was agonized, and she said, "Boys, why do you invite a curse by doing such things?"

I can narrate a string of such episodes. But you cannot say that this led to me dropping my gun and picking up my binoculars. It happened on its own as I grew up mentally. Except for the reason of being an immature youth, can any good person kill a wild animal that had the right to remain alive?

I wandered in the Sinhagad forest with my close friend Jayantrao Tilak. I wandered the forest near the Mulshi dam. I wandered on the mountains near Pune, the Daddi valley, Kondankeri, Gunjavati in Karnataka, I hunted in the reserved forests of Masoor. But most importantly, I experienced the forests deeply. I learnt to read some letters in the unbound book of Nature.

After acquiring this literacy, the pleasure I used to get in killing animals and birds dropped away. The curiosity and love that I had for them stayed. Instead of the gun, now I found greater delight in carrying binoculars and a sketchbook. I think all civilized hunters grow up in stages like this. Now I can swear that the sight of a herd of musk deer does not even remind me of the gun that is hanging on the wall of my house.

I don't want to be a naturalist or zoologist. I don't want to study forestry. But I have tremendous curiosity and eagerness to understand this great world of nature, and it will never end. These days I have thoughts of pursuing it and becoming a forest hermit.

Source

Excerpt translated from the Marathi, *Maza Shikaricha Chhanda* (pp. 49–54), Chitre Ani Charitre, January 1983, Pune, Mehta Publishing House.

16

VYANKATESH MADGULKAR'S WORK IN THE WORLD OF ART, WRITING ON ART, AND HIS ART

Vasant Sarawate
Translated by Wandana Sonalkar

In this essay, I will take a look at Vyankatesh Madgulkar's overall work in art, his writing on art, the art works themselves, and his creative writing.

While I have no problem with his writing on art, I have some reservations regarding his art works. One would have to look at all his art works, those which were published in his books as well as those which he made for his own pleasure. I know about them but have seen very few. So I will consider only those of his works which are available in printed, published form. The works that I have decided to leave out include naturescapes, portraits and, more importantly, works done in colour. His published art works are, with a few exceptions, drawings done in black ink. They accompany his own writings, and his role as an artist may be viewed as secondary here. But such drawings also give scope for an artist's creative powers, and both the writer and the illustrator may be considered as playing equal roles. James Thurber in the West and Prakash Sant in India are examples of this.

Before we look at Madgulkar's art, it will be worthwhile to consider how he was shaped as an artist. Madgulkar wanted to become an artist even as a child. He must have displayed some innate talent, he tells us, because his mother saw it and kindled a liking for drawing in him. She used to draw pictures of cobras, the chariot of the sun on the white-washed walls and fashion clay bullocks and wheat flour lamps to commemorate various religious festivals. These paintings, Madgulkar says, fascinated him. Because of his innate vision, those shapes, lines and colours remained with him even in adulthood. His inborn talent for drawing was recognised by his mother and noted by Kalal, his drawing teacher. Madgulkar's first earning came from art. From painting milestones on roadsides! He enrolled himself in the Dalvi Art Institute as a means of earning a livelihood at the time when he joined the Freedom Movement. His first proper job was as an artist for *Kirloskar* magazine. Until he was eighteen or nineteen, Madgulkar had not considered any career option except that of an artist. And had that one unexpected event not taken place, he would have settled down in the *Kirloskar* job. Or at least continued as a professional artist.

With this background, it is puzzling why, at a certain stage in life, he abandoned the calling of an artist and turned to writing. Once he took to this new path, he continued to write prolifically, for over fifty years. During this time, he produced literature of high quality and earned all kinds of honours. There is no doubt he achieved success as a writer in every sense. When asked, "How did you turn to writing when you had an inclination towards art and no small degree of skill as an artist?" he replied, "I was going through a highly emotionally charged phase of my life then, and I needed to give vent to my feelings. The medium of visual art was inadequate for that, I felt, so I turned to words and writing."

But then the question arises, what happened to the artist? Where did the innate talent disappear? Madgulkar's answer was that his love for art did not diminish even when he was writing prolifically. Art was still his first love. "I had a dream," he writes, "that I should have a beautiful tiled house. It should have a study with large glass windows. And I would stand in it for hours, wearing a white smock, painting on a canvas. But dreams remain dreams, and that is why they do not fade. Even now I draw sketches from time to time. There is nothing to compare with painting and drawing to lose oneself in." (*Chitre Ani Charitre*, "Pictures and Portraits," pp. 122–123).

In the tumult of living and his other pre-occupations, the love of art which lay buried deep in Madgulkar's mind was rekindled in 1969–1970, when he had the opportunity to visit France. He visited every museum and saw the original works of world-famous artists . . . the sculptures of Rodin, the paintings of Van Gogh, Gauguin, Lautrec, Matisse, Braque, Picasso and others and lost himself in them. In his own words, "I felt like those students of Alauddin Khan Saheb who, when they listened to their *guruji* playing the sitar, felt that God had come to them!"

But even though he fell under the spell of so many world-renowned artists, it was Vincent van Gogh who left a lasting impression on him. Not just because of his art but because of his overall personality. He was thrilled to tread the same ground that Van Gogh had. Just as a pilgrim visiting Pandharpur takes home a handful of soil, in the same spirit did Madgulkar bring back with him art materials purchased in Arles, France!

When Madgulkar stood in the cemetery at Auvers-sur-Oise, where the graves of Vincent van Gogh and his brother Theo lay side by side, he was so overwhelmed that he did something he had not done for many years. He brought out his pen and pad and made a sketch of the graves. And he had a moment of epiphany. The power of the line, which he had neglected for so long, had not left him. Suddenly, unexpectedly, a doorway opened out onto a vast realm before him. After that, throughout his travels, he continued to sketch and draw. He did not stop even after he returned to his homeland.

Many of the drawings that appear in his books were made after this revelation. I wonder about this emotional closeness Madgulkar felt with Van Gogh. For every painting of Van Gogh's is the expression of intense emotion. All his life, Van Gogh struggled to give expression to his repressed feelings through his painting. When he found that traditional styles were inadequate, he developed his own unique style. He found his own lines, his own method of applying paint to canvas. And through his non-conventional use of colours and brush strokes, he made not just people but inanimate objects like shoes, chairs, fruit and sunflowers come alive. Nature, as depicted in his paintings, is not merely beautiful. It gives us a vision of life and death.

Madgulkar has seen all this, given it deep thought. It has imprinted itself on his mind. So much so that when he describes a melancholy evening that disturbs the senses, he has a painting of Van Gogh before his eyes. He writes, "The setting sun is sinking below the horizon . . . the sky is darkening . . . over the yellow corn fields a flock of crows is soaring towards the sky." This description brings to mind Van Gogh's painting, "Wheatfield with Crows." Madgulkar follows his description by expressing the emotions depicted in the painting, "As this feeling intensifies, the mind returns again and again to past times, like cattle kicking up dust as they are drawn towards home." (*Kovale Divas*, p. 21).

If he feels thus, then why did he find visual art inadequate to express himself? The answer lies, perhaps, in the time and place when Madgulkar made the choice of turning to writing. It was 1948. In Kolhapur. There were many artists there at the time, and the atmosphere was stimulating for art. But art was seen more as a skill. Artists were judged by how faithfully they reproduced in their pictures exactly what the eye saw. That is why most painters chose landscapes for their subject, and occasionally portraits. I don't remember anyone at that time being aware that an artist has something to say through his painting or that a picture has anything to do with the artist's sensibility. Except for an extremely limited group in Bombay, this was the general understanding of art in Marathi society. I do not know if Madgulkar had seen the paintings of Van Gogh or any other modern western artist at that time. But even if he had, it is doubtful if he would have considered art as a means of livelihood. Making drawings or caricatures for the commercial elite of the Mahadwar area of Kolhapur city would hardly have enthused him.

If this was the discouraging prospect for art in Kolhapur, things were very different in the literary world. The '*nav katha*', the new short story, was making an appearance. Writers who were leaving well-trodden paths to discover new avenues were being noticed. They were receiving applause from discerning readers. In such a situation, it is not surprising that someone like Madgulkar, with his storehouse of extraordinary experiences, would find words rather than pictures a more reliable medium. Also, the new and flourishing avenues of radio and film afforded a more dependable source of income. As a consequence of all this, Madgulkar must have decided that writing was his primary vocation and drawing/painting was something more suited to the leisure hours. Writing and art were not to be paired together. I conjecture this from the fact that, in the twenty-odd years before the epiphanic moment in France, he did not think of illustrating his writing with his own drawings. Would he not have used lines to sketch the people of Mandesh whom he delineated through words in his *Mandeshi Manase?* They are all people he has known. I feel that illustrations by Madgulkar himself would have had an additional impact. Godse and Dalal have done an excellent job with their illustrations, but they only knew the subjects through Madgulkar's writing, a second-hand view at best. There was absolutely no reason for Madgulkar to doubt his own artistic ability because he had made a very telling sketch of his Bittakaka around this time.

Though much of his later writing centres around his own experiences and persons he had met, he does not illustrate it with his own drawings.

The one thing that strikes me is that when Madgulkar gives form to his experiences in words, it is that of a visual artist. For example,

> That house of his was a very simple one, tiled roof, rough and uneven mud walls, a pile of onions in one corner, an earthen stove right there like a stone mason's, various household goods, and the whole house permeated by the smell of onions and white clay. To the corners of the walls were attached spiders' webs and fluffy white cocoons.
>
> On the day of the wedding *varaat*, I was fluttering around the lamp like a moth.
>
> (Kovale Divas, p. 22)
>
> Books like Wren and Martin's grammar, and Athavale's Algebra with a green cardboard cover
>
> (Kovale Divas, p. 38)
>
> In the dark inner room, they lay sprawled like lions in the shade
>
> (Kovale Divas, p. 40)

> A flock of black and white sheep came into the dark open space nearby. They came, they scattered. Began to forage among the grasses, *harali, kurdu, shippi,* then with lowered heads briskly started chewing on them. On the embankment behind was a shepherd with a bright red turban on his head and a dark *ghongadi* on his shoulders . . .

> The great ones flaunt their official positions like a stag flaunting his antlers
>
> *(Pandharyavar Kale,* "White on Black", p. 60)

> Golinbai looked like the pictures of women in the *pothi*. She wore a huge red kumkum on her forehead
>
> *(Karunashtak,* p. 26)

On his return from France in 1969, Madgulkar's art appears to have received a boost. He occasionally did portraits and landscapes in water or oil colours but was most absorbed when he did pencil sketches. He truly loves the line in black. He comes to life, playing with lines.

He says, "If one tries to do everything, then one accomplishes nothing. A lifetime is too short to understand a subject. If I keep on drawing only lines, maybe at least a couple of them will be strong and powerful."

This dedication led Madgulkar to create innumerable line drawings. Since line drawings are more convenient for printing, he began to illustrate his writings himself in his later books.

If we look collectively at his drawings in the illustrated books that were published from this stage onward of Madgulkar's literary career, we can broadly classify them into three categories:

1. Drawings of nature and animals (jungles included)
2. Portraits
3. Occasional drawings where he is trying to express an idea

Of course, this last category includes drawings of the first two types. In all three types of line drawing, there is a basic, primary event. There is a hint of the third type in the first two since the line, the content and its expression together form the purpose of any sketch. A line by itself can rarely express anything. Only when it attains a shape or form on paper does it acquire the capacity to express something. When accompanied by a shape, the line takes on various forms and can express the content. In addition to line and shape, a third element, 'composition,' is necessary. Composition is the arrangement of various shapes on a surface. Composition makes the possibilities of expression limitless.

The different forms that a line can take are literally infinite. A line made by the stroke of a brush is different from that made by a quill or pen. A line made by a quick, intense stroke, one made fearfully and without confidence with a loose hand, a continuous line, a broken line, a rough line, a measured, contained line. A line that says only what is necessary, a line that gushes, a mischievous line, an innocent line . . . The list is endless. But to exploit the innate capacity of the line, the artist's sensibility and his drawing skills can be a limitation.

When the pulse of the writer and the artist is in sync, or when the writer and the artist are the same person, this difficulty is largely overcome; but it does not happen all the time. Sometimes the individual's sensibility to describe an experience in words and in pictures can differ. This may be true of some kinds of experience in some, while in others, it is evident in all.

In Madgulkar's case, the third type, namely the occasional drawings, does not seem to have bonded well with his writing. With the second type, portraits of people, the connection is made in many places. But with the first type, his nature drawings, the bonding is excellent. That's what I think.

In 1970, Madgulkar was writing a column for the newspaper *Kesari*. These articles have been published in his book *Pandharyavar Kale* ("Black on White"). The illustrations that accompany these pieces fall into my third category. The mischievous perspective, the playful style and the crisp language highlight the information conveyed. While his words meet our expectations, the accompanying sketches fail us. We do not see the easy flow of lines drawn with a confident hand, which characterises all of his later work. This kind of drawing would have gelled better with the ease of presentation in the writing. An unerring choice of incidents, an appropriate amount of caricature and meaningful composition would have achieved the playful effect consistent with the written content. In *Pandharyavar Kale* too we meet the people who are around him. The illustrations on pages 106, 119 and 134 are of people who have been guests in Madgulkar's home, yet they do not seem familiar. If we had seen them as they really were, it would have enriched the content. The illustration of his older brother, GaDiMa, on page 58 is a case in point.

Madgulkar seems to be disinterested in drawings of this kind. Otherwise he would not have left an article like *Lekhandarshan* ("A Glimpse of Writing"), with its immense possibilities for illustration, bereft of pictures. The artist does not seem to have become a soulmate of the writer. Perhaps because he had taken up sketching after an interval of many years. The bonding might have succeeded in his later years, but then he did not continue with this kind of writing. Madgulkar has, however, done plenty of drawings of the second type, that is, sketches of individuals. He is still doing them, and here the artist and the writer have bonded well. An excellent example of this are the character sketches of his grandmother, mother, father and siblings in *Karunashtak*. There are very few physical descriptions in his narration. But with a few precise words and selected incidents, he reveals their personality traits that leave a lasting impression on us. Here the author is telling us stories from his childhood, from a long time ago. Of those days of hardship. Not only are we moved by the pathos, we also experience the author's affection for the members of his family and the feeling of nostalgia for all that is now lost, and it leaves us uneasy.

The artist Madgulkar, using lines drawn delicately with a slack hand, using only as many lines as are necessary to provide details, or even leaving a space blank, has depicted all this effectively. The glimpses we get from those visible and invisible lines tell us that they represent people he had seen in his childhood many years ago. The illustrations add depth to the poignant experience the verbal description has given us. Another noteworthy point is that all the figures in these pictures are standing up, except his mother (*Karunashtak*). This is a more recent drawing. Perhaps the author is suggesting that no one had the leisure to sit down those days! Some excellent examples of portraits he has done are those of the father, the grandmother, his mother, his brother and Akka from *Karunashtak*.

The two sketches of Madgulkar's mother, one from the past and the other a comparatively recent one, show how effectively the changes in her personality, brought about by the passage of time, the ups and downs of life and the sad-happy occasions in the family during that time, are vividly portrayed by Madgulkar.

The pictures discussed so far are drawn for a specific purpose, to accompany the writing. But the artist sometimes doodles just to while away the time. Or because he feels like it. Madgulkar does this all the time. Some of his sketches, done while seated on the stage for a programme of storytelling (when other author's stories were being read), have been published in another context, but two such appear in *Chitre Ani Charitre*. The poses of persons in these drawings and the composition have nicely captured the mood of the audience.

In my view, an artist must have an innate awareness of composition. A good composition cannot be achieved by following rules or formulas. Different subjects demand a different kind of composition.

If we look at Madgulkar's drawings of the first category, namely nature and animals, we can discern a tension within them. Such pictures are also seen in *Sinhachya Deshat* ("In the Land of the Lion"), *Janglatil Divas* ("Days in the Forest") and *Sattantar* ("Transfer of Power"). The 1994 annual issue of *Maharashtra Times* carries many such sketches, some in colour too. In *Chitre Ani Charitre*, Madgulkar has included sketches he made in France of Van Gogh's grave, the asylum at St. Remy, Fort St. André in Avignon, a palace built from stones of all shapes and sizes collected by a postman over a lifetime, etc. As these are all on-the-spot sketches, they do not have the finish of the drawings made at home, yet one does expect to see in them a freshness coming out of the artist's spontaneity and a reflection of his mental state. These sketches do not fulfil that expectation. Probably because the habit of drawing had been broken for a long time. There is a great and remarkable difference in quality between these drawings and the pictures in the *Maharashtra Times*, *Sinhachya Deshat*, or *Janglatil Divas*.

Madgulkar had an immense love for nature and animals. His close observation of animals and the description of his experiences that arise from this love are incomparable. There are very few examples of this kind of writing in Indian languages. Forget about the artists! I cannot think of a single name that has done similar work. The most numerous of his art works are drawings of animals and the jungle, and these are artistically superior to other works. This is Madgulkar's supremely invaluable contribution to Marathi literature as a writer and an artist.

Ask any artist how difficult it is to draw animals! The list of the wild animals that Madgulkar has sketched . . . sambar and other deer, rabbits, wild buffaloes, boars, rhinoceroses, tigers, lions, elephants, giraffes, zebras, ostriches, leopards, vultures, ducks, storks, crocodiles, different kinds of birds, insects . . . is endless.

In his animal sketches, not only are their body parts correctly proportioned, there is also no distortion of any kind. He captures the unique features of every animal, such as the shyness and swiftness of the deer, the sluggishness of the rhino, the belligerence of the boar, the humanoid nature of monkeys . . .

Madgulkar uses various types of lines to achieve this effect. Sometimes it is a line lazily drawn, in one movement without lifting the pen, a line moving without care for exactitude; sometimes an economical, careful line placed exactly and quickly just where it should be (*Sattantar*, p. 67); sometimes an extravagant but hurried line (*Janglatil Divas*, pp. 65, 73), sometimes forceful, sharp but precise lines in the available space (*Janglatil Divas*, p. 80 and *Sattantar*, p. 67), and sometimes strong and firm, few but telling . . . the line in so many forms.

It is evident that some of the drawings are made on the spot, as the artist observes the animal in front of him. This is a very testing way to draw! To bring onto paper the body parts in proper proportion, the characteristics and special features of an animal in motion is a tightrope walk. Madgulkar accomplishes this delightfully. After 1970, Madgulkar's sketches show a marked progress of the 'line', from *Pandhryavar Kale* to *Janglatil Divas*.

Regarding Madgulkar's writings about art, I have read very little of them. He writes mostly about artists Van Gogh and Gauguin but mainly about the places where they spent their lives. Their paintings are referred to only in passing. We find a mention of Renoir, but Picasso and Braque, even Cezanne and Matisse do not get a mention as far as I remember. It is surprising that a lover of forests and beasts like him was not attracted to Henri Rousseau!

We find Madgulkar's views on art scattered through his writings. Many are indirect references. From them we can conclude that not only did he not like abstract art, but he was also not enamoured of art that strayed too far from realism. Of course he would never subscribe to the view of the Kolhapur artists that exactness in reproduction was the only criterion for judging an artist's worth. He believed that a picture should speak to the viewer. No wonder then that Van Gogh was his favourite artist.

In the article "Pradarshan" in his book *Pandharyavar Kale*, we find Madgulkar's views on nature drawing. He has some telling words about a particular artist. "His personality was striking. It was not rendered odd by the variegated hues of his tight clothing, his sideburns or his chin-hugging beard. His eyes were not dreamy. His face was not serious and lost in itself."

Madgulkar may not have written much about art, but as an artist whose talent for sketching forest animals has no equal, he has written with great admiration of the British illustrator Ralph Thompson, who was undoubtedly an inspiration for him. Ralph Thompson described his sketches as 'a kind of writing'. He describes the problems faced in sketching forest animals, the challenges and the attributes of good drawings. While unambiguously praising Ralph Thompson, Madgulkar says, "Only one in ten-twenty *lakh* artists can achieve this. No! Not even one in ten-twenty! Whoever is the creator of this vast world makes only one copy of someone so inspired. Only one, no carbon copy." (*Chitre Ani Charitre*, p. 225).

I would like to mention here that Madgulkar wrote, with unabashed delight, about the animal drawings of Eileen Soper in her book *Muntjac*, in the December 1988–January 1989 issue of the magazine *Lalit*.

In conclusion. one may say that though the line drawings of Madgulkar after 1970 show indisputable progress compared to the heights he attained as a writer, he rarely goes beyond being an excellent sketch artist. Except for *Sattantar*, the writer always dominates. And yet the drawings in *Sattantar* arouse greater expectations from his future work.

Source

Translated from the Marathi, *Vyankatesh Madgulkaranche Chitrakalethil Karya, Lekhan va Chitrakala*, Vasant Sarawate, from Lekhak Ani Manus, Dnyanada Naik ed., 2010, Pune, Anubandh Prakashan.

17
MADGULKAR'S DRAWINGS AND ILLUSTRATIONS

Vyankatesh Madgulkar

Figure 17.1 Kaziranga 1975

Source: Vyankatesh Madgulkar, *Janavanatil Rekhatane*. Mehta Publishing House, 2nd ed. 2012.

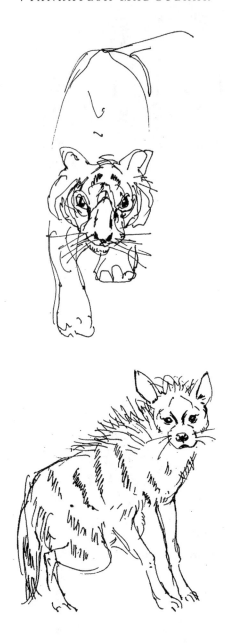

Figure 17.2 A tiger and a fox

Source: Vyankatesh Madgulkar, *Janavanatil Rekhatane*. Mehta Publishing House, 2nd ed. 2012.

MADGULKAR'S DRAWINGS AND ILLUSTRATIONS

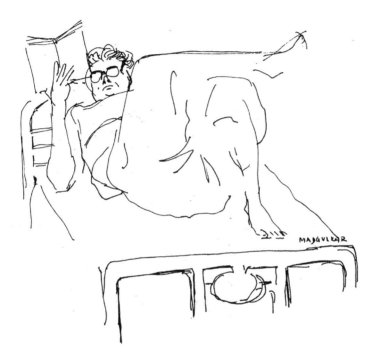

Figure 17.3 Vyankatesh Madgulkar's brother and renowned Marathi writer G. D. Madgulkar

Source: Vyankatesh Madgulkar, *Janavanatil Rekhatane*. Mehta Publishing House, 2nd ed. 2012.

Figure 17.4 Brother G. D. Madgulkar who never turned his back on the sufferings of his siblings.

Source: Vyankatesh Madgulkar, *Janavanatil Rekhatane*. Mehta Publishing House, 2nd ed. 2012.

Section 3

BETWEEN THE REGIONAL AND THE UNIVERSAL

3.1 Critical Reception and Legacy

18

THE COURSE OF THE NEW SHORT STORY AND MADGULKAR'S STORY

Sudha Joshi
Translated by Meera Marathe

The '*nav katha*', or the New Short Story, made its appearance on the Marathi literary scene after World War II. It redefined the very form and structure of the short story as it existed and made it more open and flexible. It revamped the traditional structure and the established method of experiencing the story. Similarly it transcended the conventions of plot construction and character delineation, exploring the inner world of the characters and their emotions, the purpose and the impact of the situation, the narrator and his perspective, the manner of narration, the use of language, the role of the writer's imagination, etc.

While the new short story was being created and developed, its nature was being examined and discussed by writers, critics and readers from different points of view. For example, the new story was thought to be (un) sympathetic to city dwellers, that it was a narrative without a plot, and incident was not predominant. Rather, it was character-centric and focussed on psychoanalysis. It was also accused of being abstruse and obscene.

Into this environment appeared Vyankatesh Madgulkar, one of the first generation of *nav katha* practitioners and a forerunner of '*grameen*' or rural/country literature. The country-story writers preceding him and whom he admired were S. M. Mate and R. V. Dighe. Madgulkar's own literary career began in 1946 with the publication of his first short story, *Kalya Tondachi* ("The Black-faced One").

In 1948 he moved to Bombay, "to find a life", he says. Two statements, he states, were very important for him. One was Ernest Hemingway's "The best early training for a writer is an unhappy childhood," and the other, W. B. Yeats's words that the first twenty years of a writer's life shape his writing in the future. Madgulkar says that in the first twenty years of his life, he didn't travel beyond Kolhapur, Kundal, Kirloskarwadi, and the cluster of villages within a ten-mile radius. But within this limited *'Panchkroshi'* space, he gathered a wide range of experiences.

> I wanted to write everything connected to that life. How the people of Mandesh live, how they think, what they endure, what gives them joy . . . That's what I wanted to write, with honesty, being faithful to their real life experiences.

Mumbai provided Madgulkar a congenial atmosphere for the development and advancement of his literary aspirations. Although he has depicted both rural and urban culture realistically in his stories, over 172 of them, the heart and essence of Madgulkar is evident in his *grameen katha*, his country story. And this is not merely because of their sheer number but because of their artistic merit and distinctiveness. As a writer, Madgulkar's primary area of experience, his *karma bhoomi*, was Mandesh. As Gangadhar Gadgil puts it, Mandesh was his 'Nandanvan', his paradise. While it is true that Madgulkar's fiction depicts the life and culture of a particular region, its regionality is purely geographical. The stories deal with human nature, human emotions and human life, making them universal and eternal.

Madgulkar observed the world around him with an innocent, detached, objective, interested and curious eye. He viewed human beings and their predicament as an inevitable fact of life. The good and bad, beautiful and ugly, the contrariness of life are all inevitable. One needs to be wise to understand that and accept it, according to him. This attitude is reflected in all his work. He rarely ever takes a partisan stand or a judgmental position, nor does he advocate one particular way to lead one's life.

Madgulkar was as interested in the world of Nature as he was in humanity. According to him, there is no duality between Man and Nature. Man is as much a constituent of Nature as is the tree or the deer. While he has an innate love for Nature and sees the beauty in it, he does not turn a blind eye to ugliness, nor does he try to avoid or ignore it. He recognises that human shortcomings, flaws and failings, occasional bursts of violent behaviour and criminal tendencies are a reality to be recognised and accepted. Therefore in his portrayal of the assorted characters who people his stories, we see a sensitivity and an empathy that is endearing. He also offers insights into their behaviour and suggests how one can see their point of view.

Though Madgulkar has depicted many an intense and acute experience in much of his writing, he has done so in a remarkably restrained manner, without compromising on the emotional intensity or allowing the accompanying tension to slacken. He is able to portray the melodramatic or overly emotional situations in a calm and controlled fashion whilst retaining the dramatic element.

One major feature of this master storyteller's narration is that though he tells serious stories dealing with human suffering, the daily trials and tribulations, the sadness and loneliness of the lives of the rural folk, they are not grim or uni-dimensional tales of unhappiness. Madgulkar is able to infuse into them the big and small joys and pleasures of their lives, the happiness they derive from simple things.

Though his stories reflect the heart-rending social reality and the great social injustice prevalent in society, the helplessness of the deprived classes, the exploitation and humiliation meted out to them, Madgulkar does not assume the role of a social scientist or an activist. He is non-partisan and objective in his approach and comes across as a sensitive, compassionate observer of society. Just as he shows no caste biases or discrimination in his writing, he is similarly secular in his approach to matters pertaining to religion and religious faith.

There is a strong autobiographical element in much of Madgulkar's writing. He says of his character depictions that the human body is the physical manifestation of the inner mind, and the mind is the representation of the inner body of our being. We experience this indivisibility in his literary work. Through the description of a character's physical appearance, his movements, body language and any quirks he may have, he reveals the personality of a character, capturing for the reader the soul of that character.

Madgulkar's very important and unique contribution to the Marathi short story has been his ability to highlight the different kinds of relationships that exist between man and animal. His animal stories present the same kind of human emotions and experiences of loneliness, distrust, companionship and loyalty, among others, between animal and animal and between man and beast.

While it is true that in Madgulkar's fictional world, there is a preponderance of male characters, it is equally true that his female characters are diverse and varied. He portrays them with remarkable sensitivity and poignancy. Even the child characters are interesting individuals with personalities of their own, which the author captures in a few deft strokes.

One must pay attention to the space in a story or the time, space and environment which are components of the creative planning and construction of Madgulkar's story-world. The space in his stories is not just a piece of land, it is a cultural space. Temples, schools, tall buildings, the village or town square, the *wada* and the *chavadi* are central to Madgulkar's narrative technique.

Although Madgulkar is most popular for his short stories, he didn't restrict himself to one literary form. Among his other works are word pictures of people, novels, plays, folk plays, autobiographical pieces, travelogues and many pieces on his other passion – the jungle and wildlife. He even tried his hand at poetry in the early days.

Vyankatesh Madgulkar is, in essence, an experienced and expert storyteller. He is a master of the story form, its narrative structure and technique, which are all essentially influenced by the oral tradition of story telling to which he was exposed from a very young age. It is ironic that despite being so adept at the craft of writing and so thoroughly knowledgeable about his art and craft, he has not received the kind of critical acclaim he deserves for his unique and independent style nor the contribution to the evolution and development of the Marathi short story.

Source

Abridged by Usha Tambe. Translated from the Marathi, *Navakathecha Pravaha Ani Vyankatesh Madgulkaranchi Katha*, Katha: Sankalpana Ani Samiksha, 2012, Mumbai, Mouj Prakashan Gruha.

19
THE REGIONAL AND THE RURAL REALITY IN VYANKATESH MADGULKAR'S SHORT STORIES

Ravindra Kimbahune
Translated by Manali Sharma and Sachin Ketkar

At an extremely crucial juncture in the history of Maharashtra, Vyankatesh Madgulkar portrayed an authentic picture of regional and rural life in his fiction. His stories are rooted in his own experiences and observations of social life around the river Maan in pre-Independence days. We do not come across such a truthful delineation of the extensive canvas of societal life in the village with all its minutiae before Madgulkar. He has created his world of fiction by balancing the objectivity of a social scientist and the great literary sensibility of a mature artist.

Madgulkar has created a comprehensive representation of the vegetation, the wilderness, the streams and rivulets, the wildlife, the cycle of the seasons and the changes that it brings about, extreme instances of water scarcity, the goings-on in the princely state, villages deprived of even basic amenities and order, and the people living in such places, their interpersonal relations and their lives destroyed by penury. So many seeds of the *grameen* literature that is being ardently promoted these days can be found in Madgulkar's works.

There is a geographical continuum of jungle-wilderness-village-city in Madgulkar's writing. The relationship between man and nature is portrayed with untainted realism. A purely romantic representation of the beauty of nature, untouched by nature's fearsome side and its impact on people haunted by poverty, does not attract him.

Madgulkar's writings are centred on the traditional edifice of village life. His fiction thematizes the caste system and the weak economic structure which brings about the failure of labour associated with caste. Madgulkar has effectively portrayed the more or less static village social structure comprising the wide range of castes and communities like the Brahmins, the Marathas, the artisan castes, the Mahars, the Mangs, the Vhalars, the Chambhars, the Kumbhars, a couple of Mussalman families, as well as the itinerant communities who visit the village according to the season. As his stories are mostly character-sketches, they constantly provide characters representative of these communities in the village.

His writing paints a dismal picture of family life, mismatched couples, devious people, ramshackle houses, hand-to-mouth existing Dalits, blind faith and superstitions, village assemblies, an old generation clinging to traditional values, the monotony and overall mundaneness of village life, the vice-like grip of various political structures on the villagers' minds and the sheer impossibility of societal transformation.

The torments and tribulations in the lives of good, bad and indifferent characters that one finds in the collections of his short stories like *Mandeshi Manse, Gavakadchya Goshti* and *Sitaram Eknath* are products of such traditional social structures. Madgulkar has developed a distinctive narrative style for bringing out a person's psychology that is inevitably shaped by his never-ending struggle against extreme poverty. Like the painter who selectively uses few but precise strokes to portray an individual, Madgulkar uses minute details to illustrate how people behave and speak, or how they sit and sulk without referring to the topic they want to discuss or how in spite of speaking a lot they avoid revealing their true intentions. He creates a semiotic system for depiction of his characters' minds without the use of any psychological theory. He brings to life Mandeshi characters like Dharma Ramoshi and his daughter who cannot step out of the house as she has no clothes to wear, the dim-witted Bakas of the Mulani who puts up with the cruel behaviour of his brother and sister-in-law, rugged Kondiba Gaikwad, Raghu Kaarcoon (clerk) who lives a tedious life, Banya Bapu who sells off whatever little land he has in order to keep up his reputation and the *paan*-seller's affectionate Khaala who determinedly conducts her business with a paltry capital. The ironic portrayal of Ganya Bhaptya's character is typical in the context of a stagnant village economy. Ganya, who fantasizes about acquiring fabulous wealth as if by some magic and who harms himself by falling prey to superstitious beliefs and tantric rites, appears laughable to us. It is the static and inflexible village economy that lies at the back of Ganya's wild belief that you do not need organized efforts to earn wealth. Contexts of such symbolic background in Madgulkar's character-sketches need to be examined too.

Madgulkar portrays the obdurate structure of the incarcerating caste system with the same realistic objectivity. Many of his stories depict the plight of untouchables and the 'backward' castes. We can read these stories in G. M. Pawar's edited volume titled *Oza*. We see the appalling nature of the oppressive caste system in stories like *Deva Satva Mahar, Aadit* and *Gode Pani* ("Sweet Water"). The characters and protagonists are forced to accept defeat by the establishment, even if their position is just. In the same context, the story *Zhombi* depicts a gloomy picture of the struggle for existence of the Muslim minority and the compromises they have to make in order to survive.

THE REGIONAL AND THE RURAL REALITY

Arvind Gokhale, in his introduction to a collection of Madgulkar's selected stories edited by him, complains about the lack of violence in the stories. Gokhale believes that Madgulkar diluted whatever little violence is featured in them. But the stories do have rugged, defiant, evil and stone-hearted characters too, like Kondiba Gaikwad or Bhagvantrao in the story *Dubala*. However, Madgulkar's focus is on the violence that is implicit in the social establishment, and it is understandable that this should escape Gokhale's superficial reading of the stories. Representation of extravagant violence in the inert village social structure comes from a certain urban understanding of rural society and would be alien to Madgulkar's actual experiences of village life. The depiction of the stagnant economic and social system that completely destroys inherent human virtues, abilities, hopes and dreams, creative talents and zest for life is actually nothing but a representation of real violence. And Madgulkar is by no means 'mild' in its delineation. The sheer distress that is endured while getting water for the sugarcane crop in the scorching summer heat, as described in the story *Jupi*, is worth examining. It is heart-breaking to see how Naama is handicapped when all his agricultural implements are taken away by his neighbours without his permission, the wooden axle of the water wheel snapping after he puts in a leather water bag to draw water from the well and the only carpenter in the village missing at that crucial time. Or when the exhausted old man in the story *Talyachya Paali* does not receive the money due to him after giving up his agricultural land, or Deva Satva Mahar who only gets abuses from his superiors even after he has run around the village in the hot sun and on an empty stomach, making announcements. Or when Arjunaa, who must return without having a glimpse of Lord Vitthala even after going on a pilgrimage every year because of the age-old traditional values he has imbibed, tells a tragic tale.

In Madgulkar's writings, one can discern the direct blistering impact the repercussions of World War II, though seemingly distant, had on the village. His writings also reveal the effect of erratic seasonal cycles, displacements, hardships and exiles caused by famines, violent flare-ups in the aftermath of Gandhi's assassination and the lives of the villagers who have left for the cities to try their luck. He has also written stories about how the winds of urbanization and inevitable modernization were affecting the village system. It is in this context that one can understand the condition of Gopa Vhalar. The story *Service Motar* symbolically depicts the plight of one family affected by the forces of modernization. The change described in the story is inexorable. However, it does not create an alternative system but rather destroys some of the intrinsic strengths of the existing one. Madgulkar's later stories poignantly reveal this directionless drift. He has also portrayed the generational conflicts between the older and the newer generation as this traditional village edifice begins to crumble.

We come across long-suffering men and women who have helplessly accepted their entrapment by this inert social system in these stories. In spite of the impossibility of major transformation, all the deprivation in their lives and the endless toil that will yield no significant results, these people's keen desire to survive and their simple and honest nature provide their characters with uncontrived splendour. Madgulkar's autobiographical writings reveal the influence of the Brahmin values of his home. What is important is that he never veiled them. Nevertheless, through the extensive portrayal of the wide-ranging, non-Brahmin society, Madgulkar's sensibility reveals its authenticity of experience and shows the features of a great artist whose consciousness transcends the precincts of caste and class. Portrayal of the regional and rural realities that are not conducive to leading a fine life, which leave no scope for the people to dream and which turn all creativity to dust, is the most original accomplishment of Madgulkar's fiction.

Vyankatesh Madgulkar started writing *grameen* stories which coincided with the emergence of the *nav katha* (the modernist short story) in Marathi. The depiction of wide-ranging social reality is an excellent illustration of modernism in Marathi literature. Shridhar Vyankatesh Ketkar had said that to be *ati*-Maharashtriya (excessively Maharashtrian) is to be an Indian in the true sense. In this regard, Madgulkar's writing is an illustration of his universality. Robert Frost has stated that one cannot be global without being completely regional and local. Vyankatesh Madgulkar has proved this truth with his writing.

Source

Translated from the Marathi, *Kimbahuna*, 2010, Mumbai, Lokavangmay Gruha.

20
LIMITATIONS OF LANGUAGE IN RURAL LITERATURE AND THE WAY FORWARD

Anand Yadav
Translated by Nadeem Khan

Once the writings of Madgulkar-Mirasdar-Patil had faded away, the new generation of writers of rural literature began using the rural register with greater freedom and naturalness. As a consequence, the manifestation of rural literature changed between the years 1965 and 1975. Even now, in 1978, the newly arrived writers of rural literature have been using rural language with greater felicity. This trend is welcome for many reasons and is significant from the viewpoint of the history of literature.

Many stories written in the rural language are such that the educated persona of the writer assumes the role of a neutral narrator and does his narration from that position. Therefore it is perfectly proper for the narrator to use the *'praman bhasha'* or *'nagar bhasha'*, that is, the city language as the medium of expression. Since the narrating personality is presented as an educated one, the manner in which the narrator conceives of the characters and incidents in the story and the meaning of life that is derived from this conception – is inevitably the creation of that particular educated individual. That is exactly why the person has undertaken the responsibility of being the story's narrator. In a sense, that rural story is 'a story coming out of the narrator's mind', and therefore, the use of *nagar bhasha* is not only inevitable but also artistically appropriate. Not only that, the *nagar bhasha* is a constituent of the educated person's character. A piece of literature sometimes has some very specific circumstances when the writer uses the rural language as the medium of expression. But here it does not appear either incongruous or artistically inappropriate.

At such times, the rural language used by these educated writers often brings with it traces of the city language. The sentence structure, the rhythm and movement of the narrative, the stylistic use of the figures of speech, the occasional 'city' sentences that have slipped into the rural argot are strongly reflected here. The attraction rural language has for the city becomes obvious, as a result of which the aesthetics of that work gets affected accordingly.

It's not as if this problem arises only in the case of the educated third person narrator of a *grameen* story. It is also present in the case of a first-person self-expression. The problem is not all that terrifying in prose writing because prose incarnates predominantly at the practical, realistic level. But when an attempt is made to use rural language for rural poetry, matters become dangerous. Compared to prose, poetry is far more personal. It transcends practical events and mundane realities and rises to higher poetic levels. The experiences it communicates are delicate, subtle, and usually do not relate to or concern everyday life. Therefore it becomes necessary to convey these experiences only by remaining within the bounds of the vocabulary available in the rural language. Even if the rural tongue has its own grammar, its peculiarity is that it does not allow the coining of new words through grammatical, linguistic and etymological channels. The reason is that although the rural person uses the language of his area, he has no conception of grammatical and linguistic rules. He observes them without being conscious of them. He speaks using only the vocabulary that is available to him. Since he doesn't know the rules and he does not have the need to mint new words in conducting his everyday affairs, he must manage with the words that are prevalent and of common usage even in his poetry. But to compose poetry within this limited lexicon is a difficult task.

The fact is that a rural language is the language of the life of that region, a folk language. Hence it develops only to the extent of the level at which life is lived in that community. Normally it is quite adequate to meet the needs of the ordinary people there. A person in a village lives life at a very basic level. Food, clothing, shelter, a very basic level of religion and ritual, as well as an elementary level of thoughts, feelings, passions, imaginations, etc., can be quite adequately expressed by the language available to them. At least that is the picture of the Indian villages we see today. This primary-level village-language often proves inadequate for the writer to express consciousness of a subtle, complex, imaginative kind.

It is possible for the poet or the author to coin rustic words along the rules of grammar, linguistics or etymology. For example, the rural word for *bhakt* is *bhagat,* and for *rakt* it is *ragat;* but even so, if I have to convert the term *sakt taakeed* into rural-speak, I cannot use *sagat* in place of *sakt;* or, because *naahee* becomes *nyaa-ee* in rural Maharashtra, I cannot use this analogy to convert *paahee* into *phaa-ee* for my rural language. The reason is that the words *sakt* and *paahee* do not exist in the rural language, and words that have no existence cannot be so converted, even if the conversion mechanism falls within the rules of the spoken grammar operative in that language. Since rural language is primarily spoken, it is only when a word settles into everyday use that it acquires the quality of 'spokenness'. But if such a word is used in rural literature, it will not meet the demands of propriety.

The enormous constraint that rests on the writer using rural language does not exist for the user of the city language. When the occasion demands, he may happily pick up words from Sanskrit, Persian, Hindi, Urdu and English and use them. With the help of grammar, linguistics and etymology, he can coin new words and work with them. It doesn't matter if they are not rooted in social communication. This practice is evident in urban poetry. What happens very often is that the poet mints new words and introduces them in his literary compositions. It is possible that they gain currency in the language of the community later and get incorporated into the vocabulary. But the words first get accepted in literary circles. It also happens that a poet is lauded for creating new words as the situation demands. This, however, is not possible when rural language is used as the medium. If that happens, it becomes a breach of propriety.

In the matter of rural language, therefore, the situation is the reverse of what obtains in the city language. Rural language is primarily the medium of oral communication in the spoken form. As such, words first need to get embedded in the language of speech before they can be used in poetry. Rural literature, therefore, needs to operate within the boundaries set for it by the active vocabulary of the local language. This imposes a serious limitation on the use of rural language for literary creation.

Rural language did not have to deal with this problem until now. Whatever other processes were taking place inside it, in the matter of creating new words, it had remained unchanged for centuries. A bit of stir was created when the Mughals drifted in or when the English arrived. That was when, ever so slowly, in minuscule numbers, foreign words took on their rural *avatar* – words like *gor, asar, makta, theshaan* (station) and *kantraatdaar* appeared in rural speech. But this process is the result of social changes and the introduction of new objects. No new rural word either arrived or was created to meet the needs of literature.

Rural literature in the rural language and in the written form is now being produced for the first time in the cultural history of the country. This is an important and an unprecedented offering of the new age to rural literature. But what becomes evident from the above is that however rare and however slow, the process of new words entering the rural language does go on, whatever be the forces that keep it going. If this is so, why should it matter if the linguistic gospel that 'rural language keeps providing sustenance to the standard language' is turned on its head? There is certainly no damage done if now the *praman bhasha* offers sustenance to *grameen bhasha* and helps in the articulation of the rural mind. I believe that the deliberate furtherance of this new process is extremely important.

An unprecedented, radical churning is happening in Indian society and, by extension, in the rural community. A concerted effort is being made to restructure the rural community, to carry out improvements in it and bring it on par with the urban community. An exercise is afoot to pull the rural community out of its basic level of existence. The whole village aspires to become literate and get educated so they can all live life the new way. From the linguistic perspective, this is a grievous assault on the community. At such times, the likelihood of all kinds of changes taking place in the language is real. It is this act of linguistic transformation that rural writers are trying to attempt through literature. This is what makes me believe that this attempt is loaded with historical significance.

Why didn't this process begin with the writers of Madgulkar-Mirasdar-Patil's generation or other writers of their temperament? Why did it begin with a later generation? These are questions of historical sequencing, and it is important for them to be answered in that sequence.

Grameen bhasha, the rural language, is considered to be a dialect of the mediatorial language of that region. This language is nothing other than the *praman bhasha* or standard language. Almost all written material – professional, administrative, educational, books on all scientific subjects, newspapers – use the *praman bhasha*. When a person of that region becomes educated, he tries to use the standard language. In our parts, since very early times, the upper castes have foisted the caste system on language too by conceitedly confounding the word 'standard' with 'pure'. This pure-profane polarity – of the Brahmin language being pure, therefore superior to everybody else's as being defiled and therefore inferior – has been prevalent in India since ancient times. People who know linguistics, however, know that from the linguistic perspective, the concepts of pure and profane are meaningless.

Ordinary educated people do not know this because of the hold that tradition exercises on them. Consequently, they work under the misconception that *grameen bhasha* is impure while *nagar* or *praman bhasha* is chaste. Therefore, when a person who has grown up in the rural area and spoken the rural tongue since birth acquires an education and moves to the city in pursuit of employment, he gradually abandons his rural language. He begins to consider the use of his native language below his newly acquired dignity. Nobody else in the city speaks his language. If, in an unguarded moment, a word, a sentence, or an accent of his native tongue slips out, he is sniggered at by the 'educated' people around him. He therefore sticks to the standard language, which was the medium of instruction anyway, and lets it take him over.

There is another subtler reason why he feels the need to use the standard language. Earlier, the language of his region was quite adequate for the simple, basic level of interaction in his village and also to express his thoughts and feelings. Once he becomes educated, he leaves behind that primary level of existence and rises to the next stage of greater awareness. Perhaps he finds the rural language inadequate for everyday transactions, to communicate subtler thoughts and feelings that are now part of his life. But this is an indirect reason. The true and important reason is that in his heart of hearts, he does not want to show himself up as a 'country bumpkin' through his language. He is now out to convince others that he is a cultured 'citywala'.

Along with his rustic tongue, he also discards his village customs and traditions and adopts those 'standard' practices of the city dwellers. He quickly convinces himself that it is the standard language and standard culture that are truly his own and begins transforming himself accordingly. The purpose here is not to discuss the propriety or the impropriety of this process from the sociological perspective but only to present a clearer picture of the mental journey that begins once a rural individual acquires education. The rural writer is also a person going through this same process.

This process leads us to associate 'educated' with one who uses *nagar* or *praman bhasha*. We view the rural writer from this perspective, so when we encounter the use of rural language in the third-person narration of his rural tale, we consider it an artistic shortcoming. We expect that the third-person narrator, who the author creates, is 'educated' and should make his narration in the city language. Keeping this expectation in mind, Madgulkar, Mirasdar, Patil and others of their temperament have unabashedly used standard language in their rural stories told by a third-person narrator. The only thing they have done is given the language a consistently rural flavour. And for that, they deserve our appreciation. Critics say that the later generation of writers should emulate them when writing rural stories. It is, in their opinion, not only artistically appropriate but obligatory.

This first generation of writers has unwittingly used the rural language only as a stylistic device. For the purpose of dialogues, to give the narration a colouration and to create a rural resonance, these writers used the rural language in greater measure than the earlier generation of writers did. They used the urban language as a medium of narrating a rural story because, inside their skin, they doubted the adequacy of the rural language in its native form for this purpose. Besides, in their minds, the standard language was the language of their readers, and they realized that they too belonged to the same city culture but had become writers of rural fiction. This is how their role was defined. Since they had accepted the city culture as the standard, the choice of the standard language for their narrations became automatic. And that is why their literary creations have conformed to aesthetic literary standards. From a contemporary perspective, it is a good thing.

The picture of the generation that followed is different. For the previous dozen years or so, that is, around the 1965–1975 decade, conditions in the villages changed. Compared to earlier times, the number of educated persons in district places, taluka towns, and fruit and vegetable-growing villages close to cities is increasing. With the advent of sugar factories, fruit farms and gram panchayats, cooperative societies and the administrative machinery that has arrived with them have a sizeable number of educated people working in them. This primarily rural class got its education in schools and colleges established in rural areas. The teachers in these colleges also came from predominantly rural backgrounds. Therefore, the language of the educated class in the villages of today is no longer the standard city language of Pune and Mumbai. While it may appear like the city language in written transactions, the intonation, the inflection, the pronunciation and the occasional use of particular words and idioms in their speech remain markedly rural. The picture becomes clearer when we observe the way these rural graduates spell words. Considering that this class of people was taught in rural colleges by rural teachers and their contact with the village community remained unbroken, it is quite natural that their language should also remain largely unchanged. The young rural writers of the present generation have been moulded by this system. Whatever influence the *praman bhasha* or urban literature or other related matters have upon them, it is mainly through books and not through direct transactions.

When this young rural writer begins writing the kind of rural story that has been mentioned in the beginning, the rural language he uses will certainly carry a marginal influence of the city tongue, its mannerisms, stylistic peculiarities and ornamentations. Even if this is so, the language he most frequently uses in his social interactions is that of his village tongue. Therefore, writing his rural stories in that tongue will be natural and closer to his heart.

It can be said that even if Madgulkar, Mirasdar, Patil and others like them directly chose the standard language, consciously giving up rural language, in their literary works, there are shades of the rural language in them which have either crept in inadvertently or were deliberately introduced. The younger generation of *grameen* writers, however, openly used *grameen bhasha* as the medium of their literary expression, yet the influence of the *praman bhasha* on their work, either unconscious or intentional, is noticeable. It is a good thing that the matter is discussed from a literary perspective.

Even though the rural writers of rural literature have loosely accepted the rural tongue as their medium of expression, it can be said that the influence of the city tongue continued to remain on their rural tongue. From the perspective of rural literature, it has been a good thing.

This process is of a rather delicate nature. Wherever required, words, phraseology, style, the tendency to use similes and other embellishments, the occasional expression of a subtle experience that doesn't quite suit the rural language have been brought into the rural tongue from the standard language by the writers of rural stories. New words, new phrases, figures of speech and the manner of employing them and poetic expressions have begun appearing in rural literature. A new word that has sprung up under some special circumstance in the environment gains currency because it is used in the literature of that language. For instance, the word 'television' has entered rural vocabulary as '*tele-ijun*'. The occurrence of such words is, obviously, rare, but it seems this process will gather speed from here on. This will probably lead to the development of rural language as the medium for rural literature, and there is a distinct possibility that it will be a more powerful and effective medium.

Village life has been constantly changing. Village dwellers are aspiring to rise to a higher level of life than before. The village tongue that has so far been used for transactions at the primary level naturally finds it difficult to articulate thoughts that arrive at this higher level. Therefore, only the changing rural language would be appropriate to express the changing thoughts at this new level. It shall, in due course, become the language of the educated litterateurs of the villages.

However, allowing the city language to continue influencing the rural language indirectly and helping it to develop as a medium is a risky task and needs to be handled with great responsibility. For one, while working to aid this development, we must constantly keep in mind the fact that we are doing it to develop the *'grameen bhasha'*. Therefore, only those words, phrases and sentence structures of the city language that can be easily absorbed in the rural language must be introduced. An overdose may well destroy the texture and the essence of the rural tongue.

For the creators of literature, the development of one's language as a medium is always an urgent need. Its development is closely related to its production. When the village language finds itself inadequate to express a feeling, an idea, a thought or a state of mind, this matter of development becomes vital. The litterateur does not set off with the primary purpose of developing the language as a social task. It is another matter that once the writer's job of creation is over, language does evolve in that society. After all, when he brings about a change in the language for the creation of his literature, the society is at liberty to use the novelty that has arrived in that language. It is obvious that once the society begins to use the innovations, the development of the language happens by itself.

There is no evidence to show that the first generation of rural writers contributed much to the development of the rural language. They skirted around the problem and went about with the task of creating literature. The later generation, it must be said, helped in the development of the rural tongue as a medium of literary expression. This, however, is just the initial stage of its development. At this stage, the languages of the different rural areas will certainly be woven into the tapestry of the literature of that rural landscape, and in the process, they will gain new vigour and vitality. In due course, they will evolve on their own. For this to happen, great literature needs to be created in these rural languages. Again, the writers can create great literature only when they have confidence in the vitality of their ruralness. Instead of taking the simplistic view that it is the language of the illiterate, they should look at it as the only effective medium to express their life experiences. Towards this end, they should study grammar, linguistics and etymology with an open mind. They should not forget that advanced countries of Europe and Russia are doing everything to preserve their vernaculars with pride as symbols of their cultural heritage. That is why the use of the rural tongue as a medium of rural literature is a meaningful development in the history of Marathi literature.

One fear that is always expressed with regard to rural literature and the use of the rural tongue as a medium is that in a few years' time, villages will progress and become suburbs of the cities. When that happens, rural life there will get destroyed and, consequently, the rural language too. If this is so, what future does rural literature and rural language have?

This question is spurious. For one, it is based on the process that worked upon the first generation of rural writers. Also, the question has emerged from a city-centric mindset. That is to say that when the young generation of rural writers gets educated and moves into the city, its rural language disappears from their speech, and these writers speak only the language of the city. According to this logic, therefore, once people in the village acquire education, they switch to only the city language, and the village language will simply die away.

But we have seen in this very article that a different process has been going on for about a dozen years (1965–1975) now. To assume that the educated villager will necessarily shift to the city and begin using the city language is wrong. He has been educated in the village and continues to live a rural life. Therefore, even if the influence of the city leaves traces on his language, he will not abandon his village life and continue to use the rural tongue.

We have already seen that this process will only enrich the rural language. Of course, it is likely that internal changes will take place in it. But linguists say that such changes happen all the time. Today's rural language will not be the same as the rural language of tomorrow. For that matter, no language of today can possibly be the language of tomorrow. Look at the enormous changes that have taken place in Marathi from the Yadava age to the Shiva age, the Peshwa period, the early British times right up to the present. Language flows. Rural language too will keep flowing. And therefore, there is no reason to worry about its future.

By the same argument, it is equally delusional to think that rural life will be destroyed. Industrial cities are islands by themselves. They are the centres of trade and industry, huge factories, administrative government offices, business and educational institutions. Every day we see upheavals and turmoil. A person gets deeply embroiled in time and work, and his lifestyle gets shaped accordingly. By contrast, however much the villages progress, however much they begin to look neat and tidy like the cities, however much they get infiltrated by radios, transistors and motorcycles, however well they get connected to the city, they will still remain agricultural in essence. The huge enterprises, giant factories, important government offices and the various educational centres that circumscribe city life and shape its style will never enter the countryside. At the most, these villages will look like the orchard towns of today. Nature, farming, physical labour and a small human community will continue to flourish here. In all probability, life in the villages will change, but imagining it to become a miniaturized version of city life goes against reason. Therefore, the lifestyle, the balances and the prevalent social tensions that we see reflected in the rural literature today will continue to be visible in the rural literature of the future.

Thus, even if we agree that there will be changes in rural literature, it will not be proper to say that it is the same as saying it will mean the destruction of rural literature and rural language.

The value of any piece of literature does not depend upon whether the life portrayed in that piece or whether the language in which the literature has been written is extant or not. It depends on the various facets of the human mind that have been uncovered through that language, on the fundamental values resonating in that mind that get expressed. When we read *pauranic* and historical stories, when we read Sanskrit literature, when we soak in the experience of the old Marathi poems and chronicles, we do not find either that lifestyle or that language reflected in our present surroundings. They disappeared from the community and got interred in the past long, long ago. But has that lowered the excellence or the value of that literature? In the same manner, even if the rural language of today keeps changing slowly across the centuries that lie in the future, the value and importance of the rural literature that has been created in the rural tongue (and continues to be created) will not change with the change that would have arrived in that language. On the contrary, in some distant future, it will claim importance as a cultural heritage, as 'the first individual sample of a certain rural language prevalent in a certain part of a region of those ancient times'.

Source

Translated from the Marathi, *Sahityatil Bhashechya Maryada Ani Vikasachi Disha*, Grameen Sahitya: Swaroop Ani Samasya by Anand Yadav, 2016, Pune, Mehta Publishing.

21
PLAYS OF VYANKATESH MADGULKAR: SOME OBSERVATIONS, SOME QUESTIONS

Anagha Mandavkar
Translated by Chinmay Dharurkar

"Vyankatesh Madgulkar is a short story writer and a novelist. Has he also written plays?"

"Vyankatesh Madgulkar's plays are taught in Drama schools and performed at State level competitions even today."

"Vyankatesh Madgulkar is not a serious, genuine playwright!"

"Vyankatesh Madgulkar laid hands on the play and skillfully tackled other mediums of expression as well. He had a precise understanding and awareness of the medium he deployed."

Such contradictory views were revealed to me when I began the study of Vyankatesh Madgulkar's plays. According to Rajeev Naik, drama theorist and playwright, "Vyankatesh Madgulkar is an important but a rather less studied playwright in Marathi." And he was right. I found that except for a research thesis on Madgulkar's folk plays, very little study has been undertaken of his plays as compared to his other writings. This essay therefore attempts to present the characteristic features of Madgulkar's plays while mapping the coordinates of his plays in the course of Marathi theatre and their place in his oeuvre. Through a textual analysis of the plays and conversations with the theatre artists who were closely associated with the staging and performance of the plays, this essay makes some observations and asks some questions.

Madgulkar's play writing spans two decades, from 1955 to 1976, and we are told by Ms Dnyanada Naik, Madgulkar's daughter, that several of the plays are adaptations of his short stories. Of all the plays he wrote, only eleven – *Binbiyanche Jhad*; *Janar Kuthe*, also known as "Tu Veda Kumbhar" ("Oh You Silly Potter!"); *Kunacha Kunala Mel Nahi*; *Kalabarobar Chala*; *Sati*; *Pati Gele Ga Kathewadi* ("Oh the Husband has gone to Kathewadi"); *Devajine Karuna Keli*; *Gaurai*; *Nama Satpute*; *Bikat Vaat Vahiwat* and *Devachya Kathila Avaj Nahi* – were performed. Though he contributed full-length and one-act radio plays to All India Radio, very few scripts of Madgulkar's plays are available.

For this study, the plays whose texts/scripts were available have been analysed. It is interesting to note that only excerpts from "Tu Veda Kumbhar", *Sati* and *Pati Gele Ga Kathewadi*, included in this volume, have been translated.

A Textual Analysis of the Plays

The characteristic features of Madgulkar's plays are innovation, diversity and flexibility on the levels of content and genre.

Themes

Madgulkar's plays can be classified as adaptations, folk plays, independent plays and auto-adaptations of his short stories. Some thematic genres he touched upon are tragic (*Sati*), melodramatic (*Nama Satpute*, "Tu Veda Kumbhar"), comic (*Pati Gele Ga Kathewadi*), some inspired by western literature, by plays and films that moved him, historical events and folklore.

Folk dramas, like *Binbiyanche Jhad* and *Kunacha Kunala Mel Nahi*, are based on the folk tales that are part of the oral tradition. *Binbiyanche Jhad* tells the story of a king who is cursed with a habit of eavesdropping and how he is exposed by a *nhavi*, a barber. *Kunacha Kunala Mel Nahi* is also about a king of the imaginary land of Changulpur who steps out in disguise. He meets a *dhobi*, Namu Parit, who is fed up with his drab existence. The play wittily depicts how meeting the King changes the course of Namu's life. Both the folk plays focus on the entertainment aspect. The play *Kalabarobar Chala* speaks of a Maratha nobleman, Sardar Manajirao Bhosale, who refuses to move with the times and continues to flaunt the outdated idea of Maratha lineage and legacy.

Makarand Sathe, an eminent playwright, finds Vyankatesh Madgulkar's folk plays rather naïve and simplistic. They lack a fierce critique of social evils like corruption and only make a few passing comments on contemporary issues, he adds. Interestingly, these plays were presented by the Rashtra Seva Dal, whose primary objective was to educate the masses through entertainment, even though they belied those objectives.

The play *Sati*, set during the later part of Peshwa rule when cultural conservatism reigned, weaves together some historical facts and events that Madgulkar had read about and links them to certain incidents that took place in a family of his acquaintance. The play tells of a woman who refuses to commit *sati* when her husband dies because he never gave her the due rights of a wife. However, she willingly performs *sati* on the death of the

British officer from whom she received warmth and affection, companionship and caring. The woman's defiance of the code of conduct forms the plot.

The seed of the story of *Pati Gele Ga Kathewadi* lies in a popular folk tale where a woman with her intelligence and wisdom proves her fidelity while maintaining her dignity. She also asks her husband some pertinent questions regarding chastity and fidelity which were considered virtues only in women. Several elements of folk theatre have been incorporated into the play. *Janar Kuthe* (also published as "Tu Veda Kumbhar") and *Nama Satpute* are based on Madgulkar's adaptation of his short stories *Service Motar* and *Dubala*, respectively. "Tu Veda Kumbhar" traces the changes that take place in the life of a village with the arrival of a 'service motar', which becomes a symbol of development, modernity and a money-driven economy. How this affects the interpersonal relationships of the villagers and the simple ethical values that ruled their lives are poignantly portrayed. *Nama Satpute* limns the struggle of the poor protagonist Nama and his wife, who have relocated to Nama's paternal aunt's village in search of employment. Nama faces relentless harassment from the lecherous Bhagwantrao, who has his eyes on Nama's wife. Nama's helplessness and despair are sensitively portrayed in the play.

The titles of Madgulkar's plays suggest either the main theme, for example, *Kalabarobar Chala*, which means 'move with the times' or refer to events depicted in the play as in *Sati* or carry the name of the protagonist, as in *Nama Satpute*. Some of the titles are taken from popular songs, *Devajine karuna keli*, *bhate pikun pivali jhali*, and *phirtyaa chakavarti deshi matila akar*, *Vitthala*, *Tu Veda Kumbhar*, and popular idioms that are still in use.

Plot Structure

Madgulkar does not seem to adhere to the accepted practice of plot building. Most of his plays do not follow the tamasha tradition of opening with the *gana*, an invocation to Lord Ganesha for the success of the performance, *gaulan* and *batavani*, which were compositions before the actual performance began. Nor do they end with a short prayer-like invocation. While most plays have a three-act structure, sometimes there is a fourth act in the text, but it is deleted in the performance as in "Tu Veda Kumbhar". According to Jabbar Patel, a well-known actor-director-writer, since that act expresses Madgulkar's anxiety about the introduction of a mechanized way of life into the village system, it does not fit well with the Marathi theatre tradition.

As in the stories, the events in the plays are arranged in chronological order. They generally do not have a subplot, and when there is one, for example, the story of Mohana and Diwanji in *Pati Gele Ga Kathewadi*, it merges with the main plot. Madgulkar's hybridization of music and folk theatre in this play was a unique and successful experiment. In some of the plays, songs serve as connectors between scenes and events.

Masterful writer that he is, Madgulkar makes a precise selection of scenes, offers vivid depictions of events and arranges the scenes into Acts to build up excitement, create dramatic situations, depict conflict and infuse dramatic irony, to maximum effect.

The subtle, emotional scenes between Lakshmi and Captain Ford in *Sati*, intense emotional scenes in "Tu Veda Kumbhar" where Ijappa is seen beating the driver Sakharam to death after finding him in a compromising position with Ijappa's daughter-in-law, and the several humorous scenes in *Pati Gele Ga Kathewadi* between Jorawar Singh and Diwanji, are depicted with equal skill. Madgulkar is just as adept at presenting dream sequences as realistic ones.

The endings of Madgulkar's folk dramas align with Madgulkar's pleasant and jovial personality, as in *Pati Gele Ga Kathewadi*. Although the ending of *Sati* is tragic, it is illuminated in the light of the uplifting spiritual satisfaction of the protagonist. However, "Tu Veda Kumbhar" and *Nama Satpute* end on an extremely heart-wrenching note. These endings differ from the endings of the stories they have been adapted from.

Madgulkar's plays bring different themes, different techniques, different forms and different contexts to Marathi theatre. They go beyond the established Marathi, middle class, white-collared setting of the drawing room. This difference is reflected in the concept of space and time in his plays. One can see the drama of life in the real and imaginary regions beyond the typical urban setting of Mumbai-Pune. *Pati Gele Ga Kathewadi* is located in the Kathewadi kingdom, but in "Tu Veda Kumbhar", the realistic drama, the setting is a village in Mandesh. There is only one location throughout the play, but the context of the location changes during the course of the play. The plots of *Nama Satpute* and *Pati Gele Ga Kathewadi* demand different locations for different scenes, and therefore, the directors and the stage-designers had to come up with creative options such as a revolving stage and suggestive and symbolic backdrops. One consequence of this was that flexible experimentative arrangements of props and staging replaced the established, conventional backdrops.

The time span of Madgulkar's plays ranges from four days to ten-eleven years. The references to space and time come according to the actual context of events. Sometimes the references are suggestive of some symbolic significance. For example, *Sati* opens with the joyous wedding scene of Lakshmi and Narayan in the palace but ends with the tragic incident of Lakshmi committing *sati* in the vicinity of Captain Ford's camp.

Characters in Madgulkar's Plays

Vyankatesh Madgulkar's plays do not have as few characters as were found in contemporary experimental theatre. Though numerous, his minor characters do not overshadow the main characters and serve a specific purpose in the plot. The names of the characters are appropriate to the regional and social class context and theatrical form. Some names are intriguing because of their interactive or discursive symbolic connotations. The main characters in *Sati* are named after the divine couple, Lakshmi and Narayan, but do not have a husband-wife relationship! In *Nama Satpute*, the demonic form of Bhagwantrao hovers over the truth and purity of Pavitra.

The characters in Madgulkar's plays are diverse and range from the King Shurasena to Lakshmi-Captain Ford, to Janaki-Sarjerao who are intertwined with the imaginative and historical environment, to the real, long-suffering and hardworking people of Mandesh, representing many castes, communities and age groups. There is an array of characters who complement or oppose each other in thoughts, attitudes, behaviour and roles.

Female characters in Madgulkar's plays are assertive, rebellious and individualistic. Lakshmi in *Sati* defies the coercion of custom when she declares, "My intellect doesn't agree to this." (*Sati*, p. 33), and yet chooses to commit *sati* in honour of another man in whom she finds warm solace. Janaki, in *Pati Gele Ga Kathewadi*, questions her husband on why only women are subjected to the fidelity test. While some female characters are devoted and loyal to a lover or husband, others who are dissatisfied with their husbands allow themselves to be exploited by other men. Some wives appear to be critical of their husbands' weaknesses but are actually helping them become stronger. The complex situation of a woman entering into a socially unacceptable relationship with a man is dealt with in a compassionate, non-judgmental manner in Madgulkar's plays and short stories.

A character is sometimes introduced through stage directions and the dialogues of other characters. Another device Madgulkar uses to reveal the mentality and attitude of a character is through dialogue. For example, in "Tu Veda Kumbhar", the conversation between Sakharam, the truck driver, and the cleaner is suggestive and full of double entendres. It indicates Sakharam's evil designs upon Ijappa's daughter-in-law. As in all his writing, Madgulkar's humanistic approach, sympathetic attitude and non-judgmental acceptance of people's strengths and weaknesses are evident in his plays as well. His characters are portrayed as victims of their own plight and are not categorized as black or white.

According to Vijay Kenkare, noted actor-director, Madgulkar limns his characters quite clearly, but that does not limit or confine them and allow the actor several interpretations, without compromising the disposition or the soul of that character.

Dialogue in Madgulkar's Plays

Madgulkar establishes the region, the period and the society through the language he employs. Dialogues are also used to give the back story of the character's life, manifest the character's state of mind and convey the character-to-character relationships.

Stage Directions

Madgulkar gives few short, simple stage directions except when an act or scene opens as they set the location, time and atmosphere of the scene. Sometimes a physical description and the body language of the character are suggested through the stage directions.

Verses

Vyankatesh Madgulkar wrote poetry in the very early stages of his literary career but seems to have turned to the *shahir* tradition, where an actor performs the role of a *sutradhar* or compere of his folk dramas. Other songs and poems used in his plays were by popular poets of the time.

Linguistic Features

Madgulkar's characteristic style is passionate yet tempered, with the use of few but effective words. He did not subscribe to the accepted view that characters should speak in standard language and not use colloquial forms. So the language varies according to the region, the social context and the local dialect. The characters in "Tu Veda Kumbhar" and *Nama Satpute* are from Mandesh, so they speak in the Mandeshi dialect. Since *Sati* was set in the late Peshwa period, it is natural that Sanskrit verses and mantras appear in it.

Madgulkar brings in humour through the clever use of allusions, diction, vocabulary and popular idioms and sayings. For example, the folk drama *Binbiyanche Jhad* makes a reference to the broadcast of this play on All India Radio. However, the language is always appropriate to the period and setting of the play.

Madgulkar's love of wildlife and nature is evident in the similes he uses in some of the dialogues. For example, Nama Satpute tells the old woman that Bhagwantrao "laughs like a horrible hyena, and spits, after eating a *paan*, like a snake!" (*Nama Satpute*, p. 23).

Whether it is his fiction or his plays, Madgulkar's authorial personality is clearly seen.

Adaptations of Western Plays

Madgulkar adapted several Western plays but completely indigenized them. For example, Tennessee Williams' "Rose Tattoo" was called *Gaurai* in Marathi. Bertolt Brecht's "The Good Woman of Setzuan" became *Devajine*

Karuna Keli and was set in a village in Maharashtra, with the characters using the typical local expressions. Though it was appreciated when it was first performed, some critics believe that none of the writers, directors or music composers of this adaptation had understood the essence of Brecht's plays.

The play, "Fiddler on the Roof", originally set in Russia, was located in a village on the Hyderabad-Maharashtra border before the merger of the Hyderabad State in 1948. The Fiddler is a Dhangar, a sheep-herder, who plays the flute. While the fiddler in the original quotes verses from Moses and the Bible, in Madgulkar's play, he quotes from *Ekanathi Bhagavat* and compositions of saint poets like Namdev and Tukaram!

Some Questions Regarding the Authorial Role of Playwright Madgulkar

Madgulkar's literary expression was shaped by his participation in the freedom struggle, his relationship with the Rashtra Seva Dal, a romantic humanist vision, a progressive attitude and lifestyle and exposure to various currents of world literature through extensive reading. And yet one wonders if there is a hint of orthodoxy in Madgulkar's plays like *Sati, Pati Gele Ga Kathewadi* or "Tu Veda Kumbhar", especially regarding the morality of women characters and feudalistic values. Does Madgulkar tend to hark back to the old world while presenting the old-new conflict? Was he beset by questions, doubts, qualms about modern life, and if so, why? "Was Madgulkar one of the writers on the brink of the transitional generation who depicted the conflict between modern and traditional values?" asks Rajeev Naik. Madgulkar was writing from the context of people, folklore and historical facts. Is it because of this that he draws the equations in a man-woman relationship, or a master-servant relationship, as it existed then? Does it bother us because we expect him to be different? From my own study and from discussions with theatre artists, I realized that perhaps it is not fair to evaluate the role of the writer based on the decisions and behaviour of the characters in the plays that were written decades ago.

According to Jabbar Patel, instead of looking at the external contexts that Madgulkar presents, if we make sense of the metaphor of a woman's true love and devotion to a man, Madgulkar's plays will not seem to have an orthodox tone at all. In fact, humanism leaning to the left, romanticism with a compassionate vision and forward-thinking characterize Madgulkar's plays, as do his other literary expressions. In Vijay Kenkare's view, "Madgulkar was a progressive writer, at least not consciously regressive, and some such aspects must have appeared as a part of the system that he was portraying."

Madgulkar's art of narration, which is an essential feature of his stories and novels, is not available or relevant while writing a play. The particularity and situatedness of the characters' moral world-view, rooted in the old ethos, is likely to have been mapped out as the author's personal perspective. But this point needs to be discussed and elaborated.

The Performative Aspects of Madgulkar's Plays

Vyankatesh Madgulkar wrote for magazines, radio and stage plays and films. He understood each medium perfectly and adapted the techniques for it. Madgulkar was aware of regional and group differences in language, and yet he could deliver dramatic dialogues effectively for every reader, listener and viewer. Some of the theatre artists recall that Madgulkar would present readings of his plays himself to help the actors get the accent, intonation and emotions of the character right. He even rehearsed with leading actors like Jabbar Patel!

Dramatists like Jabbar Patel, Vijay Kenkare, etc., say that Madgulkar understood the requirements of theatrical language so thoroughly that the flexibility and openness of his writing allowed the performers immense possibilities of performance. Because of this, Madgulkar's plays of fifty years ago still retain the charm and entertainment value, say the artists who perform them today.

Madgulkar's Contribution to the Marathi Theatrical Tradition

According to Rajeev Naik, there is a great tradition of writers who study Sanskrit literature and medieval Marathi literature. There has also been a tradition of studying folk art, as well as having a subtle introduction to western literature, western drama and western films through English. Vyankatesh Madgulkar falls into this tradition of local-global or domestic-foreign sensibilities. Madgulkar's plays are of a specific time, a specific region and a specific socio-cultural context, but the content transcends these particular frames of reference, which makes their appeal timeless and universal.

When his contemporaries were influenced by Ibsenian realist technique, Madgulkar was handling the genre of folk theatre. His plays, in both content and form, were rooted in the local soil and brought flexibility, simplicity, wisdom and the real rural world into the white-washed world of the middle class as represented in Marathi theatre.

Madgulkar, S. N. Pendse, and Jaywant Dalvi are similar in terms of regionalism; they are writers in narrative literary genres, and they also handle drama competently. At the centre of their plays are the people connected to the soil, their lives, joys and sorrows, trials and tribulations, and their interpersonal relationships.

Place of Madgulkar's Plays in his Oeuvre

As in all of his literary works, Madgulkar's plays reveal a deep understanding of human nature, his ability to portray events and characters vividly and crisply, to use details creatively and paint on a wide canvas. His language is restrained, the imagery realistic and the visualization definitely that of Madgulkar the artist.

Madgulkar seems to have taken to writing plays to satisfy the creative challenge of handling a different form, a different genre. "I felt that I needed a change after writing portraits and stories. When I change the form, I get new challenges, and like Bhima, whose back has touched the ground, I rise up against the odds with double the enthusiasm. I, thus, turned to plays," he says in *Pravas Ek Lekhakacha* (p. 152).

Perhaps his penchant for playwriting waned after he realized that the success of a play is dependent on too many factors other than the writer. It is also possible that Madgulkar's authorial temperament was primarily that of a narrator. Vijay Kenkare says that writing plays was not Madgulkar's first preference because the themes that he was struck by were more suited to the narrative form. Besides, a play is experienced collectively, unlike other forms of literature which are a matter of personal or individual experience.

Conclusion

Madgulkar's plays are stories of human beings deeply rooted in the soil, with picture-perfect visual portrayals of characters and scenes and judicious use of music and dance-based folk forms. The title of Madgulkar's most famous novel, *Chitrakathi*, a visual narrator, is most appropriate to describe him.

> I like to narrate stories. I feel good when I tell the stories of human beings, stories of their joy and pleasures, their sorrows and sufferings, their follies and their repentance, their wisdom and naivete, their pettiness and nobility . . . I am a Chitrakathi. There has been a thousand year old tradition of chitrakathis who used to enthral and captivate the audience with their narrations combining elements of drawing-painting, singing and music
>
> (Madgulkar, *Chitrakathi*, p. 90)

This essay is based on personal and telephonic conversations with Sunil Barve, Asha and Vrundavan Dandavate, Vijay Kenkare, Dnyanada Naik, Meena Naik, Rajeev Naik and Jabbar Patel. A special mention must be made of Sunil Barve, who gave me the unreleased audio recording of *Pati Gele Ga Kathewadi*. I thank them for their time and the valuable information they provided.

My thanks also to Dnyanada Naik and Mohan Madgulkar, Chinmay Dharurkar and Sushant Devlekar, Mandar Joshi, Uma Nabar, Nidhi Patwardhan, Deepak Rajadhyaksha, Vinod Pawar, Srirang Godbole, Saili Tharli, Amit Mhadeshwar, Vanshree Radye, Pratham Watamble, Mohsin Pathan, Khwaja Moinuddin Syed and Ganesh who supported me in every way. The staff of the Reference Department, Mumbai Marathi Library, NCPA Library, Mumbai, Pune Nagar Vachan Mandir and Digicopiers, Pune, Government Library, Ratnagiri, State Marathi Vikas Sanstha Central Reference Library, Badlapur, Maharashtra Theatre Inspection Board for prompt assistance in finding and availability of reference sources, my deep gratitude.

I Am Including Here a List of Scripts Available and Audio-visual References of the Plays

Madgulkar, Vyankatesh. *Devajine Karuna Keli*. (Samhita by Director Vijaya Mehta, Year Received – 1988), (Script-courtesy: NCPA Library, Mumbai).

Madgulkar, Vyankatesh. *Devajine Karuna Keli*. (Samhita by Music Director Ashok Ranade, Year Received – 1988), (Script-courtesy: NCPA Library, Mumbai).

Audio-visual References of the Plays

Pati Gele Ga Kaathewadi, 1968. https://youtube.com/channel/UCwR8mEwQQgS1ap360foQ5_Q

Pati Gele Ga Kaathewadi. From the personal collection Sunil Barve.

Tu Vedaa Kumbhaar, 2014. https://youtu.be/YX09JaCZAY0

22

VYANKATESH MADGULKAR (VYAMA)

Depiction of Dalit Life

Go Ma Pawar
Translated by Madhuri Dixit and Deepak Borgave

One

The works of every great author contain multiple attributes. The scope of the author's portrayals, nuances of the life he shows, his use of different narrative techniques and the conscious choice of words that he makes, as well as the rhythm of his prose and the maturity of his writing skills collectively render excellence to his work. These features may not have been recognised and acknowledged at once. If they were understood or assessed critically, it may have been in a specific time frame and from a specific perspective. It is therefore necessary to examine all aspects of the author's style and world view periodically and in a new and fresh manner in order for his works to be understood and appreciated.

Vyankatesh Madgulkar is one such author. The canvas of his depictions is very large and unique. Nature and animals form some of the subjects of his depictions, while various members of society, like Brahmans, farmers, the touchable *balutedar* castes, the minority Muslim communities and the untouchables, are featured in his stories. To understand the scope and unique qualities of his depictions and to assist a critical assessment of him as an author, we thought of reconsidering his recently compiled stories portraying Dalit life. Also because he was recognised as an author of standing, particularly after the publication of some of his stories and his novel, *Mandeshi Manase* ("People of Mandesh") in 1947–1948.

Madgulkar's literary merit earned him a place among the four short story writers identified as the *nava kathakar*, (authors of the 'new' story) in Marathi literature whose writings transformed the contemporary Marathi short story.

It was natural for Madgulkar to write about the rural life he had experienced firsthand, and his critics did appreciate the different quality of the rural life he portrayed. But they did not immediately label him as an author of the rural life. Bagul Baburao, also a short story writer, was acknowledged as an author of high standard due to the quality of his short stories based on his own experience of village and slum life. But no critic felt the need to use the soubriquet 'Dalit' for Bagul to establish his stature.

Social changes in India naturally accelerated after Independence. Rural youths and Dalits began to take advantage of concessions and reservations provided to them in the field of education. This changed the social scenario and resulted in the emergence of a sizable class of writers from the rural areas and the Dalit class. Compared to the past, a greater body of narrative literature based on rural and Dalit life began to be written.

Grameen, that is rural and Dalit literature, became separate categories in the body of Marathi literature, and labels such as *grameen* or Dalit began to be attached to these writers.

There is nothing wrong in the labels in order to project differences found in tropes of literary delineations. However, the difference in the objectives of creating such literature was also openly stated by Dalit writers. Writers who portrayed rural and Dalit life certainly enriched Marathi literature. Up to this point, their efforts may be considered praiseworthy. However, in recent times, some literary tendencies which are not so praiseworthy seem to be gaining strength. It appears that the fact that every literature has a tradition and that the literary predecessors have made certain significant contributions is being forgotten. The belief that the real literary output of a specific kind begins with their works is becoming prevalent among some authors. This arrogance is noticed in some of them. It seems as if the pernicious political tendencies that corrupt the literary field have gained strength. Sloganeering has begun to cloud the truth, I feel. Therefore, in my view, it would be fruitful, even from the point of view of improving the health of the literary environment, to cast a glance on literary history and explain the characteristic features of the stories on Dalit life written by Madgulkar by compiling them anew.

In order to clarify the literary features indicated by nomenclatures of provincial or rural literature and Dalit literature, Madgulkar is an important short story writer as he stands firmly on the common ground between the rural and the Dalit literatures. He is known as a *grameen* or rural author since he mainly delineates rural life. It is natural to expect that rural authors will portray rural life and social structure. Just as touchable middle artisan castes, known as the *balutedars* in Marathi, like carpenters, blacksmiths, barbers, etc., are inevitable elements of rural life, the untouchable castes like the Mahar, Mang, Chambhar (cobbler), and Ramoshi are integral components of rural society.

When can we say that an author understands the village well? When the author understands the farmer who is at the centre of village life, along with his occupation of farming, his love for his fields, and his emotional involvement in his work of farming. The author also comprehends the family system, caste system, and the relationship between the majority and the minority communities in the village, their religious beliefs and superstitions, customs and rituals, etc. He also possesses knowledge of the Mahar and Mang untouchable castes who have to keep contact with the villagers for their livelihood, and the nomadic communities like the Paradhis or the Nandiwales who are also dependent on the village. But it is not enough to comprehend all this merely intellectually. It is advisable to modify the comprehension with knowledge of the various cultural, economical and emotional relationships. Additionally, the author must have the potential conscience to observe them from a distant, noble authorial perspective.

To view rural life collectively and comprehensively, we need to understand that the untouchable castes are an integral part of the rural sociality. The powers of a provincial author, his originality, scope and richness can be assessed by apprehending his potential to depict the Dalit castes which interact with the entire village community. While it is normal for the provincial author to write on the theme of Dalit life, if he is unable to portray Dalit life, it can be considered an inadequacy on his part. The range of Madgulkar's comprehension of the sociality of rural life is vast, and the numerous stories he wrote based on Dalit life bear testimony to it.

Two

Madgulkar wrote nearly thirty stories on Dalit life. His protagonists are Mahars, as in stories like *Deva Satva Mahar, Gana Mahar, Kalagati, Vari, Gode Pani* ("Sweet Water"), *Bet, Akher Akanya Ghari Ala, Viparit Ghadale Nahi*, etc. The Mangs are represented in the stories *Nama Master, Gavakada, Nyay, Padaka Khopata*, etc. *Rama Mailkuli, Aadit, Vahana, Khel*, etc., are about the Vharal community; while stories like *Dharma Ramoshi, Nyay, He Paap Kutha Fedu?*, and as the name suggests, the life of the Vadars is seen in Vadarvadichya Vastith. Similarly, the nomadic communities which are mostly the de-notified tribes in Maharashtra, such as the Gadavi Sonar, the Paradhis, Nandiwale, Katkari, and Vaidu, Makadwale and Gosavi, also find themselves depicted in Madgulkar's fiction All his characters are not just members of some caste. They manifest certain special characteristics of their respective castes. His portrayals are sensitive and heart-warming since he explores their inner selves as well. The village life too comes across as real, capturing the reader's eye. The range and scope of his depictions indicate his proximity, empathy and synthesis with rural life. Madgulkar's rendering of how a village community and its *savarna* (upper caste) members treat the Dalits living on the outskirts, the interaction of Dalits with the village and the multifaceted nature of the mutual relations is excellent. One of his earliest stories, *Deva Satva Mahar* (1947), narrates the story of a good-natured, gentle and diligent Mahar, who quite uncharacteristically explodes, provoked by the *savarna* doctor's abuses. This is more than purely incidental. It suggests that the authorial vision sensed the changing times and rising aspirations of the Dalit mind. And that is why Deva's outburst is described as most natural.

This is possibly the first instance where such an outburst against *savarna* exploitation receives realistic treatment in Marathi literature. Madgulkar's other story, *Gode Pani* ("Sweet Water"), illustrates how not just a single *savarna* person but the entire village inflicts injustice on the untouchable community for their own selfish interests.

One afternoon, a few Mahars relaxing in the *takkya*, a meeting place, to talk about the acute scarcity of drinking water. There are a few wells for the *savarnas*, but they yield salty water. The Mahars don't have any provision for even that. They have to walk down to the river far away to fetch water. Vetal Nana, a wise Mahar village elder, suggests they dig a new well for their community. His inspiring words make them resolve to dig a new well. A suitable spot is selected along the stream near Maharwada, the Mahar settlement. The owner of the land, however, is nowhere to be found. A relative, Yadu Baku, is asked for permission to dig the well, and he gives it. The Mahars work hard, and in two days' time, the well yields sweet water. The Mahars are overjoyed to see this. When the *savarna* villagers hear the news, they do not believe it. First they ask Vetal Nana to swear by the god Maruti that the water is indeed sweet. Then they threaten the Mahars. "Complaint will be registered against you all. You have taken somebody else's space illegally and dug a well in it? Is this any Mughal administration that you dared to do so? Have you become greater than the village?" Following this, Yadu Baku changes his mind. The Mahars get scared at the mention of courts and cases. Vetal Nana understands the reason for this threat. He states, "All this is because the well provides sweet water . . . How can the village admit that they are drinking salty water when the Maharwada enjoys sweet water!" The frightened Mahars succumb to pressure from the villagers but obtain a promise that the courts would not be approached. Upon this the villagers generously offer Rs. 50 to the Mahars as remuneration for the hard work they had done and take possession of the well. They rebuild the wall with a barbed wire fence around the well and install two pulleys to draw water so that the well is entirely on their territory. Now the women folk of Maratha, Vani, and Brahman castes fetch water from the *takkya* well. The Mahar women are sometimes seen standing on the other side and literally begging the village women to fill their pitchers. But the upper caste women don't pay much attention to their pleas. When the piteous cries continue for a long time, some village woman fetches one pitcher of water and empties it into the Mahar woman's pot. Seeing it, all other Mahar women at once renew their plaintive appeals. The village women get annoyed by the commotion they create and say, "Look how these people are! No use doing any favour to them!"

A heartbreaking picture of collective ungratefulness and depressing injustice meted out to the untouchable people on the social fringe is the theme of Madgulkar's *Ase Chalalele Ahey*.

Madgulkar's stories show how it is customary for the villagers to always take the side of the *savarna*, even when he subjugates the untouchable, although the untouchable is not guilty. *Akher Akanya Ghari Ala* illustrates this truth. When Akanya is mercilessly thrashed for no crime except being close to the Kulkarni, his mother cries out to the villagers for justice for her son. They taunt her cruelly, "What justice are you talking of? Are they mad that they would beat someone without reason? You people utter some 'words of wisdom' here or there, then you get beaten." They even threaten her. "If anyone seeks to register a complaint against me, just remember that I will not tolerate it. I will burn the whole Maharwada." The Mahars think about it. Should they stop doing the Kulkarni's work? In the end, they make a compromise. Only Akaram voices his opposition to their decision. "You are all scared of the Brahman. I spit on you . . . This Akaram will never work for the Brahman, till his last breath. Anyone who steps into his *wada* (house) does not belong to the Mahar race." And yet, when he sees the old and frail Kulkarni chopping wood, he takes the axe out of his hand and does it himself.

It was not practical for Mahars like Akaram to sustain enmity with the Brahmans. They have to reconcile even if the other party has enraged them. Otherwise it is difficult for the Dalits to live. This is an important aspect of the relationship between the villagers and the Mahar/Mang communities. The *savarna* members disapprove of any attempts made by the untouchable to ask for equal or simple human treatment. They expect the lower castes to always grovel before them. They don't even like the untouchables to wear the special pleated turban!

Madgulkar's stories do not reveal any prejudiced or lopsided understanding of the conflict between Dalits and upper-caste villagers. He does not show that it is always the non-Dalits who treat the Dalits unfairly and the untouchables are always justified in their actions.

There is a hierarchy among the Balutedars (artisan castes) as well. The low castes like the Mahars, Mangs and Ramoshis are expected to be humble or submissive in front of the villagers, at least when they come face to face with them. The farmer community however is dependent on the cobblers and the Vharals. These people who are normally humiliated naturally look for an opportunity to compensate for their dignity. They do not think twice before insulting farmers when the farmer needs them or when they have a chance to earn handsome wages. This fact is revealed by Shida, the cobbler in the story *Shida Chambhar*. When asked if he will repair a farmer's torn chappals, he retorts, "What question is this, sir? Who will, if not me, Nana Nhavi, the barber? He too is a businessman, sir." Shida goes on to fill mud between the two layers of the sole of the thick sandals. When the customer finds out and questions him, he simply says, "Is it soil? No, you are mistaken. It is *karal*."

Gopa Vharal, in the story *Ahana*, asks Panda sarcastically, "Why did you bring this old pair for repair, sir? Even a dog will not like to sniff at it." Madgulkar's depiction suggests that the sarcastic remark has a hidden motive. It seeks to compensate for the humiliations they face everywhere and every day.

However, the relationship of the Dalits with the upper-caste villagers is not always stressful as seen in the story, *Dharma Ramoshi*. The Brahman narrator and his mother are sympathetic to Dharma and do what they can to help him. When Rama Mailkuli, in the story of the same name, is offered tasty, nutritious food, like *bhakri with* butter, *pithale* made of gram flour, lemon pickle and garlic chutney, he keeps it aside for his nephew, instead of enjoying it himself. An inevitable consequence of the untouchability associated with birth in our society is the abject poverty of the low castes. Several Madgulkar stories present a heart-wrenching picture of the squalor that embraces Dalit life but in a restrained yet very realistic, artistic way.

If working men were pushed into such bad conditions, what could one say about the widows? Yesa, in the story, becomes a widow. She can give her son nothing to eat because they have no food. Not even a grain. The entire Maharwada, Mangwada, Vharalwada – all the poor untouchables living on daily wages, were simply surviving by eating all kinds of leaves boiled with salt. Yesa, who watches her son roast a piece of dry turmeric and chew on it, embraces him and starts crying. "O God," she wails, "why didn't you kill us poor folks by making us catch some contagious disease like *pataki*, instead of putting us in such condition?" The story ends with "God did not want to kill her. She was destined to lie in the hut starving. Her only fatherless son was to suffer the pangs of hunger, eat the piece of turmeric and sleep, and she was to ask from the bottom of her heart – Oh God! Why don't you kill the poor with diseases like *pataki*?

It was to be like this, forever.

Untouchability imposed by the social system generates grief that the entire community has to bear. Additionally, it makes the poor suffer from emotional stress. The story named *Kalagati* presents the psychological upheavals experienced by a person who is Brahman by birth but has become untouchable by occupation and co-living. He joins a tamasha troupe, a profession considered suitable only for the Mahars and the Mangs. The Brahmans treat him like an outcaste, a Mahar, and he too believes in it. Pavali, a woman from the tamasha troupe with whom he lives, abandons him in his old age, so he lives out his life with a Mahar woman named Tai, who admired him when he was in his prime. The story *Viparit Ghadale Nahi* shows that a police officer, Vitthal Deshpande, Havaldar, is attracted towards Bahina Mahar, but as he believes firmly in caste hierarchy, he makes a determined effort to ignore the temptation. Bahina is equally attracted towards the young ma. She longs to be with him, but their co-living is unthinkable in their social environment. By sensitively describing the emotional tensions they undergo, the author shows a different aspect of Dalit life.

Madgulkar does not seem to believe that the injustice meted out to Dalits by the *savarnas* or their poverty is alone responsible for creating sorrows in their lives. He profoundly understands the varied expressions of human emotions and attitudes and that sorrows in Dalit life are caused by various factors. Sometimes it is our own people, our own relatives, who are responsible for a lot of the unhappiness and grief that we experience. At times it is our own faults and weaknesses, like various kinds of addictions, that are responsible. At other times, it is the inherent evil that we carry as humans. Hira, a performer in a Mumbai tamasha troupe, creates enmity between two loving brothers by setting up one against the other. Ravya and Bhavya in the story *Padaka Khopta* are another pair of brothers who care for each other very deeply, yet after a quarrel are after each other's lives and, as a consequence, all of them die. Just as Madgulkar draws an excellent portrait of loving familial relationships, he paints equally well the bad feelings like enmity which are introduced in such kith and kin relationships.

Laxmi, a vadar in the story, *Vadarvadichya Vastith*, seeks the support of Kalya vadar after she loses her father, but he cheats her. Then Laksha, an addict, dominates her life, beats her and attempts to kill her too. This is the play of destiny she has to face.

While delineating Dalit life, Madgulkar is always very conscious about its social side, but he is also aware of the subjective and sometimes even contradictory human attributes. There is a Rama Mailkuli on the one hand who asks why to migrate, leaving behind one's own village, house and people; and on the other, there is this Gana who is relieved that he left the work of *gavaki* behind and came to Mumbai. There is Hira, who is ready to sleep with anybody in order to take revenge, and there is the *jogtin* Bahina, who prefers to suffer silently and nobly for love. We see young Pavala, who leaves the Master without bothering about loyalty, while there is this old woman, Tai Mahar, who remembers the Master from his young days and offers him shelter in her hut. Everyone is destined to be poor, but each one displays individuality in fighting poverty. When the famous temple of god Vithoba opens up for all untouchables, Tuka Mahar unhesitatingly goes straight into the sanctum to bow before the deity, while Arjuna Mahar restrains himself and stops at the saint Namdeo's step, the traditional boundary for the untouchables, and pays obeisance from there. Madgulkar has shown a stark picture of the Untouchable people and enlivened his characters with different attributes and attitudes in diverse contexts. He goes beyond the physical world and highlights the spiritual impact on Dalit life.

Madgulkar's depiction of Dalit life is not monolithic. He does not portray only the poverty, squalor and injustice suffered by the Dalits at the hands of the *savarnas* but expresses its diversity and small pleasures. Though the

Dalits have to live in conditions of penury, dereliction and restraint, Madulgar's stories also bring out some delightful moments of their domestic life, as in the story *Deva Satva Mahar*.

After Rama Mailkuli's wife leaves him because of his impoverishment and his inability to fulfil her desires, Rama devotes his life to taking care of his widowed sister and nephew, whom he loves very much. Before he goes to work with the police official, he lovingly pats the nephew, kisses his dusty cheek and saves the good food the Amaldar gives him for the child. By considering the sister and nephew as his family, he makes his life bearable and worth living.

Madgulkar highlights the happiness Banda Mang, who works in a Tamasha party in Mumbai, feels when his brother Bapu comes to visit him. He is most concerned that his brother had to roam around a lot to find the address and that the journey was very tiring. He proudly introduces Bapu to the hotel manager, "This here is Bapu . . . my younger brother . . ." and orders "One *pilet* (plate) *khima*" and four *chapatya*, "You must be hungry, you eat first," Banda tells Bapu.

Not only are the untouchable *balutedars*, who are an integral part of village life, the subject of Madgulkar's stories, the other nomadic and tribal people who depend on the village to some extent for their livelihood are also featured in his stories. He has chosen his characters from the Gadhavi Sonar, Paradhi, Nandiwale, Makadwale and Gosavi castes. His story *Asa Lai Baghithlyath*, in which the life of the Gadhavi Sonar caste is portrayed, is probably the first story to have delineated nomadic life in Marathi literature. (In recent times, Charuta Sagar has written five or six great stories about the nomadic castes.) Paradhi Gangaram, Govinda Katkari, Bhau Vaid are primarily character sketches, though partly based on a fictional narrative. Similarly, Nandiwala can be called a fictional article. The important fact is that whatever and whoever is related to the village has sought the focus of Madgulkar's descriptive writings. The nomadic castes have become the object of his empathy as an author and, therefore, of his experience as well as description.

The main theme of the story *Asa Lai Baghithlyath* is how Laxmi, the daughter of a Gadhavi Sonar, bravely cuts off the nose of the lecherous Bhagwant, the Patil's son, who is a womaniser and sexual harasser. But the way of life of the Gadhavi Sonar community serves as the setting for the story. He tells how the Gadhavi Sonar families load their donkeys with their belongings and go from one place to another, camping for a few days before moving on. All their everyday matters are conducted under the open sky. The village needs them for their skills. They are much sought after because compared to the village goldsmith, who delays small work and steals gold in minuscule quantities while repairing ornaments, they are more efficient. Also, they serve the needs of rural women who, more often than not, want to make new ornaments from the money they save without their husbands' knowledge! These details of rural life do not escape Madgulkar's attention and find their way into his stories.

Although the villagers do not get to work closely with the nomadic castes as they do with the Mahars, Mangs or Ramoshis, Madgulkar's empathy, curiosity and open mind prods him to observe the nomadic tribes from close quarters, obtain information about their way of life with a sympathetic attitude and draw short character sketches that bring the people, their life and their occupations alive.

But since Madgulkar's interaction with the Paradhi tribals was close and deep, his writings about them do not remain mere character sketches. He is fully aware of the entire domestic life of Mithu Shipayi, a Paradhi by caste. He describes their temporary settlement and mentions the common names they are known by, like Mithu Shipayi, Ramjan, Faktya, Medvarya, etc. Their surname is Bhosale. Their god is the Hindu god. They take money for marrying away their daughters and treat women as objects for transactions. They use the loin cloth as a marker of caste. When caught in any trouble, they are possessed by goddess Bhavani to whom they surrender. They hunt vultures and owls and eat them with relish. They can produce the sound of a *chitoor* and by that trick can catch it skillfully. Their cows trot like horses. Their male children do not wear any clothes and run around with dishevelled hair. Such information is revealed through various incidences he describes and through the dialogues he writes. The narrator and Mithu make a deal. The Paradhis would catch a *chitoor* for the narrator, and in return, he would shoot a vulture for them. The Paradhis had killed a dog in the village to attract a vulture. The narrator shoots the vulture, but the Paradhis are not able to get a *chitoor*. They hastily move their settlement out before the narrator finds out. His friend, a Ramoshi, feels bad for the loss of two lives. This is how the author shapes the story.

Three

One may wonder how Madgulkar could write several stories that profoundly describe the multiple aspects of the life of the Dalits, the untouchable castes or how the nomadic people could become the main subject of his narrations. The development of his personality provides an answer to such astonishment.

Madgulkar's sensibility was shaped by the characteristic features of village life. Village life is basically collective life. Whether they are the Brahmans and Marathas from the *savarna* castes or Mahar-Mang-Chambhar-Ramoshis from the Dalit castes, they are all interdependent on each other. Madgulkar's formative years were spent in the village since family circumstances did not permit him to study in a city school. He developed a compassionate, helpful nature, wanted to mix with everyone, understand people and build relationships. Perhaps his poverty allowed him to interact easily with people of low status and his upper caste did not become a barrier. His mind sought influences equally from home and from the village. His home was next to the Ramoshiwada. He used to accompany the Ramoshis into the wilderness. Rama Ramoshi used to tell him funny stories. He was in close contact with Akbarya the Muslim, Lakhu the Mahar, Bali the Ramoshi guard, etc. His mother's influence enabled him to develop close relations with people of various castes. It was a custom in his house to address even the woman who supplied cow-dung cakes respectfully as Govarya *mavshi* (cow-dung cake aunty). The capacity to understand and experience the life of people of all backgrounds must have been developed because of the influence of the collective village life and the liberal caring environment in his family. He had the potential to observe the Dalit lifestyle closely and also developed a capacity to understand their minute reactions, responses and attitudes. Every now and then, we can get glimpses of how he feels: one with them in his writings. The author becomes cheerful when he meets Gana Mahar in Mumbai. "It was very pleasant to chat with Gana! After all he was from my village, a Mahar and a tamasha artist!" He says to Gana, "Come friend, let us have tea in a hotel. You are from my village, and we have met after a long time." He watches Gana play the *dholak* in the tamasha, pats his sweating back and says, "My ears are full hearing you play the *dholak*." (*Gana Mahar*). When he knows that Naga Mang has become a teacher, he embraces him appreciatively. He reacts to Nama's language from an open perspective. He writes, "Even though Nama received education, his language remained as it was, with his old accent. He must be teaching in that language, but who requires pure language there? Nama was the right kind of teacher for the five-ten children, wearing red cloth headgears and round cut shirts in that small village." Madgulkar wrote this in 1948, much before Mahatma Phule's thoughts on education became widely known. When Madgulkar meets Gangaram in a train and comes to know that he is of the Makadwala caste, he connects with Gangaram immediately. "Oh! The Makadwalas are the people who own and train the male and female langur couple, popularly called Devaji Dhasade and Bhagabai, to perform tricks while they play on their small drum called *kudbude*." By showing his familiarity, Madgulkar shows the Makadwales that, in a sense, they were on the same level. He could make anyone open their hearts to him and speak their mind.

Sensing this empathy, not only Gangaram but even Mithu Shipayi speaks candidly after the initial hesitancy. The author feels a lot of compassion for Govinda Katkari and Bhau Vaid, whom he has known for a long time. Bhau Vaid wishes to see the author's children, he feels that their next generation should also become friends. The author's kind and understanding disposition helps him understand the woes of Rama Mailkuli. His heart aches to see the terrible conditions that Dharma Ramoshi lives in. He recognises the acute injustice meted out by the villagers when they forcibly take over the untouchables' well. He understands the anguish of Deva Mahar and the vexation of Arjuna Mahar, whose thinking is heavily influenced by tradition. It is because of his real sensitivity for every kind of rural people that Madgulkar can touch their intimate thoughts and interpret their actions and various emotional responses correctly in his delineations. To say that Madgulkar comes from the same upper class as the Kulkarnis, and hence his outlook is the same, and he views his rural characters from the same perspective is to blatantly misinterpret him.

Several of Madgulkar's stories describe how some members of the untouchable community possess weaknesses due to addiction or how there are some faults like extreme wickedness or dangerous rivalry. But the stories that talk about vices of untouchables are far fewer than the stories which depict their penury and the injustice done to them. It may be Madgulkar's natural desire as author to portray the various aspects of human life; that's why he did not hesitate to reveal their vices too.

The story *Bet* shows how Sandipaan and Vithuba Mahar are disappointed when they do not get to enjoy the meat of Patil's calf that they had killed. Some readers and critics were displeased with Madgulkar for writing such a story. This story is recalled as an example of Madgulkar's outlook towards the untouchables. It points out their flaws and treats them with disregard. We should remember that Madgulkar the author has faith in every kind of human behaviour. He wants to depict every kind of human attitude and action. Madgulkar does not possess any resentment or bias towards any caste. He not only portrays the quarrelsome attitude, selfishness and meanness of the Brahmans but also their illogical, pure wickedness, if given a chance, in the stories. The story *Kalagati* portrays the poor but egotistical Brahmin Sakharam Pandurang Kulkarni, who steals the sacred cloth used in the ritual. Seetaram, in the story *Seetaram Eknath*, is the son of a Brahman Inamdar (revenue official) and the epitome of wickedness. A womaniser and a skillful conspirator, he seizes land parcels from people unethically, entices women and even cheats the widowed daughter of the malin (gardner woman) and makes her pregnant. He traps her innocent son, Shamu, and gets him arrested. Later he pretends to help them get Shamu released and grabs their land. When the mother and daughter duo find out about his evil deeds, they confront him in the wilderness and finish him off with axe and spear. It is Madgulkar's position to portray various attitudes and actions of humans as an author. He looks at all castes from the broad perspective of the author. If his literary works are read comprehensively, one finds no evidence of any bias in it. Following this reflection on his stories, it can be stated that the motivation to cover Dalit life from various aspects seems to be at the root of his story writing.

Four

Some critics fail to understand the literary standards and qualities of Madgulkar. They note that Madgulkar writes in a chronological manner, writes what he sees directly, presents much-detailed descriptions, does not deal with the character's mind but portrays the incident in a realistic manner, and his writing is not original or creative. Their views do not reflect any real understanding of Madgulkar's writing as they mislead us. His writing demonstrates classical restraint as evident in the structure, language and description of emotions in the stories.

To believe that an author writes exactly what he sees as he sees it is to display ignorance about the process of creative writing. It is the author who determines what to see and show in his writing from all that is visible to him. His potential to create lies in that choice too.

Madgulkar's story does follow a chronological timeline. In that way, he has retained the traditional nature of story-telling. A great artist like him might have considered it immature and, hence, undesirable to use the device of flashback for a certain effect. Moreover, his use of a chronological timeline is creative in the sense that though narration may appear to follow chronological time, the nature and order of events are maintained in such a manner that it makes the content poignant. The details of a description are rendered with the power of suggestiveness and are related to the content in order to enrich it. The simple ease with which his story progresses in a chronological manner may be identified as a classical feature of his art.

Deva Satva Mahar follows a chronological timeline which is very important from the point of view of the story. Deva dutifully delivers the *dawandi* (public proclamation) in the evening. Then he happily eats dinner with his family. When his wife tells him that she will not allow her youngest child to get vaccinated for smallpox, the readers get a hint of possible objection from other women in the village. Mharuti Engineer's talk in the *takkya* about changing times and about Ambedkar's honoured responsibilities in Delhi makes Deva aware that their times will be better and there is someone who will take care of their interests. This assurance makes him happy. The conversation suggests his increased confidence and aspirations. Then follows the detailed description of how his second day passes in work, which also proves that he has not neglected his duties. The particular detail that it is his day of fasting and he works hard doing errands on an empty stomach is important. Against this backdrop, the author describes the abusive behaviour of the doctor and Deva's explosive reaction to it. It becomes meaningful even when what goes on in Deva's mind is not described anywhere in the story. The message reaches the reader merely through chronological arrangement of events and suggestive detailing. For his misbehaviour, Deva is punished and sent to prison. The author's remarks at the end on Deva's belief that there is someone in the government who will care for him – "The respected Dr Babasaheb Ambedkar does not know anything about what happened to the honourable Mahar, called Deva Satva Mahar. He will never know it either." – is the most evocative way in which the author brings out the gap between reality and Deva's imagination.

The detailing in the story *Gode Pani* ("Sweet Water") is equally creative. Members of the Mahar community are relaxing in front of the *takkya* one afternoon. Gana Mahar is resting his head on the big neem root jutting out on the ground, his knees bent, and Sandipaan sitting with hands wrapped around his knees and rubbing his chin on one of his arms. They are talking about the scarcity of water and the troubles it is causing. This description of their postures effectively presents an accurate picture of the laziness of the Mahars. But even they work very hard to dig the well. Old Mahar women bring water for the young men toiling in the harsh sun, and the old men wipe their sweating backs and cheer them for their work. Details like how the youths get bathed in sweat and how their calves and forearms became numb with pain demonstrate how hard they had worked. They are significantly placed in the narration in order to bring out the irony, pathos and injustice of the forceful occupation of the well by upper-caste villagers.

The sequence of events in the story *Aadit* is made meaningful with suggestive details that enrich the content. The events take place at different times – on a morning, in the night and again on the next morning. The first morning's incident takes place at the house of Gopa Vharal. Gana Chalpate visits him to buy a male goat, but Gopa behaves arrogantly. In the night, Gopa and other Vharal caste members get beaten till they bleed at the hands of the upper caste Maratha. This violent event changes the scenario totally. The next incident happens at Gana Chalpate's house. Humbled and humiliated, Gopa visits Gana's house and urges him to buy the male goat. Now it's Gana's turn to show arrogance while Gopa bows his head to him.

In this story, the author employs details to suggest the attitude of the characters. Seeing Gana approach him, Gopa continues to look for lice in the seams of his dress. He does not greet him or talk to him. He keeps looking down, plucking his chest hair, and spitting between his feet on the ground. These details imply his haughty attitude. His dark-skinned son pulls the female goat's nipples in play while the male goat bleats all the time. These details render an adversarial impact and underline the consequence of arrogance. Such detailing is common to all his stories.

Madgulkar provides fine details to give the experience of environment, space, human existence, emotion and action and enables the experience of the event in an easy and natural way. This skill is truly commendable.

For instance, in the story *Gode Pani* ("Sweet Water"), the Mahars get up one by one from the *takkya* after they decide to dig the well. But Madgulkar does not end the narration there by simply saying that the *takkya* building was empty. He makes the readers 'see' the empty space by adding, "Sparrows started perching on the ground plastered with cow dung" ("Sweet Water").

In the same story, connecting action with space, he writes, "Yadu Baku speaks while taking down the shirt from the peg, wearing it and unfolding the cloth of his headgear on the ground."

Describing the overwhelmed Arjuna Mahar, who is about to start his pilgrimage on foot, Madgulkar writes, "Then he pulled his grandson to his chest and started kissing him fervently." The action reveals feelings more powerfully than any description of the sentiments in words.

The Mahars approach Yadu Baku to ask for his permission to dig the well at a particular spot. Sandipaan asks Vetal Nana to speak. This is followed by a description of Vetal Nana's actions: "Vetal Nana lifted himself and squatted on his legs. He cleared his throat, threw some pebbles and twigs lying near his hand out of the door, then slowly started speaking cautiously." These details are not without purpose. They represent the importance the Mahars attached to speaking with Yadu Baku, the doubts in the mind of Vetal Nana, and the delay in speaking caused by his humbleness and civility, etc. Such mixed feelings surface through the detailed description of Vetal Nana's small actions. Such creative use of detailing, as stated earlier, appears classical. It moves the reader's mind subtly and generates a muted sense of suffering there. This style is qualitatively different from some other authors who use the same words, repeat the name of the feelings and offer the same interpretation of the state of mind of a character or use disparate but disconnected images to create verbose narrations. Madgulkar impresses with his restraint.

There should be no need to specifically mention that an author can use particulars very creatively, can easily create word pictures of any kind of event. Madgulkar enlivens several different kinds of incidences and descriptions in his stories and other writings, such as the brutal beatings of the Vharals by the Maratha youth, a quarrel between two brothers, frugality of the camp of tamasha artists in Mumbai, entertainment on the street presented by Baba Khan Darveshi, Arjuna who does not dare to depart from tradition on the doorstep of the Vitthal temple, Nandiwalas who stand at the thresholds with their bull, and the process of putting up a tent for the tamasha (*Mouj*, Special Issue, 1947), etc.

Again, whether it is the description of how Paradhis settle down on open lands like a pair of foreign birds, how their cows pick up the rhythm like horses when they walk, how their naked children look with their unkempt hair, how they ride cows to hunt vultures, how Govinda Katkari jumps down into a thicket and lands on his back when a wild boar attacks him, how the highly decorated bull of the Nandiwala looks, etc., they all come alive because of accurate and relevant particulars and Madgulkar's natural language. The reader may actually 'see' the Nandiwala's bull standing in the courtyard just by reading these words, "O my bull, owned by god Shambhu Shankar . . ."

We have already discussed how the chronological sequence of events in his narration have a logic, a function and a purpose. Some other features of his narration are also worth mentioning. A modern dimension is yielded to the stories by the perspective of the narrator. The narration never becomes sentimental. Not only that, it is never even presented in an emotional manner. With regard to the times in which he started writing stories, such control on expression of emotions is unique and praiseworthy. It is also the main reason why the post-1960s generation of authors find Madgulkar stylistically closer than other authors.

The narrator in his stories is sometimes incorporated in the event and the life being described. But the third person narration is used from the omnipotent author's perspective. Both kinds of styles show equal control over expression of emotions. It is noteworthy to find even the first-person narration follows this norm. The story *Dharma Ramoshi* ends with the mention that the *dhoti* given to Dharma was worn by Baja in a saree-like fashion. In another example, the narrative ends by stating that Rama Mailkuli reserves the good food for his nephew, without any comment on his poverty and grief. It generates a strong, grim, introspective and profound impact on the reader's mind. It is sufficient to say that the third person narration in stories like *Aadit* or "Sweet Water" achieves the same impact. The story *Akher Akanya Ghari Ala* is exceptional in making a character narrate the story. On the one hand, it conveys what kind of attitude a selfish, egoist Brahman youth possesses towards untouchables, and on the other, it makes the reader uneasy with the realisation that the Mahars cannot retaliate against even the unjustified oppression; rather, they have to submit to the Brahmans. This is how Madgulkar's style of narration checks emotions and does not let the control over factual depiction ever loosen.

Another unique feature of Madgulkar's narrator is that while looking at human beings and the whole of life from the omnipresent perspective of the author, he actually becomes one with the rural collective mind and knows people and events from that perspective. Choice of words also follows the same perspective. The usage of Mahar and 'Mhara' (colloquial and disrespectful address) does not originate from his upper caste contempt of untouchables. As we can see, he also habitually and frequently uses other colloquial expressions, like 'Baman' or 'Bamna', in the flow of his narration. The real rural sensitivity representing the rural collective mind thus surfaces in his language. From the natural ease and unique power of Madgulkar's language, we may say that he seems to be gifted with it. He understands the nature and power of language very well and appears to use it very consciously. He knows the relation of language with the truth of experience. He says, "If I eat stale bread soaking in the flowing water of a stream, it would affect my language. All that I have seen, suffered and heard has gone into making of my language." His language appears powerful as it is qualified with the power of experience.

Madgulkar absorbs all the nuances of the languages spoken by the different castes. The polite tone in the language of the Mahars and Mangs is absent in the language of the liberated, free-living nomadic castes. It does not have the respectful plural form. "Have '**you**' ever eaten an owl?" is the innocent question Mithu Shipayi asks the author, as if he is an equal. "Thought I'd turn this way, but no space. Thorny bushes to the side, thorny bushes behind, thorny bushes above. And this one suddenly appears right in front . . ." is how Govinda Katkari speaks when attacked by a boar. As for the Marathi spoken by Bhau Vaidu, whose original language bears a similarity to Tamil or Telugu, it makes a complete hash of grammatical gender! By effectively using the varieties of the language used by the upper caste Brahmins or Marathas, the Balutedars, the touchable and untouchables, and the beggar nomadic castes, Madgulkar has enriched the language of narrative fiction. The other author who can be given credit for rendering the linguistic potential of dialects from different religions, castes and regions to narrative Marathi literature is Bhalchandra Nemade.

The examples quoted previously show how keenly Madgulkar employs nouns and adjectives by linking them up with the content. He describes Bahina, who is preparing to start her dance in this way: "Bahina arranged the *padar* (pallu) of her sari and thumped her right ankle on the ground. Her ankle bells sounded zuis . . . sss. . . . The single string *tuntuna* player started playing tanw . . . tanw. . . . The *chondke* (drum like instrument) began playing taang gudgud taang" (*Viparit Ghadla Nahi*). The onomatopoeic words and the verbs selected to describe the incident fully convey its sound and picturesque quality. Madgulkar hardly ever uses adjectives to describe a person, unless absolutely necessary. His style owns the skill of creating live pictures using simple words: "The kid named Mithu was slim and black as a berry. He was real smart. He had grown his hair long and had plaited them on his back. He wore a small loin cloth like the poor students who are fed by people in turns" (*Paradhi*). Madgulkar's similes do not attract our attention as merely fine images but give the reader an actual experience.

Madgulkar's sensitivity is characterised by his belief in oneness of the world of humans, animals and trees. His images show that. A hen with her chickens is described as '*lekurvali*' (a mother with her little ones). Mithu the Paradhi sits with his children around him, on his lap, in his arms, like chicks under the mother hen's wings. Describing the changes in Laxmi after her marriage to Kalya vadar, he writes: "Laxmi, who had fallen silent after her father's death, started chattering like a chirping bird and went around like a spinning top in the saris Kalya brought her." (*Vadarvadichya Vastith*).

Madgulkar's prose has a rhythm produced by simple, long or short sentences. He connects it with the content to create an emotional response. One recognises a different expression of the power inherent in the prose. This is evident in his story, *Vari*, in his description of Arjuna:

> Now Arjuna is tired. He knows he is going to die and hence he is sad and depressed. He is looking to detach himself from the matters

of domestic life. Now he is not concerned about what there is or isn't in the house. He does not grumble that he is neglected in his old age. In fact he doesn't talk much to anyone at all. He sits in a dark corner of his house, shrinking into himself, lost in thought. He eats what his daughter-in-law serves him, and strokes his grandchildren's backs.

There is a certain movement in this paragraph that is related to Arjuna's tiredness and his dispiritedness. By using only the two forms of the verb to be, that is 'was' and 'was not' (more evident in the original language), the author has created this movement. Such examples of writing prose with simplicity and power are rare! Madgulkar is such a great author that one may open any page of any of his books and be pleased.

Five

For the first time during the period 1940–1941, S. M. Mate demonstrated that Dalit life could be made the subject of literary creation by writing stories such as *Bansidhar!*, *Tu Atha Kuthey re Jasheel?*, *Krushnakathcha Ramvanshi* and *Eka Asprushyachya Diarythil Paana* (Pages from an Unctouchable's Diary) The last story, adequately proves that Mate had gained an insight into the untouchable mind. It is not that Mate wrote many books on Dalit life or that all his writing can be considered as accomplished, but it is historically important as he showed the way to make description itself a subject of narrative literature. Madgulkar expanded that trope to a great extent by writing several fine stories on Dalit life over a writing career that began in 1947. Village life being the prominent theme of his creative reflection, he typically wrote stories about people of the untouchable caste, along with some other social elements. Truly speaking, it is very natural for an author belonging to a rural area to write on both the touchable as well as the untouchable castes. For example, Baburao Bagul and Waman Hoval are the other two authors who have written on both the castes and communities. But with the exception of Charuta Sagar, there is no other short story writer who belongs to the province and writes on Dalit life, except Madgulkar.

Madgulkar's stories exhibit various dimensions of Dalit life. After Bagul, Keshav Meshram, Amitabh and Yogiraj Waghmare are the pre-eminent authors whose stories depicting various aspects of Dalit life compel non-Dalit readers to introspect. Madgulkar's depictions of nomadic castes dependent on the village demonstrate how vast the canvas of his compassion and experience is. We have already discussed that quality of his writing.

Madgulkar began to be recognised as a great short story writer soon after some of his stories and the collection of character sketches, *Mandeshi Manase* ("The People of Mandesh"), were published. Some critics use epithets like modern classics to appreciate "The People of Mandesh," but Madgulkar's allegiance is contained in the support he obtains from his own experiences of life. It was natural for an author like him, who wrote classical stories committed to experiences, to have impressed new provincial writers who aspire to write better. For instance, in the character sketches titled "The Soil below the Soil," Anand Patil confesses that he was influenced by Madgulkar's "The People of Mandesh," which he read while studying for his B.A. He felt he too could delineate people from the village and consequently wrote "The Soil below the Soil" (*Khalal*, second edition, p. 187).

Bandhumadhav, author of many excellent short stories on Dalit life, is held to be the first Dalit author. He admits that Vyankatesh Madgulkar's advice shaped his writing:

> I grew up hearing stories read out loudly and started writing my youthful, romantic narrative dreams as love stories. They began to be published in recognised, popular magazines and weeklies. Gradually I began to gain identity and fame as an author. Meanwhile I happened to meet my friend Madgulkar in Sangli. At that time, he was writing his character sketches, "The People of Mandesh," in the periodicals *Mauj* and *Satyakatha*. He was also gaining name and fame as a provincial short story writer. He had only read my romantic love stories in different magazines and weeklies. Hence in our meeting he said something like this: "What is this? Why are you writing only love stories? Write about your fellow Dalit men just as I am writing about my Mandeshi people." His advice pushed me to reconsider my writing, and since I was also thinking in that direction, I started introspecting. Thus my first provincial story, nay the first Dalit story, *Vishari Bhakri* ("Poisoned Bread"), based on the real life of my grandfather, Yetala, became the first Dalit story written by me.
>
> (*Asmitadarsh*, Diwali Issue, 1986. pp. 167–178)

No wonder Madgulkar easily became the inspiration and influencer for the authors identified as provincial and/or Dalit authors for the period to come.

Source

Translated from the Marathi, *VyaMa: Dalit Jivanche Chitran*, Vyankatesh Madgulkar: Sahitya Ani Vyaktitva, April 2019, Pune, Hermes Prakashan.

23
FEMALE CHARACTERS IN VYANKATESH MADGULKAR'S NARRATIVE PROSE

Vandana Bokil-Kulkarni
Translated by Vrushali Deshpande

In this essay, I attempt to present some of my observations on the depiction of women characters in a few of Vyankatesh Madgulkar's prolific oeuvre of stories and novels. I restrict myself to just *Mandeshi Manasa, Oza* and *Jambhalache Divas,* his collections of short stories and the novels *Bangarwadi* and *Karunashtak* in view of the word limit imposed on the essay.

Vyankatesh Madgulkar had not only understood the true man of the soil, he was able to depict him vividly and realistically in words. Numerous word pictures of the simple and ordinary, crooked and deceitful, naive and innocent people emerge from his region, Mandesh. But the percentage of women characters among them is significantly small. And the ones that are there are not drawn in strong, bold strokes. The bear-man Babukhan Aswalwala's wife and Dharma Ramoshi's daughter Baji seem to have come in as merely supporting or complementary characters in the story.

Madgulkar's characters smell of the village and the rural soil in which their stories are set. Their language and their problems are all genuinely rural. Therefore, it is but natural that the majority of his female characters are also rural. Whether it is the Dalit woman Bahina who becomes 'God's Tree' for falling in love with Vitthal, a Brahmin policeman in the story *Viparit Kahi Ghadale,* Guna who persuades her husband to become a wrestler to teach a lesson to Yelmara who thumps his arms every time he sees her, or the brave Lakshi who catches a live jackal in *Vadarvadichya Vastit.* Or it could be the Mussalaman goat-herder Chaman who comes back to her father's home because her husband turns her out, or Pawar's Vancha who opens her heart out to a stranger, Sukha Jadhav, and speaks about the harassment from her in-laws for not bearing a child in *Bazaarachi Vaat.* These women come to life in their stories as physically and temperamentally strong. While creating these characters in a very limited space, Madgulkar keeps a tight grip on the plot. Therefore, it does seem as if the author has not presented the entire life story of many of the women characters.

FEMALE CHARACTERS

The one unforgettable woman character who stands out independently, with name, colour, appearance and life story, is Tambolyachi Khala or Khala of the Tamboli family from *Mandeshi Manase*. When the narrator comes into the English fourth grade, he takes up a room in a wada in the village, along with his friends, to study. In the room next to them lives a tamboli, a betel leaf vendor, called Khala. Her husband had a good business, but as the money came in, he changed. He started beating Khala every day. Then he brought a woman into the house. Khala put up with it for as long as possible, but when it got too much, she left the house early one morning. With some of the money she had saved, Khala starts a small business selling kumkum and toothpowder. One day she gets the news of her husband's demise. She starts living as a widow, working hard and struggling to make ends meet. Khala is a dark-complexioned, short, plump, street-smart woman. The writer says, "The tamboli's Khala would stride along purposefully, holding the bunched up pleats of her sari in her hand. And when she spoke, words crackled out of her mouth like popping grain." This lonely woman with no kith or kin of her own earned her living by selling roasted gram, peanuts, popped grain, kumkum and toothpowder in the neighbouring villages. She showers affection on the narrator and his friends. She daubs the floor of their room with cow dung. Occasionally, she gives them freshly roasted gram. She accepts the life she has and lives without self-pity but with dignity. She has a simple philosophy – connect with four-ten people, be deemed good, and live in peace and harmony. She is the only female character in *Mandeshi Manase*, a collection of character-based short stories, but she leaves a lasting impression on the reader.

In the story *Vadarwadichya Vastit*, Lakshi and her old father live by themselves. Lakshi used to take the sheep out to graze throughout the day. She would collect the cow dung, make dung cakes and sell them. In the flock, there was a male sheep called Harya. He was the love of Lakshi's life, and she pampered him thoroughly. Harya had won many prizes in sheep-fights in nearby villages. One day, when Lakshi's father had gone to the village, Lakshi sees a wolf trying to drag away one of her lambs. Lakshi pounces on the wolf and grabs him by his hind legs near the mud fence from where he had entered the enclosure. She holds on to him till the people from the Vadarwadi colony come running with lathis and sticks and capture the wolf. Lakshi is greatly appreciated for her courage everywhere. From that day, Harya changes. He shows her loyalty and gratitude as if Lakshi had saved his life. A few days after the death of her father, Lakshi enters into a relationship with Kalya Vadar. In that preoccupation, she ignores Harya. Kalya, who was initially good to her, starts drinking and beating Lakshi. Lakshi endures it all and starts paying attention to Harya once again. One day, Kalya asks her to serve him Harya's flesh. Lakshi refuses. Kalya attacks Lakshi with an axe. Seeing this, Harya breaks his tethering rope, barges into the hut, attacks Kalya and kills him. Since then, the courageous wolf-catcher,

Lakshi, and Harya, the devoted animal, live happily in the Vadarwadi. Lakshi, a free spirit, like the wild plants and shrubs that flourish in the forest, and Harya have become immortal in the world of Marathi literature.

In the story *Oza*, Ladabai and her husband Soma come to the city from the village to seek work. They live in a roadside hut and earn some money by collecting garbage all day long. Ladabai is into her full term of pregnancy, so Soma persuades her to commit a petty theft or some other offence that will send her to jail. In her heart, Ladabai does not agree with this proposal, but after the life of poverty on the roadside, she thinks this is the only way she can have a safe delivery and eat a full meal during childbirth. One day, Ladabai sees the open door of a bungalow, quickly enters it and steals a silver pot and glass and puts it in her sack. Just as she is walking out, the mistress of the bungalow catches her. Seeing Ladabai's heavily pregnant form, she says, "You should actually be handed over to the police and put in jail, but seeing your condition I will let you go." Ladabai is half-dead with shame. Breathing heavily, she somehow reaches the hut and tells her husband firmly, "I will give birth in this hut here. I will eat whatever little we get but I will not go to jail." Ladabai, who though abjectly poor, leads a respectable life, must carry the shame, the burden – the '*oza*' of her crime forever.

Abject poverty and hardship are a way of life for almost all these women. In the story *Gode Pani*, Dalit women are seen trudging for miles in search of water. *Dharma Ramoshi* tells of the young woman Baji, who doesn't come out of the hut because she has no clothes! And in the same story is the kind-hearted narrator's mother who says, "Dharma Naik is from my home's side. How can I let him starve?" Rama Malkuli's Asturi, who leaves her husband because she is sick of being poor, and Raghu clerk's wife, who falls in love with another man because he cannot fulfil her desires, are some of the other strongly portrayed female characters in Madgulkar's stories.

In many stories, it is the narrator's mother who stands out as the embodiment of a woman's tenacity, her innate wisdom. Dagadu Teli's wife, in the story *Maza Baap*, is a similar example. The teacher in her son's school is trying to get the boy vaccinated against smallpox. But the boy's father is adamant. He will not agree to it. Finally Dagadu Teli's wife, understanding her son's conflicted mental state, has him vaccinated without his father's knowledge. These women who stand by their children are very important. Ignorance, when accompanied by stubbornness, gives rise to bitter entanglements. It becomes impossible to act with reason and understanding. Words become useless. And these women know it. Madgulkar is adept at portraying the characteristic traits of courage, fortitude and wisdom that the women of that time showed while finding a practical way out of difficult situations and workable solutions to problems.

The mother in *Karunashtak* is a person that one should take cognisance of. *Karunashtak* is an autobiographical novel, and the title *Karunashtak* suggests that the deep sense of compassion his mother possessed is also present in the character of the mother in the novel. She is rich with life experiences and innately wise. The novel begins with Dada, the father, being transferred and the family preparing to move to the new place. The author gives a very telling description of the mother behaving as if she is the mother to all. It shows the toughness in her personality. The woman has eight children. Ashtak – eight. Significant. Here the author describes a female sparrow lining her nest of twigs and sticks with tangles of soft hair so that her babies can lie comfortably in it. But in the end, she gets entangled in the tangles herself and dies. With this metaphor, the author tries to make sense of a mother's life. The metaphor is apt for the mother in *Karunashtak*. She is religious by temperament, ever caring for humanity by nature, hardworking and practical in her behaviour. The extreme poverty of her home compels her to beg for some flour from the beggar who comes to her door seeking alms! But she also expresses the confidence that "Today my children are small but when they grow up they will earn 'with ten hands' ".

> My mother was not a pandit, but she was convinced of the importance of education. So she helped the needy children who wanted to study. Helpfulness was inherent in her nature. She used to keep such children at home even though they were poor, saying, "You are the seventh of my six children."

This is what Madgulkar has written elsewhere. One sees this trait in the mother in the novel too. Being useful in times of need, extending a helping hand whenever required shows the generosity of her spirit. She gives her children a legacy of noble values, high principles and a good conscience. She refers to her husband, who is utterly detached from the household, as 'Tukarambova'. Like the saint Tukaram's Avali, this mother too is completely involved in the children, people and matters of the world. In this sense too, the metaphor of a bird is relevant. This character is very practical and also emotional, representing many women of that time who had practical wisdom but led very miserable lives due to circumstances and a lack of education.

The female characters in his very famous novel *Bangarwadi* are memorable. Rajaram Vithal Saundanikar, a very young protagonist, is on a temporary appointment in a school in a Dhangar, a sheepherders' settlement. The daily routine of the shepherd women is to take the sheep and goats out for grazing and wander about the forest behind them all day or work as labourers in the surrounding fields, return home in evening to make *bhakris* and weave raw wool *ghongadis*.

Among these simple hard-working people, Shekuba dhangar's 'four-hands tall' wife stands out. She towers over the thirty-five-year-old Shekuba, who is very small-made while she is strong and sturdy. She does all the work in the field like him, even yoking herself to the plough when Shekuba cannot find an ox at the crucial time of sowing. In a rare show of sympathy and gratitude, Shekuba massages her sore back that night.

There are two other female characters in the same novel. One is the Karbhari's Anji and the other Jaganya Ramoshi's lover. But they only play subordinate roles in the narrative. They give impetus to the story, and through them, the author reveals the customs, beliefs and traits of human nature. In the same novel, the mother of the protagonist reveals her strong and sensible nature through a small incident. Rama Bangar from the village gives the hero three hundred and forty silver rupee coins with the imprint of the Queen and asks him to get change. The protagonist gets the change, but the bag with the money is stolen. It was a very big amount those days. The protagonist spends sleepless nights worrying about how he would return the money. But more importantly, he is anxious about Rama's trust. His conscience doesn't allow him to eat or drink. The protagonist's mother notices this. While the father tells him, in a matter-of-fact way, to confess the whole truth and goes away, the mother questions the young man about all the details. She is worried too, but when the protagonist is about to leave for the village to take up the job, she reassures him that they will raise the money by selling the house her father had left her. This relieves the hero's anxiety somewhat. The thought that his mother supports him, that they can give Rama's money back comforts him. Eventually the money is recovered, but the peace that the hero gets from the strong support of his mother in difficult times is invaluable.

In the stories *Bai* and *Dhar*, Madgulkar has taken a keen and perceptive look at the mental world of a woman. Not as psychoanalysis but with the view to depict the details of her everyday life!

The story *Bai* is about a school teacher in Mumbai. Having become a widow at a very young age, she has a latent hope of fulfilling all her unfulfilled desires; but she is confused about what exactly she wants and how to get it. The author captures the subtleties of her behaviour in that confused state. Valimbe, a schoolmaster, shows interest in her. He extends the hand of friendship. They get more acquainted . . . they go through the various stages like going for a walk on the beach, etc. After that the woman marries him. For four to six months, the teacher comes to her place every evening and goes back to his home in the morning. The woman, however, does not leave her room and go to him, nor does she invite him to stay with her. This shortlived marriage dissolves without anything special happening. The loneliness of the woman, the attraction she feels towards men, but the curtness with which she deals with them is captured in fine detail. Madgulkar's narrative literature contains very few characters living in the city. This exceptional woman is one of them!

Bazaarachi Vaat is one of Madgulkar's most outstanding stories. Like gentle moonlight, the story talks about companionship, attraction and yearning. Pawar's Vancha is striding along towards home after selling her crop of chillies in the bazaar. It is late in the evening and she is all alone. Sukha Jadhav, who hails from the same village and is a respected family man, is riding past when his cycle gets punctured. Sukha is forced to wheel his bicycle alongside Vancha. The circumstances, the surroundings and the comfort of a 'safe' companion lead Vancha and Sukha on a different path for a short while that night. The author's ingenuity in catching the drama of the moment and the turmoil in the feminine mind evokes a convincing, deeply moving picture of the sadness deep down in Vancha's heart. This brief interlude comes as a cool breeze to soothe her.

Basically, Madgulkar's writing does not take delight in analysis. Although he has a socio-political consciousness as a human being, its direct relationship with life does not seem to appeal to him as a writer. As a result, there is no socio-political element or analysis of the trials and tribulations of the characters' lives.

The strength of his narratives is the authentic, dramatic, meaningful and subtle details with which he draws his characters. As much as the variety and diversity of different castes and occupations that appear in his writing, so much is the diversity and variety of temperament, attitude and thinking of the characters! On the whole, though, Madgulkar's narrative world is more male-centric!

Source

This essay was written for this volume.

24
RECONNOITRING CASTE, LANGUAGE AND FOLKLORE IN THE NOVELS *VAVTAL* BY VYANKATESH MADGULKAR AND *FAKIRA* BY ANNA BHAU SATHE

Baliram Gaikwad

Though several authors have painted the canvas of Marathi literature employing myriad literary colours, few have managed to maintain their distinctness. As Suresh Bhat's lines underscore, 'My colours are distinct, even if I am mixed in all colours', Vyankatesh Madgulkar and Anna Bhau Sathe have unarguably carved and retained their uniqueness in the world of Marathi literature. One was born in Madgul, the land of the impoverished, drought-stricken people of Mandesh, while the other was born in the fertile Warna river valley with lush green hills around it. Both were part of a strict caste-segregated society.

Comparisons are always odious, especially between any two greats, be they persons or books; however, the two novels *Vavtal* by Vyankatesh Madgulkar and *Fakira* by Anna Bhau Sathe may be compared to facilitate a refined comprehension by the readers.

Vyankatesh Madgulkar's *Vavtal* ("Winds of Fire", 1985) and Anna Bhau Sathe's most acclaimed novel *Fakira* (1969) have become iconic works in Marathi literature. Coincidentally, both have been translated into Russian. *Vavtal* was translated into English and Kannada as well as Russian (Raduga Publishers). *Fakira* was translated into Hindi, Czech and Russian, and most recently into English. Though the novels were written sixteen years apart, *Fakira* takes place in the pre-independence period of the 1920s, while *Vavtal* takes place in 1948, a year after Indian Independence. Both are based on real-life incidents. The setting of *Fakira* and *Vavtal* is the Sangli district of Maharashtra.

Fakira is Anna Bhau Sathe's third novel. The socio-political portrayal, the fight against injustice, caste-based cruelty, social profiling, augmented torture of Dalits during British rule in India and the Dalit's ceaseless quest for collective welfare through martyrdom are the salient features of this novel.

It reflects Anna Bhau's own socio-political concerns and his later activism for the rights of Dalits and all marginalised people.

The protagonist, Fakira, a Dalit belonging to the lowest caste of Mangs, revolts against both the rural orthodox caste system and the British Raj to save the people of his village from utter starvation, humiliation and death. He loots the British treasury and distributes the treasure equally amongst all starving Dalits. British authorities leave no stone unturned to capture him but fail in their efforts. As a last resort, they take the whole village hostage and torture the villagers by denying them food, curtailing their mobility, and declaring that all the hostages will be killed if Fakira, who has gone underground, does not surrender. To save the lives of his villagers, Fakira gives himself up. Two hundred villagers are released. Fakira is hanged.

Fakira's sacrifice for the sake of his villagers reflects the philosophy of humanism. Patriotism, social awakening and the fight against age-old caste discrimination are the distinct landscapes of the novel. Facing all extremes of hardship in their lives, Anna Bhau's heroes fortify and energise human life. Fakira becomes the symbol of the crusader for justice for the Dalits and epitomises the qualities of Dalit magnanimity, valour, the spirit of fair play, honour and an unquenchable thirst to live life with dignity. All these values are amply evident in the novel, not just through Fakira's character but that of the supporting cast as well. Another salient feature of the novel is the portrayal of the Mang-Mahar unity. Throughout the novel, they stand united to wrestle with the adversities in their lives. The misfortunes are tackled collectively with the deepest faith and belief. Also important is the fact that the whole community, comprising all castes and classes, takes immense pride in their land and their village and is willing to sacrifice their lives to protect and uphold its honour. Fakira's struggle is the assertion of identity accentuating caste, class, gender, ethnicity, language and region, and the criminalising as well as stereotyping of the Dalits. Fakira resists the prevailing norms imposed by mainstream society and the British rulers and nurtures a voice against multi-layered oppression. It is symbolically an attempt to rediscover and reconstruct the socio-cultural history and defy the dehumanising oppression.

Fakira is part of a powerful literary genre of Dalit writing that brings collective accounts of Dalit life and their struggles based on the principle of justice and equality. It develops the narrative of resistance against caste domination. This narrative of pain encompasses both historical and contemporary reality, the truest human emotions and situations with the lived-up reality of the Dalits. Starvation and deficiency govern this narrative with a dominating sense of community, where crime has sanctions on its social merit.

Though the upper castes here have piled up inflictions, exploitation and torture, the Dalits love their country, India, equally, and the incident that triggers off the novel – the recapture of the jogini – can be viewed as a mark of their larger patriotism.

The character of Vishnu Pant Kulkarni, a staunch supporter of the Dalits, who appeals to them 'not to give up to famine but exhibit grit and be alive' reflects Anna Bhau Sathe's vision of social justice, equality and brotherhood.

Vyankatesh Madgulkar's novel *Vavtal* (1985) underscores the social tensions after the assassination of Mahatma Gandhi when the author was working in Pune. The mourning, evidently visible all over, was also accompanied by anger and incidences of violence against the upper castes, mainly Brahmins, which were recorded too.

Vavtal is a powerful novella that gallantly deals with the sensitive subject of the assassination of Mahatma Gandhi and its aftermath, particularly the violent protests against Brahmins whose houses were set on fire and innocent people attacked. This contagious social rage soon spread nationwide, and how it reached the shanties around Pune city and corrupted the common minds has been psychoanalytically diagnosed in *Vavtal*. Shankar, the protagonist of the novel, and countless Brahmin families experience the same insecurity and vulnerability that certain castes felt when they were criminalised during the British Raj. Madgulkar delineates how the anger against Brahmins was mounting, and at that moment, the entire Brahmin community was indirectly held responsible for the unfortunate assassination. Madgulkar outlines Shankar's journey from Pune to his native village and the live experiences of violence he encounters in Nandavadi of Atpadi taluka. The experience becomes deep-rooted in Shankar's consciousness. He faces mistrust in his own village, and all those who had been living a life of trust, brotherhood, mutual respect, from time immemorial, suddenly start suspecting each other. This eventually leads to riots. Avoiding any exaggeration, holding truth at the centre, Madgulkar deftly deals with the striking bitter truth, the socio-political tensions, psychological trauma, the timid responses of many innocents and mob psychology in the novel.

By comparing the novels *Fakira* and *Vavtal*, the readers are familiarised with incidents of targeting certain communities in the past. During colonial rule, the Britishers declared the Scheduled Castes and Scheduled Tribes as 'criminal castes', and for many years, those castes lived a life sans dignity, pride and basic needs. Anna Bhau Sathe portrays the caste-based collective experiences of social exclusion in *Fakira*. Madgulkar too has drawn on the homogeneous experiences of caste-based discrimination in *Vavtal*. While dealing with the main theme, both Anna Bhau and Madgulkar employ nature as a powerful tool. They devote many lines to descriptions of forests, trees, the local birds and the transition of seasons using powerful sensory images.

Both Vyankatesh Madgulkar and Anna Bhau Sathe have rural life as the central theme and setting in their writings. Madgulkar's short stories like *Ojha* ("Burden"), *Gode Paani* ("Sweet Water"), *Deva Satva Mahar, Aadit, Dharma Ramoshi*, and *Vadarwadichya Vastit* reflect rural Dalit life, issues of caste, social pressure, and superstitions which he had observed since his childhood.

Both authors concentrate on the rural lifestyle and the deep-rooted value system that prevails in the life of the village. How closely caste, religion, customs and rituals, festivals and superstitions are associated with the lives of the people is faithfully described by both Sathe and Madgulkar. The value systems operating in urban life that are reflected in the writings of both authors also bear close resemblance.

Although the language style of Anna Bhau Sathe and Vyankatesh Madgulkar looks similar, we can find the caste consciousness in it. Being of the Mang community himself, Anna Bhau Sathe had complete understanding of the Parushi language, which only members of his caste use, as well as the Marathi spoken in western Maharashtra. The nature of Madgulkar's Mandeshi dialect however is different from that of Parushi and the Marathi of western Maharashtra. The difference is noticed in the dialogue between the characters. For example, in the Warna region, '*ga*' is used, while in Mandesh, '*ra*' is common in conversation. And yet the similarities between the dialects of the two regions are palpable. The tone used in both languages appears rough and coarse, yet it has its own melody and rhythm that is reflected from that soil. Both authors have toiled to maintain the sweetness of their tongues.

The manner in which a writer conveys what he or she wants to say is roughly called the narrator's style. While studying the narrative style of Anna Bhau Sathe, we realise that he paints the nature around him elaborately and consumes much space describing forests, trees, rivers, trails, seasons, imagery and embellishment. Madgulkar is a little different. His narrative style is more autobiographical, even though he often uses the third-person narrator. His language is simple and direct, with shorter sentences and few figures of speech. Madgulkar does not allow his readers to think beyond the storyline. The strength of his narrative style lies in his most accurate portrayal of reality.

The starving group has no caste, religion, sect, language or any identity other than hunger, and the group inspired with the motive of vengeance has no such thing as kindness. Love, sin, virtue is largely the thematic and ideological concern of both *Vavtal* and *Fakira*. Since Anna Bhau Sathe was born into a Mang caste known for its fighting spirit, the context of misery, poverty and caste discrimination is underscored starkly. And as Madgulkar was born in a Brahmin family, his experiences and references of misery and poverty are also underlined. But the background in both novels, *Fakira* and *Vavtal*, paints a grim picture of rural life and caste reality. *Vavtal* is based on a real event, whereas *Fakira* is the 'epic struggle' story.

Based on the previous arguments, it can be said that Vyankatesh Madgulkar was presenting the reality of the grief of Dalits in general, and Brahmins in particular, in *Vavtal*, while Anna Bhau Sathe was looking for a remedy to cure the grief of Dalits. Both of them were sensitive to the same pain, but in a different way and to a different degree.

Select Bibliography

Atre, Supriya. 1998. *VyankateshMadgulkar: A Critical Study*. Mumbai, Suras Publication.

Bhatt, Suresh. 1973. *Roopgandh Rang Majha Vegala*. Mumbai, Elgaar Publication.

Ghughe, Sangita Ganpatrao. 2003. "*Vyankatesh Madgulkar hyanchya sahityacha Lokatatviya Abhyas*", Ph.D thesis, Swami Ramanand Tirth Marathwada University, Nanded.

Ghughe, Sangita. 2015. *Folklore Study of Vyankatesh Madgulkar's Literature*. Pune.

Madgulkar, Vyankatesh. 1983. *Vavtal*. Pune, Utkarsh Prakashan.

Sathe, Anna Bhau. 1959. *Fakira*. Pune, Suresh Agency.

Source

This essay was written in English for this volume.

25
NATURE OF POLITICAL CONSCIOUSNESS IN VYANKATESH MADGULKAR'S WRITINGS

Bhaskar L. Bhole
Translated by Madhuri Dixit

There has hardly been any attempt to analyze the political content in Marathi literature from the interdisciplinary approaches of sociology and political science. Some of the few available studies of fiction and drama in Marathi understand the 'political' on a superficial level. Any literature can be submitted to political analysis even if it does not explicitly address a 'political' subject or have political characters, events, questions or ideology because the author does respond in his own capacity to the socio-political milieu in which his writing takes place. It is impossible for any author to be a-political by completely neglecting socio-political changes in his/her environment because the socio-political reality is an integral part of the human environment.

Well-known Kenyan novelist Ngugi Wa Thiong'o reiterated the point in different words in his address to a session of the Sahitya Akademi Conference in 1994. He stated, "Every author writes politics. The only question is what and whose politics he writes about!" (The Times of India, 12 February 1994). No author's works can escape the influence of the existing power structure in class terms that incidentally shapes his everyday life. One or more aspects of the continued intense socio-political struggles are bound to find reflection in the author's works. The only choice that is available to the author is to stand on any one side: either of the people or of the oppressing social classes or powers.

In order to inquire into political content in the literary works of an author, one should critically examine his response to the socio-political realities in which he lives. Things like the author's perception of the reality, his awareness of the changing nature of that reality, his interpretation of the same and his own position regarding those changes require minute consideration. It is also necessary to see how he reconciles tradition with modernity. If politics is understood as 'when, who, how and what does one gain', the conceptualization of politics cannot remain restricted to political institutions, power politics, political parties and ideologies. It rather encompasses the entire social life. No author can remain inattentive to such politics. It is necessary and possible for the literary critic to search for the socio-political interpretative worth of literary works without compromising artistic values.

It is obvious that imaginative literature is not a mere report of socio-political processes. At the same time, it is equally clear that no artistic creation originates in a vacuum, away from the society. There is no difference of opinion that literary values should be applied first to a work of art in the process of critical analysis. Still, it cannot be denied that the work of art is required to be submitted to socio-political critique when it becomes a part of social life. This is because literature is not a mere social creation, it owns certain social power, and just as it is the result of some social reasons, it is rendered with an agency of desired or undesired social impact. All these factors call for socio-political analysis of literature. Such a perspective informs the present analysis of short stories and novels written by Vyankatesh Madgulkar. Nonetheless, it should be noted that this is not a merely base-superstructure perspective or that it does not attempt to create a simple and easy equation between Madgulkar's writings and his caste-class-race status.

Madgulkar began writing stories and novels around the time of the attainment of political independence. He was in his prime as a short story writer during 1945 and 1950. The period was also crucial for Marathi literature and society as it was embedded with several new possibilities. Important events like the two World Wars, the assassination of Gandhi and the riots following the assassination had stirred up urban as well as rural life. A new social awareness about rights of citizens had emerged through the new Constitution, new judiciary and new schemes for development, particularly among those social strata which had newly entered the political scenario by way of the right to vote provided constitutionally. Therefore, they gained self-confidence and self-expression for the first time in history. New dimensions of social change, new concepts and new political leadership had emerged. Innovative approaches of leadership were emerging from the lowest to the highest-level politics. These developments naturally influenced literature. Old literary conventions were abandoned, paving the way for new experiments in composition. The stereotyped nature of plot relaxed to allow handling of many new subjects. Such a metamorphosis was evident in both the streams of Marathi literature: the rural as well as the urban. False moralizing or idealism retreated, and real-life struggles began to be captured in words. Nuanced oscillations of mood and emotion in the subconscious replaced the coarse dramatic conflicts between stereotyped characters. Symbolism in writing was gradually substituted by objectivity. Madgulkar's literature represents these changing times in many respects.

Madgulkar's way of life seems to have had a positive impact on his literature. He could come out of his Brahmin-middle-class cocoon and experience the social life of the low classes flanked with maturity and understanding. His acquaintances criticized him for being 'a wasted youth'. He had to spend his crucial years with this belittling public perception, working hard and doing jobs of different kinds. He could sympathetically mingle with former untouchables and nomadic tribes by transgressing the superiority of his high caste. He preserved impressions of the lives of members of various castes and communities from the Mandesh region that he actually co-lived with, listened to and experienced sensitively. He made his dream to achieve something different come true by substantiating these 'humans' in his literature who had accompanied him in the exasperating moments of his life. His literary works come across as natural since he remained loyal to his own experiences. Readers gladly agree with his own view of his writing: "Narration flows as smoothly as thread from the spinning wheel. Words settle down in exact places. Sentences balance themselves finely. Everything flows together to come alive." (*Mazya Likhanamagachi Kalsutre*, "The Formulas behind my Writing"; *Gavakadchya Goshti*, "Stories from the Village", third edition, 1982–1988). He could effortlessly imitate the language used by members of different castes. He earned this skill through whatever he had suffered from, seen and heard.

Madgulkar had participated in the 1942 Quit India Movement. He was introduced to some important political prisoners who had escaped from the Sangli prison. Madgulkar wrote stories of their valour. The revolutionaries printed thousands of copies of the stories and distributed them. For three years, Madgulkar accompanied them wherever they went in order to write stories of their bravery and sacrifice. During those years, he witnessed several critical moments, met with several people (*Suruvatichya Athvani*; *Hastacha Paus*, 1965, pp. 14–15). He later narrated these experiences in his book *Kovale Divas* ("Tender Days") through the eyes of a young freedom fighter. But for a long time, his aggregate mood remained one of disappointment and dissatisfaction. He finally came out of the nervousness when his story writing received good response and publicity. Then he continued to write more and more stories. He was the first author to present the functioning of mutually inter-dependent village life that was in operation for generations of farmers, the twelve *balutedars* and twelve *alutedars* (labour or artisan castes), the Patil-Kulkarni *vatandars* (revenue collectors), the minorities, as well as the nomadic tribes and communities.

Going by what Go Ma Pawar, the editor of an anthology of his short stories on Dalit life, *Oza* (G. M. Pawar (ed.), Saket Publication, Aurangabad, 1987, pp. 4–35) says, "Madgulkar also shows mistakes committed by the erstwhile untouchables while realistically delineating atrocities committed by the upper caste members in their personal or collective capacity." Madgulkar's stories do not appear lopsided in any respect because just as he shows various kinds of conflicts and tensions between the upper and the lower castes (the *savarnas* and the *a-varnas*), he also mentions their historical cohabitation and mutual reliance. Madgulkar is well aware that there are several other reasons responsible for the outcries and woes of the Dalits, apart from poverty and atrocities by the *savarnas*, and he does search for them in his writing. Some of them, as suggested by his stories, are addiction, human tendencies, personal wickedness and so on.

Madgulkar portrays the life-world of not only the labour castes in the village structure but also of the nomadic tribes and the Adivasis in an exhaustive manner by penetrating the core of their life. It is definitely important that he approaches the life of these exploited subaltern social groups with compassion while they remain excluded from the literature of many of the rural authors of his time. Rural life can be appreciated only if we understand its inevitable constituents like the touchable and untouchable labour and artisan castes. Madgulkar could accomplish it since he possessed true rural sensitivity that is required for understanding the comprehensive nature of the rural life and vast compendious sympathy for all elements of the society. Such observations by the editor mentioned previously are agreeable.

Though Madgulkar engages indirectly with several political undercurrents on the ground while portraying Dalits in his stories, his political writing appears prominently in two of his novels, *Vavtal* ("Winds of Fire") and *Sattantar* ("Transfer of Power"). *Vavtal* portrays the riots that broke out in some of the villages of Maharashtra following the assassination of Mahatma Gandhi. It describes the prolonged physical and psychological consequences the Brahmins had to endure. It extensively depicts all that can possibly happen in such a rampant social agitation. "We are the true publics . . . the Nehru government has ordered us to burn the houses of Brahmins . . ." rant the hooligans who take the law into their own hands as self-proclaimed leaders. Theirs is a crude and irrational display of physical power in the name of Gandhi, Nehru and the motherland. "Your actions cannot be guaranteed. You bamans (Brahmins) can bring pistols in handbags and shoot at us", "All these bamans want to get together to grab the power" or "Someone from this community had distributed sugar or played music [to celebrate the assassination of Gandhi]". Spreading such baseless rumours about the Brahmin community, targeting it as a social enemy, becomes a routine activity of the rioters. An attempt to take conscienceless advantage of the situation is apparent in the extensive looting of houses and shops. There exists a casual fearlessness as seen in the trampling of victims along with criminals. But at the same time, despite the rampant mood of destruction, there are a few people who carefully safeguard the basic tenets of humanity. Both kinds of people from the victimized community are seen in the novel: those who are ready to introspect their mistakes, and others who wish to benefit from the opportunity by making loud noises about their non-occurring losses. There are some villagers who offer support and help to others in the crisis, while there are others who fight to gain space in the temporarily erected shelters. Similarly, there are some leaders and well-known members of the society who offer fake promises and show false sympathies, while there are those who are made strangers by their own people, forgetting the real or made-up relations.

In the riots that broke out following Gandhi's assassination, some people sought an opportunity to settle private scores. A few poor people took out their anger on the rich ones, like the Deshpandes and the Inamdars, and the goons saw an opportunity to create a ruckus. But the innocent and politically neutral ones also had to bear the brunt of the event. The lower classes and castes (*bahujans*) had retained disgust and anger for the vices and oppressive practices of the Brahmins, like money-lending, untouchability and display of pride in their caste status. Such anger found an easy outlet during the riots. The bystanders showed false empathy to the victims of the riots. All such obvious and not-so-obvious aspects of the riots find an expression in *Vavtal*. The author describes the situation realistically through the experiences and perspectives of three youths who are returning to their villages from Pune. He writes, "The vagabond and agitated mob is like the demon from the Ramayana called Kabandh: headless, one eyed but with such long hands that can reach across 12 miles." Those who are enjoying the sight today will be vulnerable tomorrow. The statement of a Brahmin character that "tomorrow the Mahar and other low caste public will burn their houses" does not remain a painful, anxious utterance but proves to be the authorial comment on the present political situation.

Though *Sattantar* apparently is a story of transference of power in two tribes of langurs, the intention of the author to symbolically sketch conflict among human attitudes and tendencies is revealed in many of his statements in the novel. According to the author, continuous conflict is a natural part of the enormous universal order of life. It occupies the whole natural world. It ebbs and tides as time passes. For instance, when there are more mouths to be fed, when life becomes unstable, when a species' survival is threatened by other species' encroachment, then the conflict reaches a climax. Conflict for power is not found only among humans, it is present in other species too. The nature of conflict and its tools may be different every time. Such extensive universal references seem to be kept in mind while writing, and hence, several statements are found scattered throughout that refer to the language of the universal truths about power and the struggles for power. Strength is the only support of power, and those who sustain the competition enjoy the power; others who do not remain in the competition are doomed. This is the formula behind this writing. It may be called 'the social Darwinian perspective on power'.

The framework for the struggle for power in *Sattantar* is constituted by interactions among a ruling troop of gray langurs, its neighbouring troop and a community of landless nomadic tribals called pendharis. There are two external forces which can frighten these troops: the powerful tiger and the hunter, who can even kill the tiger. Muda, the strong, aggressive warrior langur, who has retained control over his troop for the last four years, is a symbol of the sovereign might. Lalbudya rules over the neighbouring troop. His troop clashes frequently with the troop led by Muda but avoids the final battle. It appears that the clashes provide the reason to stay organized by evading destruction. Muda had ousted Moga four years earlier. Since then, Moga wanders aimlessly with his four expelled fellows and is on the lookout for regaining control over the troop. This serves as a symbol of the physically intruding power. Moga is defeated a few times, but once he succeeds in conquering Muda. A robber leader of a group of langurs acquires the status of the chief of the troop again, along with the rare pleasures that accompany the power. Following the death of Lalbudya, Muda and the nomadic robbers compete to gain hold over the troop. The nomads win it.

The multi-layered struggle for power is described with nuanced details by the author. It contains all the checks and balances of power, strategies and shrewd planning for rebellion. A particular example of internal contradiction that needs a special mention here for its dramatization is about transformation of power in the troop led by Lalbudya. The female members of Muda's troop do not wish Muda to get the power, but the females from Lalbudya's troop want him as leader to protect themselves. The story ends on the note of Tarani's pregnancy from the dethroned Muda. If the baby survives, he would kill Moga after six years to become chief of the troop and would establish his own rule. It appears that this juncture actually suggests a new beginning of dramatic conflict.

The author wants the readers to realize that the inspiration, nature and instruments of competition for power are the same everywhere, be it in groups of monkeys or among humans. It is with this intention that the following sentences occur during the narration: "It is not in the capacity of an individual to capture power, it requires thousands of hands", "Real or imagined danger brings people together, makes them live together . . .", "Extreme control gives birth to extreme, ghastly beings", "Nomads and robbers of yesteryears rule today", etc. The author's use of proper nouns for the langurs and application of other terms that are normally used to indicate human relations, like "girls" and "boys", point out that there is no difference between species with regard to acquiring power.

A manifestation of political awareness in Madgulkar's writing is apparent through the conceptualization of the institution of state by his male characters (since there are no female ones). In reality, the common man generally entertains an overall bias about government employees like the Faujdar, Kulkarni and Mamaledar. It can be said that Madgulkar's characters hold and confirm the same bias. The Faujdar, in the short story *Karani*, opines about the Lengar who practices black magic, that he "is not a human but a shaitanit is pronounced saitan in Marathi. So this is correct", and that the

Faujdar is powerless in front of Lengar. The Faujdar advises a villager to confront and challenge Lengar if possible or else yield him the land and end the matter. Another story, *Kalagati*, narrates how Kulkarni functions in the most corrupt manner for five years when he gets the authority. The story titled *Kaay Sudik Gela Nhai* shows how some thieves rob Babalal's money, jewellery and even clothes that he had acquired by selling his land. The thieves beat people and destroy many things. Yet Babalal declares that nothing is stolen because he knows very well that if he informs the police in the tehsil town, he would certainly have to repent that decision. He would have to bribe the peons and constables and give them treats, apart from travelling to the tehsil town frequently and giving statements to the police. He would have to take loans to pay for all such expenses, and even after that, there would be no progress in the case.

In the flow of narration in *Vavtal*, the author mentions how the representatives of power showed similar carelessness and inactivity even after Gandhi was assassinated. For example, he writes, "The Brahmin Mamaledar and the judge in the tehsil town were afraid and ran away. People could not find them. The Faujdar and the police could not do anything as they did not have the orders. They played the role of helpless observers. Within an hour or two, some thirty to thirty-five homes in the village were set on fire." (*Vavtal*, p. 83). Faujdar Shinde, who is insulted by the Brahmins in the village, takes revenge wrongly on a youth who is looting on the streets by shooting him and killing him (ibid., p. 84). Even when prestigious people from the village meet with officers in the capital, the district police do not reach the village for three full days (ibid., p. 94).

Madgulkar's political content is distinguished by his acquired sensitivity towards the outcaste communities, his knowledge about the interrelations among different elements in the village social system, and a short-lived and direct participation in politics. Nevertheless, his inadequacy in expressing the political awareness in words is also evident. He could not capture the essence of political processes happening in the post-independence period. He describes the limitation in his own words while explaining the modus operandi of his writing: "My creation is not the process of what I have found, rather it is a journey, like Columbus, to search for that which has attracted me" (*Gavakadchya Goshti*, Utkarsh Publications, Pune, third edition, 1982). Thus the limitation emerges from his restricted role as an author. He rendered the status of the hero to an entire village in his novel, *Bangarwadi*. But even there, rather than paying attention to currents of contemporary change in the village, he busies himself with a kaleidoscopic picturization of festivals, village customs and nature. There are many examples of characters in his writing who submit themselves to their fate. For instance, the elder son of Momin in the story *Zhombi* suffers a thrashing till he bleeds like a fully bloomed Palas tree because he fears that the Maratha anger will butcher them like hens. Aknya Mahar, in the story *Akher Aknya*

Ghari Aala, also returns submissively to the home of a Brahmin who had insulted him before.

Arvind Gokhale raises a few questions in his foreword to a collection of Madgulkar's stories that he has edited: "Why is the overall nature of the stories so 'tame' – why is there so little violence, not only in terms of physical fights but also in terms of expression of aggressive and harsh human emotions?" We meet many villagers belonging to different castes in his stories who are all very tolerant and straightforward, while in real rural life, they are quite active; Gokhale wonders whether the characters are actually lenient or is it the pen which creates them that goes in a straight direction? He answers the question a little later: "These stories would have earned a different dimension if the author had possessed a deeper awareness as an artist, about social consciousness, logic behind a particular behaviour of people, and the invisible relation of an event with the everyday life of the village. The stories would have then become more intense." (Arvind Gokhale (Ed) Stories by Vyankatesh Madgulkar, Continental Publication, Pune 1964, p. 15).

A static belief in the status quo, which appears to say that "everything follows a set pattern, big transformation is impossible", seems to be functional in Madgulkar's entire oeuvre. Madgulkar writes about the customary practices and conventions in the rural world as well as the biased standards of ideal behaviour that originate from those conventions. For instance, he mentions how individual fights immediately take on caste dimensions, how a Dalit displays vulnerable submissiveness in front of the *savarnas* (the upper castes) and how suppression of the exploited human mind occurs in the village system. But since his role as author favours the status quo, no major footprints of social change ever find place in his writing.

It is difficult to agree with Pawar's view in his criticism of Madgulkar's story *Deva Satva Mahar* that Madgulkar's vision notes the changing socio-political milieu and aspirations of the Dalit mind. When the movement by Dr Ambedkar was stepping forward, Madgulkar's character, Deva Mahar's, protest remains merely emotional and incidental. Madgulkar's suggestion towards the end of the story that consequences borne by Deva Satva Mahar never reached Dr Ambedkar renders his protest as undeserved. Madgulkar composed his next novel titled *Pudhacha Paul* (Saket Publications, Aurangabad, 1989) by clubbing select details from his previously published stories with Satva Mahar and making some minor changes in them. But even in this new novel, the Dalit protagonist does not evolve. Deva, from the original story, becomes a part of the establishment, and Krushna, his son, takes on the role of a rebel. The novel shows that Krushna goes to Mumbai as a drum player, along with his brother Gana, only to be cheated and to come to terms with life.

The entirety of village life, characterized by mutual reliance that is referred to by Pawar as having been internalized by Madgulkar's real rural sensitivity, had actually been broken down even before the English rule settled in this land. It was totally destroyed in the post-independence period. If an author depicts the *savarna-avarna* dependence without referring to the inhuman exploitation embedded in it, then it should be noted as weakness in his writing. How would it be possible to say that Madgulkar is 'reasonably aware of sociality' if his writings do not show any influence of the extraordinary politicisation of former untouchables by the Ambedkarite movement? There seems no option but to say that while he delineated individuals from the Dalit community, he refused to see the associated social transformations.

When some critics opine that Madgulkar's works have greater potential than those of Dalit authors, they count on Madgulkar's qualitatively better depiction of the relations between Dalits and *savarnas*, as well as his delineation of the human virtues and vices among Dalits. It is said that he did not portray Dalit life from any one side. The grain of truth in these statements is surely acceptable. But if it suggests discrediting the politics of independent existence of Dalit literature and its different purpose of creation, explanation becomes mandatory. Madgulkar's sympathetic representation of Dalit life is qualitatively different from the life portrayed in Dalit literature. Compared with the status quo position in Madgulkar's works, the flight of Dalit literature soars high. There is no reason to interpret this fact as a request to forget Madgulkar as the predecessor. There is no intention here of denying existing problems and constraints of Dalit literature. But there should be no hesitation in acknowledging that the first expression of protest against the hierarchized social inequality is by this stream of literature. Nothing like the crystal clear loyalty of Dalit authors to new values, their unambiguous support for social transformation or their breach of conventional symbolical depictions of the stereotyped and traditional world of experiences – can be seen in the literature created by non-Dalit authors about Dalit life. Despite the recognition of all its restrictions and faults, there can be no difference of opinion that Dalit literature is the literature of the movement. It stands tall by taking inspiration from the enormous mass movement that sowed the seeds of self-awareness and new life amidst the Dalit community. The mould from which Dalit literature emerges is different from the one used by non-Dalit authors. It is obvious that the potential of such literature has to be different, especially when it is bent on organizing burning protest against an oppressive culture that plays a false cheating game with the former untouchables and stamps their foreheads with a sign of slavery under the sheen of religion.

Madgulkar does not consider power as a socio-political reality while portraying the struggle for power. He imagines those forms of power as were pertinent in the remote, almost Paleolithic past of mankind: the cyclical and macro level biological and muscular power. Rather, it may be argued that Madgulkar artistically presents the fascist conceptualisation of human power (survival of the fittest). Therefore, his gesticulation of presenting an eternal theory of the struggle for power proves hollow. That his awareness about the socio-cultural power which keeps Dalits under slavery gradually grows weaker, perhaps because his world of writing gradually shifted from village to the wilderness. It appears that his creative imagination could not embrace the nuanced political struggles because he emphasized the struggle for power as seen in the pre-colonial or (pre-nation state) period. He did not consider tensions in urban life and embedded trends of modern politics in it as the subject of his writing, even though he lived in a city replete with various active fields like journalism, radio, scriptwriting, and so on. The cause for this non-consideration may be looked for in his concentration on the macro forms of power struggles. Due to this reason, perhaps, he also remained aloof in his writing to the subtle struggles in women's lives. One thing is quite clear: by portraying the relationships among animals in a symbolic manner, *Sattantar* does not render the experience of comprehending a period of human history with its nuanced details. Madgulkar writes. "The cycle of struggle for power operating for thousands of years, was going to be in motion forever" (*Sattantar*, p. 77). The statement offers a deterministic understanding of fatalism which may be said to be the root cause of his indifference towards the modern, transformative political processes.

Another constraint of political content in Madgulkar's writings originates from the ambiguity of his thoughts. The point can be further explained by taking the example of his novel, *Vavtal*. Even though he wrote this novel after a long period of 16 years following the assassination of Gandhi, its narration does not offer anything beyond a mere word portrait of the sequence of events, which disappoints the reader. The author does not take the trouble to perceive, at least through an artistic gaze, the political reasoning of the event. He does not research the ideological relationship between the assassination of Gandhi, subsequent riots and the politics of the Congress party, as if no ideology has any role to play in it. He seems to assume that the events result from a fight between two groups, between different individuals, and express private or familial revenge. It suggests that the author could not finally transgress the influence of white-collared, middle class urban sensitivity even after observing Dalit life at close quarters. He is not prepared to stand by any ideology or even to protest against any. Naturally his ideological positions come across as ambiguous, due to which his search for interpretation of events remains at a superficial level. He cannot offer a more insightful reference than the relationship between various individuals. It is possible to say that just like other members of the middle class, the author entertains a repulsive perspective for modern kind of politics organized by the low castes and classes and that his tendency is to remain away from the so-called 'dirty game' of politics. Similarly, it cannot be denied that, consciously or unconsciously, he attempted to make his writing appear a-political.

Nevertheless, as a consequence, the writing has become political writing that indirectly propagates status quo instead of remaining a-political as the author might have liked it to be.

Source

Bhole, Bhaskar. *Sahitya Pratyay*. 2001, Aurangabad, Swaroop Prakashan.

26

TATYA: A TRIBUTE

Vinay Hardikar
Translated by Chinmay Dharurkar

Dear Tatya,

It was a morning in August, two years ago. The sun was shining over 'Akshar' and casting a golden glow all around. Your body was laid out inside, but actually, you were hovering around the house with a blissful, 'Finally, I'm relieved!' look. A crowd had gathered there, mostly well-known personalities.

Even if their cliched comments 'Madgulkar bestowed upon Maṇdesh a fame not only in Maharashtra and India but in the entire world', 'He lived life – free and on his terms', 'Despite having no formal education, the prolific writer has made the pundits think', etc., differed, they all wore the same face! I would have said to you, 'Tatya, give them all a *tappal* on their heads!' And with a twinkle in your eye, you would have smiled and said, 'Really?' Actually, you must be planning to write a brief, tongue-in-cheek article about them, I thought.

I first got to know you when Pune Akashwani (All India Radio) broadcast a radio play based on your *Bangarwadi*. Then I read 'Jhelya', about the naive young man who was planning to slay the British Government by 'gouging out his eyes with a red hot iron rod.' He was a lovable character, but his aggression had the raw strength of an ironsmith. Of all the unforgettable characters from your Mandesh, my favourite was Kondiba Gaikwad, who said, 'I will dig your eye out and place it in your hand'. The scoundrel Shida, the cobbler, who looted Brahmin households after Gandhi's assassination and then taunted them, saying, 'If you don't mind using utensils touched by a *chambhar*, take them!', the diabolical Narsu Babaji Teli who believed that as neither he nor his father had died of small pox, his son wouldn't either and Ganya Bhaptya who believed that farming would only get you carrots, but to get rich you had to find the *kukudkunbha* bird! And of course, Khala, the tamboli's wife who made an honest living selling roasted gram and peanuts after her husband deserted her. Weren't all of them also your favourites? You have shown the abject poverty of the Mandeshi people, yet none of them wanted anybody's sympathy to get rid of their poverty. They believed that only shrewdness, daring, hard work or even *jadutona*, magic and witchcraft would rescue them.

You became a real favourite when I read *Vaghachya Magavar* ("On the Trail of the Tiger"). Bhanu Shirdhankar's hunting stories, regularly published in *Kirloskar* magazine, were about the battle between hunter and hunted, and the jungle was their battlefield. They showed how both sides used the jungle to overcome the other. When you wrote that hunting was a hobby, the jungle a large playground, where killing is only to serve a need, it follows the law of nature, it is much more thrilling to trail a tiger than put a bullet through it, to make friends with the tribals who are adept at this, and the Katkaris who roam the jungle as if it was their backyard. From them you can learn to read the jungle very closely, it was entirely new for readers of the Marathi short story.

You introduced Jim Corbett to Marathi readers in the penultimate chapter of *Vaghachya Magavar*. Corbett was exceptional, you said. He loved India, loved the jungles and animals in India. Like you. I think of you as the Corbett of Marathi or Corbett as the Vyankatesh Madgulkar of English.

I have read almost everything you wrote – short stories, novels, plays, essays and articles, but I enjoyed your accounts after a visit to a sanctuary or a forest. The sketches accompanying them were precise and minimalist, yet they captured the anatomy of the bird or animal, its mood and habitat, all seen through your sensitive eye. Sometimes I thought your sketching outshone your writing. I believe you are essentially an artist. If art had brought in enough money during the early days, you might have enriched the art world more than the literary! Your interest in photography, along with your painting and drawing skills, brought to life the word pictures you created. I sometimes nurtured the foolish hope that if I spent enough time in the forests, I would be able to write like you. How juvenile a thought was that!

Though we lived in Pune, we had never met. My first encounter with you was at a seminar in a Sangli College on 'The consciousness of the local in Indian literature' after your novel *Sattantar* won the Sahitya Akademi award. The word 'nativism' had not yet caught the people's attention. At this seminar, though, there was a group in the audience that was bent on labelling your writing as nativist. To me, referring to you as 'the writer of Maṇdesh' was limiting your identity. I fervently hoped that you would not become a victim of the nativists and hold on to your individuality. Besides the theme of *Sattantar* was something else. During the question-and-answer session after a paper was presented, I blurted out, 'Just because the novel *Sattantar* is set in the period before human civilisation began, it would be incorrect to see in it a nativist sensibility. To be called a nativist, Madgulkar would have to go even further back and write a novel on the amoeba. My remark did not go down well at all. You suddenly looked grim, as if you were displeased. When another paper attempted to co-opt you into the nativist coterie by establishing that 'Madgulkar keeps returning to his roots.' I couldn't help myself. Again, I countered, 'Stories, articles like memoirs, character sketches of family members, *Bangarwadi*, *Kovaḷe Divas*, *Karuṇaṣhṭak*, etc., have more or less the same import. In which case, how many times should we read Madgulkar's autobiography under the guise of a "pursuit of his roots?"' You turned red with rage. 'Have I ever said that all of this is Vyankatesh Madgulkar?' you asked. 'So what if you never said it. What difference does it make?' I retorted. Everyone was shocked by my impertinence. I was truly remorseful all the way back to Pune. What I had set out to do and what a hash I had made of it! Hurt my favourite author forever! Forget friendship, would we even acknowledge each other, I wondered.

We often bumped into each other at the British Council library. Except for a desultory sentence or two, there was no communication between us. I had just finished reading *The Sindbad Voyages*. So when I met you, I recommended it to you. Puffing your cheeks, you replied, 'I have already published an adaptation of it!' Shamelessly, I continued to speak to you. A few days after your long-running daily column *Parvacha* was discontinued, I said to you, 'Tatya, you are relieved and so are we!' You broke into generous laughter. And my hope that I would gain entry into this 'fortress' was rekindled.

I started visiting you regularly after that, forcing my company on you sometimes! Your table always had a stack of notepaper and the drawing board a thick sheet stretched across it. I wanted to understand how you rode the twin cycles of drawing and writing simultaneously. I wanted to make you really talk. Because your responses to any personal remarks were a laconic, 'Really?', 'Maybe, *buwa*,', 'Don't know *buwa*'. But that's what happened then. However, if the conversation was about something you had witnessed, a landscape, the playfulness of an animal, the shape of a tree or people like Usain Vaidu, who lived on the intersection of nature and human civilisation – you would be most eloquent. Your illness notwithstanding.

You rarely spoke about other writers. After you'd read my book on Mardhekar, you narrated several instances to show he was not unsocial, misanthropic or haughty and rude. He had gone out of his way to be cordial with you. I came to you very excited after reading your rendering of George Orwell in Marathi. All you said was, 'Don't know *buwa*, someone suggested I read Orwell, so I did. Someone asked me to write on him, so I wrote.' Even about Corbett you were reticent.

The label – the writer of Mandesh – has stuck to you so fast that the lands you traversed beyond Maṇdesh, through words and sketches, are often ignored. For a while, you were known as the '*grameen kathakar*'. But those who grew out of your arbour themselves rid you of that label. A left-handed compliment? Good thing you didn't remain long in that coterie. In order to take the *grameen* story to the people, they made it 'funny' by creating caricatures and farcical incidents around village life.

You have written a lot about urban life too. You always strived to lead a rural life while living in the city. And when the city closed in on you, you purchased a farm near the city. You appreciated the comforts and conveniences a city had to offer and admitted so. You were not a hypocrite who enjoyed driving a car in real life but mourned the loss of the bullock cart in your writing!

Your story *Deva Satva Mahar* and Gangadhar Gadgil's *Kadu Ani Gode*, joint winners of the competition organised by *Abhiruchi*, went on to represent the two major streams of Marathi literature later.

Your literary journey started at Mandesh but took off to gather all kinds of experiences in the small and large cities. Your travels around places of scenic beauty across India changed and developed your sensibility. Your extensive reading during this phase is reflected in your writings. Save for economics and politics, your writings are full of unexpected yet apt allusions from subjects as varied as history, folklore, philosophy and mythology, sociology and zoology! The poetry of the Marathi saints and even Sanskrit literature sometimes. It's a good thing you didn't go to a college! Your reading wouldn't have been so varied or eclectic! Your translations of Manuel Komroff's "Big City Little Boy" (*Mantarlele Bet*), Grzimeks' "Serengeti Shall Not Die" (*Sinvhachya Deshath*) or your travelogue about your Australian sojourn (*Pandhari Mendhe Hiravi Kurane*) reveal your ability to traverse diverse landscapes with ease. Whether it is the rural or urban, the Marathi or Indian, local or international, natural or mechanical, innate or cultivated, you have experienced them all. As such, any kind of labelling becomes meaningless.

You seem to be doing a tightrope walk between being a nature-lover and an abject nature worshipper. Your literary world is peopled by animals, birds, insects, plants and shrubs (but never the sea, owing to Mandesh's geography) and also with humans, who live with tenacity and perseverance, with the belief that to live is their birth-right, who struggle to find happiness, simple folks who give easily and spontaneously. This is your beloved world. Ironically though, except for the first twenty-odd years, your life was spent in exactly the opposite environment. Some authors bestow human attributes on animals to establish that they too have human emotions. You, however, describe humans with analogies of plants and animals.

It appears as if the novel *Sattantar* is a metaphor for establishing a human world through the world of apes. It is perhaps a limitation imposed by linguistic conventions. Right from the title of the book, this limitation takes over, and immediately, the reference to power struggle in the human world swiftly attaches to the narrative. The struggle there was not exactly for power, certainly not in the sense of what 'power' means today. Struggle was not a means to an end but a part and parcel of life. When human civilisation began, neither oppression nor subjugation remained a natural inclination. Both became a means to assert superiority.

While many of your contemporaries were trying to establish that 'Man is basically an animal and no matter how far civilisation has progressed, the bestial instinct remains in him. I write to show how this instinct may be curbed so a better human being emerges,' you were saying, 'Let us first understand animal behaviour and study it.' The essay *Lekhak Darshan* in *Pandhryavar Kale*, which presents different kinds of writers through the analogy of birds, is a masterpiece.

It takes skill and a sense of balance to put different areas of knowledge together. You were deeply interested in agricultural and pre-agricultural history, but trade and mechanical civilisation that developed after it held little interest for you. Pre-agricultural life could offer space and opportunity for a certain kind of living. Natural inclination, tenacity to sustain and survive, assiduity to gain happiness – these are the true endowments of mankind and determine man's way of life. Your favourite character, Usain Vaidu, may be called a representative of this life in the twentieth century.

The novel *Bangarwaḍi* was translated into English and other languages for its fine sociological detailing. It is not the story of a completely agrarian society but of one caught between displacement and settling down. To take up farming, one needs to settle down in one place. There has to be a social structure. And laws that everyone follows. If a rebel like Baḷa Bangar or Jagnya Ramoshi emerges, there has to be some clear conventions that are fair, just and proportionate for their punishment and rehabilitation. A sense of proportion, balance and justice should prevail. You don't cut off your thigh if the baby pees in your lap! A temple for people to gather and exchange the events of the day, a house, even one with a thatched roof, a threadbare *ghongadi* to cover oneself, and a hardworking, dusky wife are all that one needs! This idyllic position you took was not naïve. I understand that. But I noticed your wonderment at the bustling transactions of a changed world driven by commercial considerations. You were caught in a dilemma . . . The squirrels must survive, but the fruit on the trees so lovingly planted must not get eaten! However, you didn't moan about the damage they caused. You accepted them.

Your novel *Vavtal* ("Whirlwind") talks about how a misdeed by one man disturbs the rhythm of the entire village. How did feelings of animosity erupt in a community that had co-existed for generations? How did the conflagration of violence begin? How did it spread? These questions greatly disturbed you. You were in your twenties when the incident took place. You wrote about it in your mid-thirties. But the shock had not diminished even then. The unrest continued in a different context, but you seemed to be in denial of the present reality. Of course you knew that the answer you got from every village was the same – 'Outsiders came and burned the village.' You understood the impossibility of this, but your mind wasn't ready to accept the altered contexts. So, despite the theme of *Vavtal* being so very

TATYA: A TRIBUTE

apt for a sociological novel – and had the seed of a grand novel just as *Bangarwadi* had – it assumed the form of a narration of events. I wonder why.

Were the violent tendencies seen in *Vavtal* different from those portrayed in *Sattantar*? Man may have some of these animal instincts latent in him, and he will be rid of them only when he is freed from a life of mechanical drudgery. But to say that is not true. Nature has this system of predator and prey. It is Nature's way to control numbers and ensure balance. Mankind too has these instincts. It is not simply by chance that some people are strong, aggressive and domineering while others are either tolerant or submissive. When this instinct becomes violent or exploitative, society takes note of it, talks of morality and declares that bestial instincts should be wiped out. But this is possible when human beings assume the roles of predator and prey. When bigger acts of violence occur, the faces of the predators are blurred, it becomes difficult to point out who is at fault. At this point, the whole community experiences the hunger of the predator. They say men are cruel, but man is kind. The violence doesn't last long, but it leaves behind hurt and wounds that go deep. This is the kind of violence that erupted in Maharashtra after Gandhi's assassination. Perhaps, in your pre-agricultural civilisation, there was simply no place for such an event. You were disturbed all right. But were you confounded as well?

Actually, I wanted to ask you all these questions. But time was running out. Our conversations were guided by how you were feeling that day. Even if I had asked, you might have said, as usual, 'You think so?' and then told me something and sent me off looking for the proverbial flame in the forest. And I would return better prepared to talk to you.

Tatya, you fell ill, you became tired, you aged, but your writing style remained fresh, robust and consistent. It was never verbose, always precise. Your readers always felt, 'Madgulkar should have written a little more on this, elaborated on that!'

To use one of your favourite sentences, 'The forest looks after the animals, the house protects the child. If necessary, the walls move aside so no harm befalls the child.' Your style was like that. Its honesty, its flexibility lent authenticity to your voice, allowing you to express everything – subjects, narratives, character sketches, observations, deep emotions, mischievous playfulness, questions with no answers, unforgettable memories – allowed them to develop in just a few words. Wild animals are not disorganised or careless, their movements are strong, supple and purposeful. That's how your style is – graceful and elegant.

Last year, I had visited Gangadhar Gadgil. We happened to talk about Pu La Deshpande's incredible popularity. So Gadgil said, 'Why are these people so enamoured of Pu La? During his lifetime, there was a colossus of a singer like Kumar Gandharva, and a greater writer than him, our own Vyankatesh . . .'

There could be no higher praise, I think. Had this happened a couple of years ago and I had told you about it, Tatya, you would have narrowed your eyes and, with a half-smile on your lips, said, 'Really? I have no idea, *buwa*!'

I cannot help but ask, "Had Madgulkar not taken birth in Mandesh, would he not have become a writer?" However impactful and zealous or sentimental your belongingness to Maṇdesh is, it is only a consequence of your accidental birth in that region. This sensibility was innate to you. Comparing the writings of your illustrious brother – his provincial short stories, poems and novels with yours, one can say he was GaDiMa, and he remained so. You became Vyankatesh Madgulkar.

Source

Translated from the Marathi, *Priya Tatya*, Devanche Ladke, January 2015, Mumbai, Rajhans Prakashan.

27
THE INSEPARABLE RELATIONSHIP BETWEEN MAN AND WATER-CULTURE AS SEEN IN MADGULKAR'S WRITINGS

Rajanish Joshi
Translated by Nadeem Khan

There is this ancient belief, strongly held, particularly in rural communities, that there is an omnipotent power that brings down the rain that reanimates the entire earth. People send up fervent prayers during famine and in rain-deficient regions for the rains to fall. Similarly, people living in flood-prone areas pray for the rain to spare them its wrath. Various civilisations have thrived on the banks of rivers. It is rain that has also wrecked them. In a primarily rural, agricultural country, rain carries immense importance. As per the Marathi almanac, almost every date is attached to some festival. Agricultural activity is dictated by the position of the rain-bringing stars. Fairs and festivals are celebrated, important events, social and political held, and travel plans made, keeping the rainy season in mind. Which is to say that *jal-sanskruti*, water-culture, is central to everyday life.

In Marathi literature, as in most Indian literatures, there are rain-related poems and stories, *abhangas* and *ovis* by saint poets, folk songs and tales, idioms and sayings. So for Vyankatesh Madgulkar, who spent his entire childhood in the drought-afflicted region of Mandesh, playing with children of all castes, communities and tribes of his village, roaming the wilds with them and learning their native skills, the environment and water became a part of his consciousness. He translated all these experiences, all that he saw and heard, into his short stories and novels. Water and the environment became as integral a part of his prose writings as the humans and animals he wrote about.

When Madgulkar writes about his native village and its surroundings, he does so after making a detailed investigation of the environment, the flora and fauna and the human relationships as they exist in Mandesh. It is necessary to look at his writings from the perspective of water-culture as it will lend a new dimension to his work. Although man and his behaviour and the

DOI: 10.4324/9781003159315-31

omnipresent environment lie at the centre of his writings, their roots lie in water. When we see a massive tree spread over a piece of land, we cannot ignore the fertile seed that gave it birth. It is always there by implication. It can be said with certainty that the seeds of Vyankatesh Madgulkar's writings can be found in the water-culture of the Mandesh region.

Through Vyankatesh Madgulkar's writings, one can see the human culture of famine-prone regions from the perspective of water. Let me present exactly what this water-culture is from the specific perspective of a story and two articles that Vyankatesh Madgulkar has written with the rains as their theme. His article *Paos*, from his collection titled *Paritoshik*, throws light on the various constellations, the hereditary *Bara Balutedar* tradition (the practice of paying the labourers on the farms seasonally), the notions of the farmers with regard to rainfall, their understandings/misunderstandings, their terminology, their mentality and the turbulence of their feelings. You can find in it the corroboration of the saying 'Water is life'. As the Mrignakshatra (the Orion constellation) begins to come closer, queries related to rainfall begin to dominate. The excited question thrown at anyone coming from another village is, 'Has it rained in your part?' After the Mriga rains, the black land turns rich green.

> The Ardra *nakshatra* (Betelgeuse star) is called the *aad-dara*, the obstacle creator. The belief is that sowing done during this period will meet with problems. The *bajra* millet is sown during the Pushya nakshatra, or Punarvasu, i.e. 'Puka'. People refer to it as the 'young Puka' and the 'old Puka'. The young one is energetic, the old moves slowly, tapping his stick. The energy that animates the young does not exist in old bodies. There is a saying, "When Puka arrives, there is contentment for the paid hands."

This description by Madgulkar is revealing. He also talks about the superstitions that village people harbour. If lightning flashes in the north, rain is guaranteed to fall. Also, if it flashes on the head, it rains to douse the village fire, lighted on the festival of Holi in the summer. It pours on *Champa Shashthi*, a festival dedicated to Khandoba, an incarnation of Lord Shiva. And when '*Bendarache khat*' begins, it will be a steady drizzle.

In his article *Parjanyaat anna-sambhav* from the collection titled *Dohateel Savalya*, Madgulkar states clearly that it is the rains that have created our culture. His stories delineate the reality that it is only on account of water that one experiences either sorrow/poverty/misery or happiness/contentment/vivacity in life. The short story *Gode Pani* ("Sweet Water") illustrates this concept poignantly and brings out the unfair and unjust social practices that operate in rural societies. In western countries, farming is seen as a means to acquire wealth; the people of Mandesh (and all across the villages in India) see farming as an inspiration to live, for life. Success is when the harvest is good; failure is when the crops let them down. Madgulkar gives examples of popular folk tales to corroborate his statements. The father-in-law who comes to drop the girl at her mother's house asks the children a riddle: "If nine is subtracted from twenty-seven, what is left?" They immediately reply 'eighteen'. He tells them it's the wrong answer. The right answer is 'zero'. "If out of the twenty-seven *nakshatras*," he explains, "nine of the stars of the rainy season go dry, what's left in hand? Zero. Which means famine." Songs that lure the rain, like "*Ye re Ye re Pavasa, Tula detho paisa . . .*" ("Come, rain, come, I'll give you a coin"), or the *ovis* that women sing while grinding, like "The rain of Rohini precedes the rain of Mrig; the progeny of the sister precedes the progeny of the brother", all demonstrate the presence of the water-culture.

Madgulkar recalls a play he had seen by Saavala Dharma Khude in which the King asks three questions to the aspirants for his daughter's hand: "Who is the biggest raja?", "Whose is the biggest son?" and "Whose is the biggest tooth?" While the scholars assembled there do not get the answers right, a man dressed in rags says, "The biggest raja is meghraja, the king-cloud. The biggest son is the calf of a cow. The biggest tooth belongs to the plough." The princess chooses this son of the soil as her husband. These three are symbols of water-culture, village life and agriculture.

In a story titled *Hastacha Paus* ("Hasta Rain") in a collection of the same name, Madgulkar presents the viewpoints of two donkeys through a human perspective. When one reads the way Madgulkar has linked the torrential rain, raging flood waters and the fate of the donkeys, all symbolic of village life, one gets an insight into why Madgulkar's writing transcends his times. Environment, nature, human beings all are destructible. Culture too can meet its end. But human behaviour is eternal. 'Human-ness' passes from one generation to the next on its own. That men are fatalistic, their belief in destiny is also a blessing of rain. Illustrated poignantly in the story *Hastacha Paus* ("Hasta Rain"), it tells of the two donkeys who run away from their master, a mason, to escape carrying heavy loads. They get caught and are thrown in an animal pound. Gyanu the potter buys them in an auction. He cuts fresh grass for them, takes them out to graze in a bid to make them strong. One day during the period of the *Hast nakshatra*, the rain-bringing star, the donkeys and Gyanu are caught in a flash flood. Gyanu is washed away by the muddy waters as they rush ahead, roaring, screaming, disgorging froth. The donkeys lurch and flounder but manage to reach Gyanu's house and stand by the wall, leaning against each other. "The Hasta rain continued to pour. Relentlessly." This story, which delineates the intense triangular relationship of man, beast and nature, shakes up the reader.

The hydrologist Dr. R. S. Morvanchikar has said, "A culture that has been created on a water-centric social structure is called water-culture." It has spread all across human life. Water-culture has also besieged Madgulkar's writings. The question as to why this aspect of his writing needs to be studied is simple. The context of Madgulkar's stories may appear to be dated, but the issues he deals with are eternal and universal. Early one morning, Madgulkar took a walk around the newly created Buddhehal lake. He saw an old man sitting under a prickly bush and staring intently at the water. When Madgulkar asked him what he was looking at, the man pointed to the water. "My hut . . . there it was . . . once . . . The lake gives water to acres all round. Lots of people benefit. But who will understand the grief of someone who has lost his home?" Who can remain unmoved by the old man's anguish!? All of Madgulkar's writing is imbued with pure compassion and honesty and a reiteration of man's relationship to his environment.

Source

This essay was written for this volume.

28
VYANKATESH MADGULKAR'S NATURE WRITING – A LOVE AND A PASSION

Suhas Pujari
Translated by Meera Marathe

English Literature and British Rule gave Indian writers a new and modern awareness about looking at Nature. That is not to say that this knowledge was not available to us earlier. Our ancient rishis and munis have recorded valuable information about Nature in books like the *Bruhatsanhita* and the *Mrugapakshishastra*, among many others. But the dawn of a green perspective happened only after Indian Independence.

Among the first to attempt a personification of Nature and give it an independent identity were Vyankatesh Madgulkar, Kusumavati Deshpande and Durga Bhagwat. There was a new realisation of the role of Nature in people's lives, and this permeated the writings of Bhagwat and Madgulkar.

Madgulkar's *Bangarwadi, Sattantar, Janglatil Divas, Nagzira*, Durga Bhagwat's *Rituchakra, Bhavamudra, Kadamba, Nisargotsav* and Shrinivas Kulkarni's *Doha* and *Sonyacha Pimpal* are some examples of Nature writings in Marathi of that period. It was a completely new approach to literary writing. Once this trend caught on, it paved a green path for many new writers to follow. Nature and an experience of Nature started to manifest itself prominently in Marathi literature. Nature is passionate, she has her own independent personality, she is adorned in various ways. Just as she is youthful and tender, she can be fierce and even cruel. We experience a whole gamut of emotions through Nature's varied forms. The splendour of Nature and the manifestation of her many emotions must be presented . . . is what these writers felt. Thus Nature's variety and grandeur began to find expression and depiction in literature. Nature should not be used as a metaphor for human feelings or as a symbol or a backdrop for human actions. Instead, its vivid and multi-hued personality should appear in prose for its own sake and sometimes take centre stage. Of the writers who subscribed to these views were Shrinivas Kulkarni, Vyankatesh Madgulkar and Maruti Chittampalli. Besides them, writers like Ravindra Pinge, Sharadini Dahanukar, Shanta Shelke, G. N. Dandekar, Madhu Mangesh Karnik, Shirish Pai,

DOI: 10.4324/9781003159315-32

Father Francis D'Britto, Sureshchandra Varghade, Aruna Dhere, Dnyanada Naik, Satish Pande, Ravindra Bhavsar, B. S. Kulkarni, Lakshman Londhe, Vidyadhar Mhaiskar, Kiran Purandare and Krishnamegh Kunte chose topics related to Nature and wrote with feeling and intensity about them. Therefore, forests, seashores, riversides, the animal world, the life of birds, the cycle of seasons, the vegetation, light and shade, human forest dwellers and the marvels of Nature have all found their place in Marathi literature.

Vyankatesh Madgulkar, the pioneer of such writing, seems to have had an inborn love for Nature. His sensibility was blessed with the fragrance of the Mandeshi soil since his childhood was spent amidst cattle and cowherds, sheep and shepherds, the young tribals and nomads with whom he explored the scrubland and jungle around him. Birds, animals, wild and domestic, insects and reptiles, none of them escaped his attention. He absorbed all that his companions taught him, the stories they told him of exploits in the jungles, the knowledge and skills like catching fish with bare hands or trapping monitor lizards or picking out baby parrots from the hollows of trees, among other things. He was equally curious about the thorny bushes as he was by the magnificent trees, about lakes and ditches and all the forest produce that sustained the forest dwellers. These experiences enriched him and are reflected in his writings. In fact, his descriptions of Nagzira are like a film that moves through the pages of a book instead of on a screen.

Madgulkar admired and respected the Nature-loving Thoreau for his ascetic life style and passionate writings. He was also impressed and influenced by Nature writers from across the world and from all languages. They gave him a deep understanding of Nature and enhanced his appreciation of it.

In an interview with Vidyadhar Pundalik, he says, 'Nature doesn't mean only the lush greenery. The rough grass of the wide plains is also Nature, as are ants and insects, worms and reptiles that crawl over it.' Vyankatesh Madgulkar declares that he was irresistibly drawn to the great outdoors. He always had one foot in the house and the other in the jungle, as the Marathi saying goes. The peace of the jungle, the birds and animals forever beckoned him. His interest in hunting and love for farming kept him closely connected to both. Although he lived in the city, his heart was in his village or in the wild. His life turned from the rural to the jungle life. He searched for the connection between man and the wild very assiduously.

When Sudhir Rasal examines Madgulkar's personality, he says, 'Madgulkar lived in the city and enjoyed the conveniences of city life, it is true, but his heart was in the village of Mandesh. Gradually his mind left the village and he became a forest dweller, like the monkeys of *Sattantar*, the tigers and wolves, the teak, ebony, and acacia trees! These major stops marked the important stages of his journey, but he never forgot his connection with the world of Nature.'(p. 1).

Madgulkar had an intense desire to write about his experiences, which arose from his innate love of Nature. And he had the ability to verbalise and pictorialise them. Maruti Chitampalli, a noted forest officer-writer and a friend of Madgulkar's, has expressed this accurately when he says,

> The marshy forests of Konkan are unique. After travelling through them, he (Madgulkar) wanted to find unusual experiences, to see fishes that climb trees, the reddish-black, vulture-like birds . . . (He wanted) to wander among the deodar forests of the Himalayas, the chinar trees, rhododendrons in full boom, paint pictures of the multi-hued flowers and birds, visit the island of the golden eagles, look for their nests and capture the moments of their giving birth, observe the wild sheep and goats of that region, get a glimpse of the snow leopard, if possible . . . These are the plans and dreams he had even during his illness, which he used to tell me about.
>
> (p. 38)

Writing about Chitampalli in his collection of character sketches, *Ashi Mansey Ashi Sahasey*, Madgulkar calls him a *'vanspatikulathil manoos'*, a 'man of the vegetable kingdom'. That epithet could very well apply to Madgulkar himself!

Vyankatesh Madgulkar has the honour of being the first to present the animal world in his prose. Animals and their lives was a subject dear to him. One of his earliest stories, *Kalya Tondachi* ("The Black-faced One"), is about the sorrow of a black-faced dog and the humiliation she suffers because of the superstition that a dog with a black mouth is unlucky. He could write sensitively about the two donkeys in *Hastacha Paus* ("Hasta Rain") or about a smart pony who refuses to be sold as in *Maaza Guni Janawar* ("My Virtous Beast"). The story *Vyaghri* about a shape-shifting *bibalya* – the panther tiger – reveals Madgulkar's keen observation of the behaviour of animals and his ability to convey it in a gripping story format.

Cows, bulls, sheep, goats, monkeys are handsomely delineated in his novels and stories. The life experiences of these common animals find description in unusual ways. Monkeys, wild dogs, boars, deer, elephants, rhinoceroses, leopards are all incisively and empathetically depicted. As are the birds like the cuckoo, dayal, bharadwaj, haroli, kotwal and trees like palash, moha, shalmali, banyan, tamarind, peepul, laburnum, as well as the lakes, tracks and mud paths. The very life-like pictures Madgulkar has presented with love, curiosity and diligent research.

The veracity of his experience can be felt in the depiction. There is no artifice in it. As he experiences the jungle creatures, he describes them in his elegant prose. Entirely natural, life-like. They are remarkably simple but, at the same time, replete with vivacity. Minute observation, apt and pleasing description, simple style and narration make the portrayal of animal life appear natural and artistic. Madgulkar unfolds the whole gamut of animal behaviour – their food habits, their characteristic features, idiosyncrasies, their struggle for power, family life and other such varied secrets of animal life. Animal sounds, their body structure and physique, their movements, their individuality and their differences are captured in words. This is Madgulkar's magical touch. It becomes his paintbrush.

Madgulkar's descriptions are the result of keen observation and provide information in a pleasing manner. 'Four feet in white socks', 'the wild ox is the gem of the jungle', such simple descriptions enliven the narrative so that it never becomes monotonous, repetitive or boring. The life of animals is presented like a movie in his prose. Nagzira is an outstanding example of this.

Madgulkar declares that there is not a forest in Maharashtra where he has not left his footprints. According to Avinash Sapre, Madgulkar chose not to be a stay-at-home but dared to explore hitherto untrodden paths. And that enabled him to find and show his readers a whole range of Nature's wonders. His aim was to record the beauty of the neglected animal world in literary writing. He says he would like to share all the joy he gains from Nature with his readers, like '*til gul*' – the mixture of jaggery and sesame, distributed during the Makar Sankranti festival, for goodwill. (*Nisargavishayi Vata; Vata*, p. 85).

Madgulkar felt very strongly that we must save and preserve our environment and all that inhabits it. This sentiment comes through very powerfully in all his writing as naturally as the breath we take. There is not a hint of hypocrisy or artifice there. That would be unthinkable for him. This idea of preserving and caring for the whole environment is the essence and beauty of all his prose. 'If I can get to the Tadoba Lake, I will be happy to spend my life there by the lakeside as a fist-sized kingfisher,' Madgulkar says in *Magar Ani Vanar* ("Junglatil Divas", p. 101). Such a great love and deep attachment for Nature has resulted in Vyankatesh Madgulkar's invaluable contribution to Marathi Literature.

References

Avinash Sapre, "Vyankatesh Madgulkaranche Lalit Lekhan", Vyankatesh Madgulkar, *Mandeshi Manoos Ani Kalavantha*. 2000, *Satara* First edition *(pp. 112–113)*.

Maruti Chitampalli, "Tatyanchi Savali", Sakal Divali, spl issue 11 November 2001 (p. 31).

Sudhir Rasal, "Characharach Vedha Ghenara Lekhak", Dainik Sakal, 9 September 2001, Pune edition (p. 1).

Suhas Pujari, "Akshar Bhetichi Shrimantha Sandhyakal", Antarnad, September 2015 (p. 24).

Vidyadhar Pundalik, "*Sammelan Adhyaksha Vyankatesh Madgulkaranchi Mulaqat*", Lalit, February 1983 (pp. 44–45).

Source

This essay was written for this volume.

3.2 Remembering Tatya

29

LOVING YET DETACHED

Dnyanada Naik
Translated by Meera Marathe

Right from my school days, since I was very young in fact, I was always aware that my father was a great writer, that our home was a great writer's home and that I was the daughter of a great writer. Once, when I got 9 out of 10 marks for an essay in school, the teacher said, "Your father seems to have helped you?" as she returned my notebook to me. I thought to myself, What does *she* know? When guests come to our house and ask in which class I am studying, he turns towards the kitchen to ask Aai, "*Aga* Vimal, in what class is Babi?" He used to call me Babi. So I was really cross when the teacher made that remark. I turned to Manik, who was sitting next to me, and said, "When *you* got 8 marks, much was made of you. But when I get 9, she asks me if my father helped me!" Manik said, "*Aga*, your father is such a well-known writer, that's why she may have felt that." I was most upset then that my essay wasn't appreciated just because my father, Tatya, happened to be a great writer.

Once, when I was in the 6th class in Modern High School, I got angry with my mother for some reason and went off to school without my lunch box. I was still seething with anger even after I reached school. To make matters worse, Kulkarni Madam made me stand on the bench during her lesson for not having done my homework. Soon it was the lunch break. All the girls opened their boxes and started eating their lunch. I was ravenously hungry. I was furious with the whole world and kept fidgeting as I sat on the bench. After a little while, some of my friends who were playing in the ground ran to me, saying, "Maadey! Your father has come." Even in that angered state, I was extremely surprised.

There had been many occasions when I had wanted Tatya to come to the school to appreciate at least some of my successes . . . Me receiving an award for acting and dancing, a prize for scoring the highest marks in class, etc. At least that's what my child's heart wished for. I'd wait and wait for Tatya to come. The other girls' parents would be there. My mother would come too. But Tatya never came. Somehow, I thought it was Aai's fault for his not coming, and I would be mad at her!

So how was it that he was here today?

I ran out of the classroom and found my father standing by the school gate, my lunchbox in hand. I felt awfully guilty and began to cry. Tatya held me close and said, "Aai said that you went off in a huff without eating your meal. *Aga*, one should never take one's anger out on food. Now eat up your lunch quickly." That day it struck me that he may be a great writer and all, but he was my father first.

When I was young, Tatya was my encyclopaedia. I felt nothing was beyond him. If our teacher fumbled for a word during a lesson, I would think, if Tatya were here now . . . When I was in the third class, he brought me some volumes of the Arabian Nights. After two days, he asked me the meaning of "ashuk mashuk" and "natak shala." I said, "I didn't understand those words, so I skipped that part and read further." Tatya firmly believed that reading had no ill effects on young children. They skip what they can't understand or what doesn't appeal to them, choose what they like, read it and remember it.

He wanted us children to read a great deal. When my cousins Kumar, Deepa (children of my famous poet uncle G. D. Madgulkar) and I were setting off to see a movie once, Tatya remarked, "You kids have a great future ahead of you. You should read a lot. Acquire knowledge of all subjects. Think deeply about it. I can't understand why you like to see films and plays all the time. Probably sitting in a cool place watching colourful images without troubling your minds pleases you more. But is it of any use?"

He himself read widely. Russell, Descartes and other such eminent writers and philosophers. We often saw books on medicine, economics and other strange subjects in his hands. Almost all the classics were available in his study. Papa, that is my uncle Gadima, would say to him, "You read only Jean-Paul Sartre and Albert Camus, which is why your thinking is warped, your thoughts are strange." But when there was a gathering of people he would tell them, "Our Tatya's reading is deep and comprehensive. Even I have not read as much as he has. I doubt any one of us has."

A number of writers visited our home during those years, and there used to be interesting and animated discussions on literature and literary matters. Tatya was often engrossed in writing or reading, often late into the night when I returned home from my job at the All India Radio station.

I was once invited to participate in a discussion on "Reading and the Young Generation". I mentioned it to Tatya. He narrowed his eyes. Then, as if he remembered something, he chuckled to himself and said, "I will tell you an interesting point. Schopenhauer writes, 'Just as a man who constantly rides on horseback forgets how to walk, similarly a constant reader forgets how to think.' Just wait a moment. I will give you the right books to read." Saying this, he brought me books by Russell, Schopenhauer and Priestley. "These three have written very beautifully on the subject of your discussion," he said. "You must read them for the purpose of that debate."

On one occasion, when Tatya had gone hunting, a thorn pricked his foot and broke inside. It stayed in his foot for a few days. Then it began to fester. The doctors said they would have to cut out a lime-sized piece of dead flesh from the sole of his foot. The surgery took place. The foot was bandaged. And Tatya, who was always on his feet, travelling either to sketch or to hunt, was completely bedridden for weeks. He would say, "It is my foot that has made me lame . . . on all fronts." During this period, he read an even greater number of books. When he read something interesting, he would narrate the story to my mother and me.

Among the many people who came to visit him then were the well-known writers P. L. Deshpande, Gangadhar Gadgil, B. B. Borkar, D. B. Mokashi and P. B. Bhave. They used to have long conversations. Tatya was unable to sleep. He lay in bed all day, somehow bearing the excruciating pain. On his bedroom wall above the book cupboard, there was a semi-circular niche. A sparrow couple had begun to build a nest there. This cupboard was to his left, just above his pillow. Tatya would lie on his side and watch the construction progress.

One day he said to me, "I don't see any twigs in the sparrows' beaks now when they come in. The male sits alone on the window sill. At the time of your birth, I stood in the veranda of the maternity hospital, a poor, helpless fellow. That's how the male sparrow waits outside his nest."

A few days later, a faint cheep-cheep was heard above the cupboard. Tatya watched very fondly as Mr and Mrs Sparrow went out frequently, brought food and called out to their babies from the door. He would report to Aai and me news of their well-being.

One afternoon he called out to my mother, "*Aga* Vimal, why aren't the babies chirping today?"

Aai replied, "It is very hot. They must be sleeping quietly." But Tatya was not satisfied. "All day there has been no sound. Go look, see if you can see them," he insisted.

So Aai climbed on a stool. "Are they there?" he asked. A moment later, Aai screamed, "*Aga bai ga*! A handful of ants have got on to them. They've eaten up the poor babies!"

On hearing this, I burst into tears. I couldn't stop crying. Tatya said, "Babi, don't cry. *Aga*, we feel miserable and sad, but in the lives of birds, there is neither regret nor sorrow. They are not deterred by tragedies. They go on living, with determination, accept whatever comes their way and continue to soar and sing in the skies!" At that moment, I saw the sparrow couple flying in, and my tears disappeared.

The grit and perseverance which Tatya had observed in the avian world, which he was sensitive to, was there in him as well. He too overcame many ups and downs and stumbling blocks in life. Once, when he was a little boy, he fell into a well and was literally hauled up with a rope, like a pot of water, by his father. He told me, "After that I fell into many wells several times, but there was no one to pull me to safety like that." He must have come out of the wells himself by sheer dint of his determination and effort.

Tatya used to tell the story of a Masai warrior. The man had been attacked by a leopard. Many of his bones were broken. Some of his tribesmen carried him to a faraway hospital in a cloth sling. It was a long and arduous journey over a rocky path. Yet this brave warrior didn't utter a whine or whimper. He didn't moan or groan. He bore his pain with great stoicism and courage. Tatya was like that Masai warrior. All his life, he endured pain and suffering with fortitude and courage and set us an example of how to deal with troubles.

Tatya had close friends from all sections of society. Human suffering moved him deeply. His heart overflowed with compassion for all humanity. But it went beyond human beings. It embraced trees and creepers, birds and beasts, even annoying insects and lowly worms. In fact, everything in nature, lakes, mountains, rivers, valleys, were part of his kind and caring world. This sentiment is evident in all his creative writing.

He used to say, "Be truthful to your experience and let good taste be your guide. Do not follow the oft-trodden, muddied paths. Let your feet carve out their own. This earth is so vast that she has place for new paths to be forged every day. Don't waste your efforts trying to be like someone else. Strive to find, to recognise yourself."

I have inherited these two traits from Tatya – compassion and a sense of purpose. Much like one gathers pretty flowers, colourful leaves and sweet juicy fruits in one's skirt, I have been collecting experiences, reading, travelling, watching and listening in Tattya's company. Even today I nurture this habit of recognising all that is beautiful and precious in life and carefully preserving it.

From a very young age, I strolled along the riverside with Tatya. As a grown-up, I wandered about the farm he had bought at Dhayari. I saw and experienced the strange and wonderful world of flowers and leaves, of birds and insects. It developed into a love for exploring the wilderness.

I began to understand the innocence and simplicity of life in the wild. I tried to pass this legacy on to my daughters. I bought rabbits, turtles, birds for them as pets. I took them to reserve forests and taught them how to study the jungle. I bought them expensive books, sometimes on instalments, to inculcate a love of reading. From Tatya I had learnt to draw and paint. I became aware of colour combination and composition. To enable my daughters to appreciate art, I took them to exhibitions, bought biographies of the great artists whose work I had admired.

As an adult, I dabbled in many activities. Tatya always said, "Any art demands total dedication. If one says I will do a little of this and a bit of that, then one can't reach great heights in anything." I heard Tatya but didn't listen to him. Like a cat that pokes its head curiously into every pot it sees, I "peeped" too. I acted in plays performed by the PDA Theatre Academy.

I tried my hand at running a handicrafts shop, got into commercial ventures, made documentary films, wrote books for children, and finally, around the age of thirty, I accepted a post in the State Textbook Bureau as the editor of *Kishore*, a magazine for youth. My extensive reading, my knowledge of art, love of nature and Tatya's moulding of my life-style all helped me in my work.

There was an unusual mixture of involvement and objectivity in Tatya's writing and attitude. This quality that I had got from him was my greatest strength as an editor. I never faced a problem with planning the layout of the magazine, deciding the cover design, choosing articles for publication. Whenever an issue received praise for a particular article or a picture, I felt the same joy one feels when one is shown one's progress report in school.

Just as nature is rich with many things, our home was also rich with people. It was rich with books, large tomes on diverse subjects, encyclopaedias, dictionaries, gazettes, serious books, reference books. I was introduced to them when I was in school. If I was stuck for a word, confused about the meaning of another, had insufficient information, I turned to the dictionary. The determination never to write something incorrect, never to accept anything wrong, turned out to be an invaluable asset in my editing work.

Chekhov, Gorky, Guy de Maupassant, Lokmanya Tilak, Agarkar, all Rajwade's literary works, Tukaram, Ramdas, Namdev's compositions, the Upanishads and other religious texts, Garcia, Marquez, the Spanish Loyes, the Irish Liam O'Flaherty . . . Why did I read all these great writers? I read them because of Tatya. He used to say, "A good reader is a potential writer. One should read the experiences of those writers who have examined life from its very roots, understand them according to one's capacity and live life meaningfully."

I have been reading since childhood. Some things were explained to me, and others I comprehended according to my ability at that time. I have come across many outstanding books. Most that came my way I read rapidly. Speed-reading has become a part of my personality. Some books I have re-read many times. I met so many great people like Thoreau, Jane Goodall, Burton, before whom hills and mountains are dwarfed, through my reading. Always refusing to tread the "muddied" paths and discover my own . . . that was who I was. I managed to achieve some significant heights in my life, to weave my own web like a spider. I have since lived purposefully.

My mother died of a brain haemorrhage. In her depressing hospital room, Tatya stood for a long time, his trembling hands stroking her withered face gently, his eyes welling up with tears. His lips quivered, his shoulders sagged. Watching him, I couldn't control myself. At that moment, it struck me that from now on, our roles were going to be reversed. Earlier, Tatya had taken care of us. Now I would have to look after him. He was weary. He had faced many of life's calamities bravely, handled numerous frightening incidents with his own strong arms. I would have to face such challenges with the same strength in future.

A huge uproar had erupted in the literary world when Tatya wrote *Sattantar*. He was accused of plagiarism. Tatya said, "Not fighting is accepting defeat. One shouldn't get into the habit of running away. One should stand up and fight back. At least once in ten times." Tatya fought and continued writing. He was not one to accept defeat. All through his life.

After Aai passed away, it was difficult for him to run the house on his own, so I came to live at 'Akshar', his bungalow. Tatya's final illness had also started to show up. He had a kidney problem and was on dialysis. But even when he had to go to the hospital, his clothes were crisply ironed, his shoes polished, hair neatly parted and his handkerchief dabbed with perfume!

During this period, Tatya and I became very close. As the days grew shorter, Tatya's study would be filled with the sweet fragrance of the prajakta flower. Like birds sitting quietly on overhead cables, many books sat in silent rows on the wooden shelves. In the soft light of the room, we, the father-daughter duo, sat chatting. Tatya was of slender, wiry build. His normally fair complexion was now darkened with age, his snowy hair well-parted as usual . . . and on his face, shone the joyousness of life.

One day Tatya said to me, "Babi, I want to talk to you. I want you to be aware of everything. Listen carefully to what I say."

We were just the two of us in the house then. The magnificent water-colour painting of the temple at Wagholi by Dénglé; a double-barrelled gun leaning in a corner; a substantial writing table and on it some writing paper and a golden Sheaffer's pen, a plump, maroon-cushioned chair, on a shelf a Greek porcelain statue of a sinewy discus thrower, a carved statuette of Lakshmi-Vishnu from the Chola period, a shiny brass head of Buddha, an Adivasi arrow and three weapons from the stone-age on a window ledge – they were all silent.

Tatya, who had probably never, in all his life, spoken much to anyone, spoke to me that evening. He spoke for a long time. In the end, he said, "Whatever I have written in my life, I have always been true to myself and to my experience. I am proud of it. I am content."

Source

Translated from the Marathi article, *Jivhala Ani Alipthatahi*, Abhalamaya, Loksatta Team, 23 February 2019, Mumbai, Indian Express Group.

30

DEAR TATYA

Ravi Mukul
Translated by Chinmay Dharurkar

Dear Tatya,

I have written two letters to you earlier. This is the third. The first I wrote when I was quite overwhelmed after reading your *Kovale Divas* ("The Tender Days"). I was a student of Fine Art then. I used to feel rather lonely in a huge city like Pune and was comforted when I read *Kovale Divas*. I felt like, here, quite nearby, dwells a giant writer whose childhood has been just like mine. Later, during one of our conversations, I asked you, "You are of my father's age. How come then your childhood is so similar to mine?"

"Villages haven't really changed that much yet, see!" That single sentence of yours spoke volumes.

You had replied to that letter in your beautiful handwriting. I had asked you only one question. Was *Kovalee Divas* a novel or an autobiography? "It is indeed a novel," you had written. "It is the story of a boy in his tender youth who, in his pursuit of colours and lines, goes through a series of intense experiences like fear, love, death and birth, etc. He realises that colours and sketches were not enough to convey all this. He would need words. And so he turns to writing. That is the subject of that novel, the story of that boy."

My second letter to you was written many years later when we had developed a much closer association. It was meant to show my appreciation and praise for your article *Binbhintichi shala* ("A School without Walls"). Actually, it wasn't as if I had wanted to praise it! You had, in a way, compelled me to do it. There was something quite unusual and amusing about that letter. I had asked my questions in purple ink, and you had scribbled your pithy replies in red ink wherever you could find the space. That was true 'communication' through letters.

And now this is the third.

There won't be a reply to this one. There is no expectation of one. And yet I am writing it. Mainly to create some memories for myself.

When I used to visit Apex Colour Lab to get prints or rolls of film, I would always notice the ash grey bungalow named 'Akṣhar' right at the corner. I didn't know that the owner of the bungalow was my own favourite author.

The architectural design of the bungalow said much about its owner – some big shot with a great aesthetic sense. Also, the name 'Akṣhar' suggested that someone connected with words must be residing there. That's what I used to think.

However, the first time I saw you, you were at your other place – the flat in the fifteenth lane of Prabhat Road. Joshi of Utkarsh Prakashan and I had come to you one evening. I was excited at the thought of meeting a famous author, the great writer whose stories were lessons in my school textbooks. Let alone that, the fact that I was supposed to design the covers for the books by this giant author was quite thrilling.

You were at the table, writing something in the light of the red table lamp. Darkness pervaded the rest of the room. A golden yellow glow fell partly over your face and partly on the paper in front of you. Some highlights glinted off your spectacles. The two of us stood in the dark. Mr. Joshi introduced me to you.

"There are two books – *Gavakadchya Goshti* and *Kali Aai* – read them first, make your drawings only after that."

"I have already read these books. And *Kali Aai* was a chapter in one of our textbooks in school."

"That's good then. Show me the pictures as you finish."

You turned back to your paper. The meeting was over. Barely two-three minutes long.

That's how you were. I learnt that over time. You wouldn't get into a casual conversation with someone unless you knew them well.

The picture I drew for *Gavakadchya Goshti* was the first cover I designed for your books. With a black ink pen, I had drawn an old man with laughter coming through the slits of his eyes. You too used to laugh like that. I thought that's how I could depict the ease of your writing. On seeing the picture, you had exclaimed, "Joshi! This is what you call a picture!? Give the rest of the cover designs to him."

I still remember the expression of sheer relief on Mr. Joshi's face. He had seen the wrath of Jamadagni in you when an eminent artist of the time had been asked to draw a picture for this same book. You had immediately rejected it. My drawing was then super-imposed on the card which had carried that artist's sketch.

We met often after that in connection with subsequent cover designs. Every cover brought us closer. We talked about art and painting. Then we began to meet for no particular reason.

Having read your article *Ek Ekar* ("One Acre"), I said, "Tatya, I want to see your farm. Let's go there someday."

"Let's go tomorrow morning itself." You did not believe in 'someday'.

You had been pacing up and down the veranda of 'Akṣhar' waiting for me. Dressed in a denim jacket, a pair of jeans and sports shoes, you were all set to go.

I thought you would ask me to park my motorbike inside the compound, and we would perhaps take an auto or something. But your youthfulness outshone mine, and you said, "Great! The motorcycle is such an excellent, smart-looking vehicle! A scooter is no match for it." You were the comfortable pillion rider, while I was the cautious driver. After all, you were on the back seat! Soon your joyous spirit seeped into me too, and I opened up to show you the delights of the Yamaha. We reached the farm.

I am also a farmer. So when I saw the place overrun with tall grass and weeds, I was dismayed. "What is this, Tatya!?" I exclaimed.

"When Vimalabai was around, this farm was lovely, a completely different place. We would both toil on it together. She would put in more effort than me."

Naturally.

"Tatya, you were a farmer. But not of this land. Of Holland," I quipped. On hearing my words, Tatya, your laughter spilled through the narrow slits of your eyes.

You accepted praise with great pleasure.

A tulsi *vrundavan* stood on a raised square platform in front of us. On it were etched the words Vimalabai Vyankatesh Madgulkar. Below were the dates of birth and death. "This was your first marriage, Tatya. An inter-caste one. You were a Deshastha Brahmin. But the Deshastha complexion and colour were inherited by your brother Anna – Gadima (G. D. Madgulkar). You are a fair, light-eyed Kokanastha. How did this marriage take place then? Who was Vimalabai?"

You replied with a question. "Do you know who is a Jinagar?"

I knew. They were craftsmen who worked with clay.

"Vadilbandhu, my elder brother (Tatya rarely called him Gadima), thought it was utter stupidity on my part. But you know what, Ravi, there exists an orbit. Once a man is caught in it, there is no escape. That's what happened to me. I tell you, she was not a bad woman."

Then you kept on talking about that marriage. It was a still sultry afternoon.

You continued, "Big brother was trying to convince me. Finally, he said, 'Arrey, debate and marriage can happen only between equals! Don't you understand a simple thing like that! Okay, go get married. But I shall see to it that you go begging from door to door.'" You said this on that blazing hot afternoon, mimicking his voice. For a while, both of us remained silent.

I then took a big bite. I dared to ask a bold question. "Tatya, your books *Kovale Divas* and *Karunashtak* are based on your personal experiences. Then why haven't you written about this?"

You replied, "I had written about it, re! For the Diwali issue of a magazine, sometime back. But many people were hurt by it. So, I didn't bring it out as a book."

When I suggested to you, "But now much time has elapsed. Several characters have departed this world. With some minor changes in the names, etc., it can be published . . .", your reply was, "First you give it a read. Then we can decide. The point is all these years, I have delivered good stuff to my readers. The graph should not go downwards."

I avidly read the clipping from the Diwali issue. The narration possessed the same gracious flow of all your writings.

After much insistence on my part, the book finally came out – *Chitrakathi*.

I was delighted to do the cover. I used your sketches in a collage on the cover. I even did the proofreading.

Enjoying good food, roaming around, watching movies . . . all of these fun activities continued. We went to Prabhat theatre and watched *Bangarwaḍi*. I'd sent a friend of mine to buy the tickets so that the theatre management wouldn't know that you and I were going to watch the film. During the interval, the people in the balcony kept turning around to look at you. Some young boys and girls came to take your autograph. The expression of satisfaction on your face was worth seeing.

For the 13–14th edition of *Bangarwaḍi*, Shri Bhagwat of Mauj Prakashan had asked you to do the cover sketches. One fine day, you said, "I don't think I can do 'on the spot' sketches anymore. Let's pay a visit to a Dhangar settlement. You take as many photos as you can. I shall make my sketches based on them."

The two of us went to Rehekuri in Ahmednagar district. Stayed there for three-four days, finished five-six camera rolls. We wandered through the sheep-herders' settlements during the day, and in the dead silence of the night in the Kalvit sanctuary, you talked. Exclusively to me. Listening to you was a rare treat.

You drew pictures based on these photographs. The artist in you – in perpetual pursuit of excellence – made you draw the sketches again and again. You would show them to me, "This too isn't up to the mark," you would say, and discard it. "Let me do it once more."

Finally *Bangarwaḍi* was finished.

And your illness took over. The torture called dialysis began. Rounds of Joshi Hospital, Prayag, became frequent.

In August 2001, some of us went to Delhi to see the then Prime Minister Atalji. I was there because I was the artist for his book *Jananayak*. On the way back, at Bhusaval railway station, I read the news of your passing.

Though it was not unexpected, it was still grievous.

I too spoke at the condolence meeting held at Sahitya Parishad.

The following morning, my phone rang. "Shri. Pu. Bhagwat here. Your condolence speech yesterday was very moving," he began.

Actually, it was Bhagwat's own speech that was outstanding. But still, it was very kind of him to look for my number and call me to express appreciation of my words in your memory. He continued, "The photos that you took for *Bangarwadi* are still with us by mistake. I shall arrange to send them across. But with your permission, I would like to keep one of them."

"Permission! What for? It's my pleasure! Actually no. Don't keep that photograph. I have made an enlargement of it. I will bring it over."

"But how do you know which one . . ."

"I know," I interrupted him.

In the evening, I had the enlarged photograph framed and went to meet Shri Pu. He was very happy to see it. He even offered me some money. But when you like something, and someone who is a connoisseur likes it equally, how can you put a price on it?

Tatya, in our association of 15–20 years, I have clicked several photos of yours, but all those were close-ups. This one alone is a long shot. You are standing on a narrow winding path in the sprawling grassland of Rehekuri, with your back to the setting sun and casting a long, long shadow.

Everything is serene and still. You and the entire universe . . .

What more can I write!?

Yours,
Ravi Mukul

Source

Translated from the Marathi article, *Priya Tatya* (p. 6), Loksatta daily, Sunday, 3 April 2005, Mumbai, Express Group.

31

THE RUSTIC JOURNEY OF BANGARWADI

Amol Palekar
Curated by Samiha Dabholkar

'You should give up looking for lost cats and start searching for the other half of your shadow.' If anyone has lived the gist of this parable of Murakami's, it is Tatya!

I was first introduced to Vyankatesh Madgulkar, affectionately known as Tatya when I was in the seventh grade through a character sketch from his collection, *Mandeshi Mansa*. Before long I had managed to devour the entire book. I, with my urban middle class sensibilities, was completely oblivious to the life struggles, the uncertainties and the forces of nature on which hinged the survival of his characters. I was indeed zapped.

Later on, when I read *Bangarwadi*, I was fascinated. His style facilitated actual visualization of the long-suffering Dhangar tribes and their sheep and their exodus due to the perennial droughts. The never-ending struggle with Nature ignited compassion and a strong urge to epitomize that content on celluloid. Around 1994, a producer offered me the opportunity to realize my dream. By then, *Bangarwadi* had been translated into almost all Indian and some foreign languages. I was a three-to-four-films-old director.

I met Madgulkar for the first time at his bungalow in Pune to discuss making the film. Within no time, the difference in our ages and personalities vanished. He showed me his water-colour paintings and pencil sketches with childlike enthusiasm. When I requested him to write the screenplay with dialogues for the film, he already had a big file ready. "Let's keep aside your popularity as an actor. I want to know more about you as a painter." With these words, he bid me farewell. That was the beginning of a robust friendship!

After reading the file, with an uneasy mind, I confessed that I didn't quite like it. Instead of being offended, he appreciated my honesty and asked for my reasons. The entire structure of the screenplay followed the traditional narrative pattern infused with linearity and songs, etc. I would rather juxtapose the inter se warmth of the characters on the drought-ridden arid background than project the characters as dry. The starkness of their contingencies should be etched on the audience for which the treatment ought to be realistic. Not only was he convinced, he agreed with my thought process.

For about two weeks, every morning at 9 a.m., we set to work in a tiny hotel in Pune. I reiterated my vision of how the film should unfold, and he sat down to rewrite. He arranged his papers and a pen on the table and began to weave in the screenplay from my, the director's, perspective. He had only one condition . . . that I sit with him while he wrote. He hummed as he wrote and, after a few scenes, would say, "Let's grab some tea." Then he would narrate the scenes. If I liked them, we moved to the next ones. If I didn't, we debate on those. By then the formalities had withered away, and I had started calling him "Tatya," which was his nickname. I was overwhelmed by his sincerity and the respect with which an established writer like him dealt with a youngster like me. His professional approach left a lasting impression on me.

During one of our chats, he mentioned to me that the rights for *Bangarwadi* had been acquired by Shantaram Bapu (V. Shantaram). Apparently, he had worked extensively on it, but the project had been shelved. Later, Basu Bhattacharya expressed his desire to make a film on the novel. With that impetus, Tatya bought back those rights. However, Basu's interest in it, too, waned after a while. Despite all these incomplete endeavours, Tatya started with me with a renewed vigour. It was this contagious optimism that stayed with me, prevented me from losing hope even later when I had to struggle for 10–12 years to make *Kairee* ("Raw Mango") on a story by G. A. Kulkarni, another doyen of Marathi literature.

On completing the script and dialogues, we travelled across the landscape of *Maandesh* which was the setting for *Bangarwadi*. I identified locations for different scenes. I felt the need to show luscious green shades preceding the droughts, just to highlight the contrasting moods of nature. I wanted to capture the palette imbued in Tatya's lines – the sheep, like stains on a dirty carpet, dotted the earthen blanket and the bright red turbans of the hard-toiling *Dhangars* scorching in the sun. "See! This is the painter in you talking! Not the director!" Tatya's pat on my back encouraged me to plan shooting the film in two different seasons. Throughout our journey in *Mandesh*, I soaked in Tatya's tales of hunting. A writer, painter, hunter, story teller and many more facets of his personality were revealed.

I decided to cast fresh new faces in the leading roles of master and Anju. I saw 81-year-old veteran Chandrakant Mandhre in the role of Karbhari. The villagers were all given roles to play. Even the crew members, like the costume handler Hiralal, were ready to perform rustic characters in the film. All this was possible only because of the lucidity and specificity in Tatya's writings!

The first shooting schedule started in the pleasant weather with occasional rains. Our film industry follows rituals of puja, like breaking a coconut before the *muhurat* shot. I, an atheist, never did! Tatya gave the clap for the first shot. For me, what could be more auspicious than the writer's presence!? The second schedule started in the blazing heat of April-May. Shooting in that extremely dry weather proved to be physically very challenging. A few crew members got ill; I was suffering from acute varicose veins. Apart from such difficulties, there was yet another one. The producer backed out during the second schedule. It looked like the cat was lost once more. I was so immersed in the film by then that nothing could have stopped me from completing it.

I procured the financial support from National Film Development Corporation (NFDC). The film was ready after a couple of months' post-production work.

Bangarwadi was first screened at the Karlovy Vary International Film Festival. It received a standing ovation. And tremendous critical acclaim. Despite our measly budget and absence of digital colour correction tools, etc., we had excelled in our cinematography and sound design. As a director, the most satisfying part was that the international audience felt their connection with a tiny unknown region in India. I rushed back home and shared my excitement with Tatya. He responded with a deep breath and a minute of silence. Probably, it was a sigh after finding the other half of his shadow!

A grand screening of the film at the prestigious National Center for the Performing Arts theatre in Mumbai was planned. Tatya could not make it for that, so I scheduled a special screening on Labour Union day in his city. He praised our effort in maximizing the film's reach. The film was also theatrically released. Upon completion of 100 days in theatres in Pune, Tatya praised the entire unit and expressed his desire for us to work together again.

We didn't have to wait too long for this opportunity. Veteran music director Hridaynath Mangeshkar urged me to make Charuta Sagar's novel *Darshan* into a film. I requested Tatya to come on board as a screenplay writer. Once again, we did recce together with the same enthusiasm. However, the project didn't take off. Tatya and I got busy in our own worlds.

Tatya's ability to recognize the strength of visuals and the power of the cinematic art form is what drew me close to him. While reading *Bangarwadi*, each reader has their own imagination to identify the characters. As a filmmaker, I had to give a face to those characters. I am glad that I succeeded in that process. I am also glad that I could paint the landscape that Tatya had sketched. I feel fulfilled that, in a way, my film could immortalize *Bangarwadi*!

Source

This essay was written in Marathi for this volume.

32
MEMORABILIA AND IMAGE PHOTO GALLERY

Figure 32.1 'Chitrakathi', Madgulkar's Art Studio
Source: @Dyanda Naik, 'Akshar', The Vyankatesh Madgulkar Museum, Pune.

Figure 32.2 Vyankatesh Madgulkar (a photo on the cover of his books published by Mehta Publication House, Pune)

Source: @Dyanda Naik, 'Akshar', The Vyankatesh Madgulkar Museum, Pune.

MEMORABILIA AND IMAGE PHOTO GALLERY

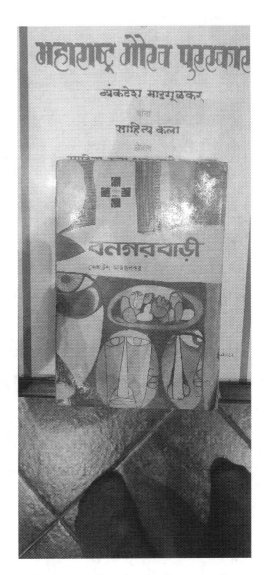

Figure 32.3 Maharashtra Gaurav Puraskar for *Bangarwadi*
Source: @Dyanda Naik, 'Akshar', The Vyankatesh Madgulkar Museum, Pune.

Figure 32.4 'My Life as a Hunter', Madgulkar's Gun
Source: @Dyanda Naik, 'Akshar', The Vyankatesh Madgulkar Museum, Pune.

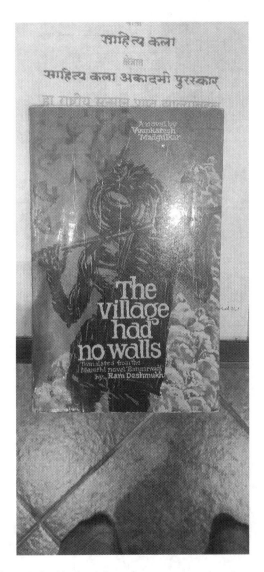

Figure 32.5 Sahitya Kala Akademi Award
Source: @Dyanda Naik, 'Akshar', The Vyankatesh Madgulkar Museum, Pune.

Figure 32.6 Cover of the German translation of *Bangarwadi*
Source: @Dyanda Naik, 'Akshar', The Vyankatesh Madgulkar Museum, Pune.

MEMORABILIA AND IMAGE PHOTO GALLERY

Figure 32.7 Vyankatesh Madgulkar accepting an award at the hands of Shri Sharad Pawar

Source: @Dyanda Naik, 'Akshar', The Vyankatesh Madgulkar Museum, Pune.

Figure 32.8 Vyankatesh Madgulkar with the renowned actor and director Shri Amol Palekar

Source: @Dyanda Naik, 'Akshar', The Vyankatesh Madgulkar Museum, Pune.

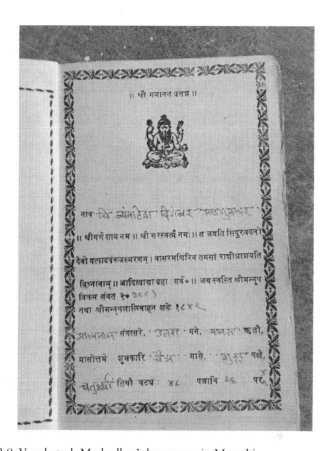

Figure 32.9 Vyankatesh Madgulkar's horoscope in Marathi
Source: @Dyanda Naik, 'Akshar', The Vyankatesh Madgulkar Museum, Pune.

Section 4

BIOCHRONOLOGY AND BIBLIOGRAPHY

33
A BIOCHRONOLOGY

Vyankatesh Madgulkar
Compiled by Chinmay Dharurkar
and Sachin Ketkar

April 1927: Vyankatesh Madgulkar is born in a Brahmin family in Madgul village in Sangli district. Madgulkar spent the first eighteen years of life in this desolate, arid region, studying up to the fourth standard. His father was a manager in the princely state of Aundh.

1936: Madgulkar discovers the pleasures of reading. When he was nine, Madgulkar's father was transferred to a village called Kinhai. There Madgulkar came across a massive wooden box, and when he opened it, against his father's wishes, he discovered a huge collection of Marathi books that included Hari Narayan Apte and Narayan Hari Apte's novels, popular books like the Panchatantra in Marathi, "Veer Dhaval" novels of Nath Madhav, the Ramayanas by Marathi poet Moropant, the *Hitopadesha, London yethil Badya Lokanchi Gupta Krutye* (a translation of G. W. M. Reynolds's "Mysteries of London") and so on. (*Pravas Ek Lekhakacha*, henceforth, *PEL*, 130–131). Discovery of this treasure left such a deep impact upon him that he would lovingly recall it several times in his interviews and reminiscences. Madgulkar also came across oil paintings and portraits of royal figures in the Kinhai palace, and he aspired to be an artist, but as he could not afford to buy brush, canvas or colours, he turned to illustrations and drawings in ink. He would say,

> I aspired to be a painter but ended up being a writer and like the portraits of royal figures I saw in the palace of Kinhai, I tried to portray my family members, acquaintances, the Ramoshis, the Mahars and Derveshis in my writing. I picked up a pen and turned a blank sheet of paper into my canvas and painted portraits and landscapes
> (*PEL* 147–149)

1941: After completing seventh standard Marathi Vernacular Final examination, he found himself a job as a teacher in the nearby Nimbwad village. The school was a 'single-teacher school' with hardly any students. His elder brother, G. D. Madgulkar, who later became an immensely popular poet, film lyricist and script-writer, also taught in a nearby 'single teacher school' in a *dhangar* (itinerant shepherd community). Madgulkar would draw upon these experiences for his future short stories and novels (*PEL*, 30).

When he went to school, he discovered works of renowned writer of rural life, Shripad M. Mate, which would also influence his sensibility.

1942: At the age of sixteen, fired by revolutionary nationalism of '*karenge ya marenge*', he joined the Quit India Movement. He was considered a criminal and had to be on the run, hiding from the government. This involvement also brought his formal education, as well as his training to be a painter, to an end.

1947–1948: Tries his hand at writing poetry and publishes in the journals *Abhiruchi*, *Satyakatha* and *Samikshak*.

1946: His first short story, *Kalya Tondachi* ("The Black-faced One"), published by *Abhiruchi*, a prestigious journal, found him early acclaim.

1948: He moved to Pune, where he heard of anti-Brahmin riots that exploded after the assassination of Mahatma Gandhi. Some houses and buildings in Pune were burnt, and curfew was enforced. He started with his friends for his village after the curfew was lifted and the journey back to his village and his experiences of anti-Brahmin rioting in the villages are described in his later novel *Vavtal* (1964).

His second short story, *Deva Satva Mahar* (included in this book), dealing with the continued oppression of the Dalits and their resistance, won the first prize in a short story competition organized by *Abhiruchi* in 1947. He shared the prize of Rs. 200 with Gangadhar Gadgil, another pioneer of '*navkatha*' movement in Marathi.

1948: From Kolhapur, he went to Mumbai in 1948. As he had no place to stay, he had to stay with assistant editor of *Satyakatha*, Gajanan Kamat, who was doing his Masters at Ruia College, either at Kamat's hostel or in the office of the periodical, *Mau*. He met renowned contemporary Marathi writers like Vishram Bedekar, Gangadhar Gadgil, P. B. Bhave, Sadanand Rege, and B. S. Mardhekar, among many others. He was exposed to world literature in Mumbai.

1948–1949: He wrote his famous *Mandeshi Manase*, which was serialized in *Mauj* and went on to be a classic.

1948–49: Madgulkar also started writing for films. The first was *Santa Namdev* (1949). He probably wrote for twenty-odd films. It is in this period that he met Vimal Mistry, an actress who worked in Marathi films, and they were married against the wishes of their respective families. This was his first marriage.

1950: Returns to Pune. The only skills he has, in his own words, are "drawing and writing." Publishing one story would earn him seven rupees (*PEL*, 1–2).

Based on his stories *Gavakade* ("Towards the Village") and *Deva Satva Mahar*, Deccan Studios Pune makes a film called "Pudhache Paul" that earns him one thousand rupees. In his own words, "A miracle brought about by my elder brother G. D. Madgulkar, P. L. Deshpande and Raja Paranjape" (*PEL*, 2). Madgulkar wrote a novel called *Pudhache Paul* based on the film.

1951: The short story collections *Gavakadchya Gosti* and *Sitaram Eknath* published.

1952: Noted Marathi scholar S. G. Malshe edits ten stories of Madgulkar titled *Vyankatesh Madgulkar yanchya daha katha*.

1954: The novel *Bangarwadi* is published in the Diwali issue of *Mauj*. Renowned anthropologist Irawati Karve writes to Madgulkar, asking him to translate this book into English and that it would make him famous. Noted cultural historian T. S. Shejwalkar, in reviewing the book in December 1955 issue of *Navbharat,* wrote:

> The shepherds left behind in the progressive movement of time are essential part of Marathi culture. Madgulkar has gathered the history of the last of the dying generation of this essential dimension of Marathi culture. Hence, as it is a representative account, one can imagine it will occupy an eternal place in literature. . . . The history of the royal dynasties is the history of those who live off the people and hence cannot be considered as true history. Nevertheless, one cannot be an imitator of the writer like Madgulkar as these things cannot be accomplished by imitation. One should have a naturally developed being of an author such as Madgulkar and genuine patriotism should be in his blood. Education is of no help here and this kind of thing is not possible for just any tom, dick and harry.
>
> (PEL, 35)

1955: The play *Bin Biyanche Jhaad* is published.

Joins All India Radio as producer for Rural Broadcasting.

Is awarded the first prize for literature by the Government of Maharashtra for *Gavakadchya Goshti*.

1957: The short story collection *Jambhalache Divas* (the folk play – *Kunacha Kunala Mel Nahi* published later in 1960) is first broadcast on AIR.

1958: Becomes President, Zilla Sahitya Sammelan, Mangalvedha.

Bangarwadi wins the First Prize in Literature given by the Government of Maharashtra.

The play *Janar Kuthe* was first performed by Progressive Dramatic Association. This play was based on his short story "Service Motar". After seven years, the play was published under the title *Tu Veda Kumbhar*, which then became popular.

Bangarwadi is translated into English by Ram Deshmukh as "The Village had No Walls" and published by Asia Publishing House.

1959: Madgulkar wrote the film *Sangte Aika* which was released in 1959 and went on to be a phenomenal success. It ran for almost two years across the cities in Maharashtra, a record that was later broken by the Hindi blockbuster *Sholay*.

Jambhlache Divas is also awarded the first prize for literature by Government of Maharashtra.

Visits Australia on deputation from the Department of Broadcasting.

A Danish translation of *Bangarwadi* was published by the Danish Missionary Institution, Copenhagen.

1960: The short story collection *Umbartha* is published. The play *Kunacha Kunala Mel Nahi* was also published this year by Rashtra Seva Dal Prakashan. The play was produced by Rashtra Seva Dal Kalapathak.

1961: *Tu Veda Kumbhar* is published. The first prize for literature given by Government of Maharashtra goes to *Umbartha*.

16 Modern Marathi Short Stories published by Kutub-Popular Prakashan, Bombay, has a story "Planning a Feast" translated by Bal Gadgil.

Sees the release of the film *Chota Jawan*. There is a long short story with the same title to Madgulkar's credit.

1962: The semi-fictional *Waghachya Magavar* ("On the Trail of the Tiger") published

Bangarwadi is made into a play and performed in Mumbai, directed by Bhalba Kelkar of Progressive Dramatic Association (PDA), Pune.

1964: *Vavtal* ("Whirlwind"), based on Madgulkar's personal experiences of the anti-Brahmin riots, is published in the Diwali special issue of the renowned periodical *Mauj*.

Contemporary modernist short story writer Arvind Gokhale edits *Vyankatesh Madgulkar yanchi Katha*.

1966: Stories "Back from the Market" and "School Inspection" in *Rough and the Smooth: Short Stories* Translated from the Marathi, selected and translated by Ian Raeside. 1966 Bombay: Asia Publishing House.

1968: The play *Sati* is published, and it goes on to win the first prize for literature given by Government of Maharashtra.

1969: The film *Mukkam Post Dhebewadi*, for which Madgulkar wrote the script, is released.

Visits France where he visited the galleries and museums and saw the works of great European painters. He was greatly affected by the paintings of Van Gogh and was inspired to revive his passion for painting.

1970–1980: The National Book Trust, New Delhi, brought out *Bangarwadi* in Gujarati, Hindi, Urdu, Tamil, Telugu, Kannada, Punjabi, Bengali and Odia translations for which Madgulkar was given two thousand rupees.

1971: His semi-autobiographical novel *Kovale Divas* revisits his involvement with the Quit India Movement.

"The Monkey God" translated by Ram Deshmukh in *A Treasury of Modern Asian Short Stories* ed. Daniel L. Milton and William Clifford 1971 New York: New American Library.

1971: *Pandhryavar Kale* is published.

A BIOCHRONOLOGY

1972: The play *Devajine Karuna Keli* is performed, produced by Rangayan Mumbai and directed by Vijaya Mehta. This is an adaptation of Brecht's *The Good Woman of Setzuan*. The play was never published.

1974: Madgulkar translates Bernard and Michael Grozimek's *Serengeti Shall not Die* as *Sinhachya Deshat*. This translation is considered important as the issues of conservation of wildlife and ecology were introduced to the Marathi world through it. As Madgulkar was passionate about animals, birds and the environment, he travelled widely in search of wildlife and nature, visiting several sanctuaries. This provided him experience which he wrote about in his books like *Ranmeva* (1976), *Nagzira* (1979) and *Jangla-til Divas* (1984).

1974: The novel *Vavtal* is translated into English by Pramod Kale as "The Winds of Fire" and published by Hind Pocket Books, Bombay.

Madgulkar is President, Audumber Sahitya Sammelan.

1975: Madgulkar is appointed Member of Advisory Board, Marathi Sahitya Akademi. Also, President, Gomantak Sahitya Sammelan.

Published a collection of short stories, *Dohateel Savlyaa*.

Gaurai – his adaptation of Tennessee Williams' "The Rose Tattoo", was first staged by Avishkar, Mumbai and was directed by Asha Dandawate. The play has not been published. Another play, "*Nama Satpute*", an adaption of Madgulkar's short story "*Dubala*", was performed by Progressive Dramatic Association, Pune and directed by Bhalba Kelkar.

1976, 19 October: An adaption of "Fiddler on the Roof", called *Bikat Vaat Vahivaat*, directed by Sai Paranjape, was staged in Mumbai.

1979: Madgulkar presides over the Grameen Sahitya Sammelan, Vita.

1981: Visits Seoul to attend the International Drama Festival for which his play *Sati* was selected to be performed.

Madgulkar is nominated as a member of Sahitya Sanskruti Mandal – a nodal advisory body of the Government of Maharashtra for the promotion of Marathi literature and matters related to literature and literary culture.

1982: An exhibition of his sketches is arranged in Bal Gandharva Art Gallery, Pune.

1983: Madgulkar is elected President, Akhil Bharatiya Marathi Sahitya Sammelan, Ambejogai, also of the Maharashtra Sahitya Sabha, Indore.

His novel *Sattantar* wins the Sahitya Akademi Award. Also receives the N. C. Kelkar Award for *Karunashtak*.

1984: Gunther Sontheimer translates *Bangarwadi* into German.

Madgulkar visits UK and USA to attend the publication ceremony of a book titled *Kumpanapalikadche Shet* ("A farm outside the fence"), an anthology of writings by overseas Marathi writers.

1985: Retires All India Radio as Senior Producer. Is appointed honorary Professor of Sociology, University of Pune.

The novel *Vavtal* is translated into Russian, along with the works of Gopinath Mohanty, Shri Krishna Aalanhalli and Krishna Sobti,

1986: The Ga. Di. Madgulkar Award (named after his renowned older brother) is awarded to Vyankatesh Madgulkar for his contribution to Marathi Cinema.

1989: Nominated as member of Sahitya Sanskruti Mandal, Govt. of Maharashtra.

1994: *Pravas Eka Lekhakacha* is published.

1995: Is awarded an honorary D. Litt by Tilak Vidyapeeth, Pune. *Bangarwadi* is made into a film by Amol Palekar.

2001, 28 August: Vyankatesh Madgulkar passes away in Pune after a prolonged, unspecified illness at the age of seventy-four.

2017, 8 and 9 April. Madgulkar's family, in association with National Film Archive of India (NFAI) and Aashay film club, Pune, organized a retrospective of four of Madgulkar's films. The films shown were *Manini, Mukkam Post Dhebewadi, Sangate Aika* and *Bangarwadi*.

VYANKATESH MADGULKAR: A SELECT BIBLIOGRAPHY

Short Stories

1. *Mandeshi Mansa*, 1949, Bombay: Abhinav Prakashan.
2. *Gavakadchya Goshti*, 1951, Bombay: Mauj Prakashan.
3. *Seetaram Eknath*, 1951, Bombay: Majestic Book Stall.
4. *Vyankatesh Madgulkaranchya Dashakatha*, 1952, Mumbai: Majestic.
5. *Hastacha Paus*, 1953, Baroda: Abhiruchi Prakashan. Vyankatesh Madgulkar.
6. *Jambhlache Divas Ani Itar Katha*, 1957, Pune: Continental.
7. *Umbartha*, 1960, Mumbai: Mauj Prakashan.
8. *16 Modern Marathi Short Stories*, 1961, Bombay: Kutub-Popular Prakashan.
9. *Kali Aai*, 1962, Mumbai: Mauj Prakashan.
10. *Vari*, 1962 (1981), Pune: Continental.
11. *Vyankatesh Madgulkar Yanchi Katha*, 1964, Pune: Continental.
12. "Back from the Market" and "School Inspection" in *Rough and the Smooth: Short Stories Translated from the Marathi*, selected and translated by Ian Raeside, 1966, Bombay: Asia Publishing House.
13. "The Monkey God" translated by Ram Deshmukh in *A Treasury of Modern Asian Short Stories*, ed. Daniel L. Milton and William Clifford, 1971, New York: New American Library.
14. "Nirvana" translated by Pramod Kale in *The Untouchables in Contemporary India*, ed. Michael Mahar, 1972, Tuscon: University of Arizona Press.
15. "The Pilgrimage" translated by Gunther Sontheimer in *South Asian Digest of Regional Writing, South Asian Institute*, 1972, Heidelberg: University of Heidelberg.
16. *Dohatil Savlya*, 1975, Solapur: Deepak.
17. *Valucha Killa*, 1976, Pune: Anmol.
18. *Vata*, 1976 (1989), Pune: Anmol Utkarsha.
19. *Kangarooche Changbhale/Vaghachya Magavar*, 1977, Pune: Kulkarni Granthagar.
20. *Bajar*, 1977, Pune: Shri Sahitya.
21. *Paritoshik*, 1983, Pune: Utkarsha.
22. *Janglatil Divas*, 1981, Mumbai: Majestic.
23. *Oza*, ed. G. M. Pawar, 1987, Aurangabad: Saket.
24. *Goshti Gharakadil*, 1990, Pune: Utkarsha; Solapur: Deepak.
25. "Bakas Mulani" translated by A. N. Pednekar in *Modern Indian Literature: An Anthology* (Vol II), ed. K. M. George, 1993, New Delhi: Sahitya Akademi.

Novels

1. *Bangarwadi* (9th ed), 1955 (2004), Mumbai: Mauj Prakashan.
2. *The Village Had No Walls* ("Bangarwadi"), trans. Ram Deshmukh, 1958, Bombay: Asia Publishing House.
3. *Vavtal*, 1964, Mumbai: Mauj Prakashan.
4. *Landsbyen*, D. M. S. Forlag, Hellersup, 1969 (Danish Translation of *Bangarwadi*).
5. *Winds of Fire*, trans. Pramod Kale, 1974, Delhi: Hind Pocket Books.
6. *Pudhche Paul*, 1960 (1978), Pune: Indrayani.
7. *Kovale Divas*, 1979 (1990), Pune: Utkarsha.
8. *Sattantar*, 1982 (1985), Mumbai: Majestic.
9. *Karunashtak*, 1982 (1986), Pune: Majestic.
10. *Das Dorf Hiess Bangarwadi*, trans. Gunther Sontheimer, Verlag Worf Mersch, Frieburg, 1986 (German translation of *Bangarwadi*).

Plays

1. *Bin Biyache Jhaad*, 1955, Pune: Chitrashala Prakashan.
2. *Kunacha Kunala Mel Nahi*, 1968, Pune: Rashtraseva Dal.
3. *Tu Veda Kumbhar*, 1962, Pune: Continental.
4. *Pati Gele Ga Kathewadi*, 1970, Mumbai: Manoranjan.
5. *Bikat Vat Vahivat*, 1978, Pune: Continental.

Other Prose writings

1. *Marathi Sahitya Darshan*, 1960, Pune: A. V. Gruha.
2. *Vaghachya Magavar*, 1962, Pune: Continental.
3. *Ranmeva*, 1964, Pune: Shri Vidya.
4. *Chota Javan*, 1968, Nagpur: Adarsha.
5. *Pandhryavar Kale*, 1971 (1983), Ahmednagar: Mohak; Pune: Utkarsha.
6. *Sinhachya Deshat*, 1974, Pune: Suparna.
7. *Pandhri Mendhre, Hirvi Kurne*, 1979 (1990), Pune: Indrayani; Pune: Utkarsha.
8. *Nagzira*, 1979 (1984), Pune: Shri Vidya.
9. *Chitre Ani Charitre*, 1983, Pune: Utkarsha.
10. *Ashi Manse Ashi Sahase*, 1989, Pune: Utkarsha.
11. *Janavanatil Rekhatane* (2nd ed), 1999 (2012), Pune: Mehta Publishing House.

Translations by Madgulkar

1. *Sumita* ("Shadows from Ladakh" by Bhattacharya, Bhabhani) 1970, Bombay: Manoranjan Prakashan.
2. *Mi Ani Mazha Baap* ("Laughter with My Father" by Bulosan, Carlo), 1967, Pune: Sanmitra Prakashan.
3. *Sinhachya Deshat* ("Serengati Shall Not Die" by Grozimek, Michael and Bernard), 1974, Pune: Suparna Prakashan.
4. *Mantarlele Bet* ("Big City Little Boy" by Komroph, Manuel), 1963, Bombay: Majestic Book Stall.

Screenplay/Dialogues/Stories

Sant Namdev, 1949.
Pudhche Paul, 1950.
Johar Maibaap, 1950.
Wanshacha Diwa, 1950.
Marda Maratha, 1951.
Jashas Tashe, 1951.
Dhakti Jau, 1958.
Sangate Aika, 1959.
Sakhya Savar Mala, 1960.
Vaijayanta, 1960.
Chota Jawan, 1963.
Deva Tujhya Sonyachi Jejuri, 1967.
Nandini, 1969.
Mukkam Post Dhebewadi, 1969.
Paij, 1980.
Bangarwadi, 1995.

Select Secondary References

1. Bhole, Bhaskar. *Sahitya Pratyay*. Aurangabad: Swaroop Prakashan, 2001, is a collection of essays on literature by the leading political scientist in Marathi. His writings bring in much-needed interdisciplinary perspective on literature, and his important essay on Madgulkar is included in this book in English translation.
2. Gadgil, Gangadhar. *Khadak Ani Pani*. Bombay: Popular Book Depot, 1966. Gadgil is another leading pioneer of the modernist Marathi short story, and this collection of his critical essays has a chapter on Vyankatesh Madgulkar.
3. Gokhale, Arvind. *Prastavana*, Vyankatesh Madgulkar, Yanchi Katha ed. Arvind Gokhale. Pune: Continental Prakashan, 1964 (2011), 6th ed. One of the most important anthologies of Madgulkar's short stories, introduced by another renowned pioneer of the *nav katha* movement. Gokhale's introduction complains that the author's depiction of life is surprisingly without any depiction of violence.
4. Hatkananglekar, M. D. *Sahitya Vivek*. Shrividya Prakashan, 2017. This collection of critical essays by a leading Marathi academician has an essay on Madgulkar's literature.
5. Jahagirdar, Chandrashekhar. "Animals and the Power-Game". A review of Madgulkar's Marathi novel *Sattantar*. *Indian Literature*, Vol. 27, No. 5 (103) (September-October 1984), pp. 121–126. Published by Sahitya Akademi, New Delhi.
6. Joshi, Sudha. *Katha: Sankalpana Ani Samiksha*. Mumbai: Mauj Prakashan Gruha, 2000. A major critical study of the evolution of the Marathi short story with a chapter on Madgulkar as a modernist short story writer. Selections from this chapter are included in this book.
7. Kimbahune, Ravindra. *Kimbahuna*. Mumbai: Lokavangmay Gruha, 2010. The essay on Madgulkar from this collection of critical essays is included in this book.

8. Kulkarni, G. G. *Grameen Kathecha Manadanda: Vyankatesh Madgulkar*, Sahitya: Dalit Ani Lalit. Pune: Nutan Prakashan, 1977.
9. Mangrulkar, Latika. A review of Pramod Kale's translation of *The Winds of Fire* by Vyankatesh Madgulkar. *Journal of South Asian Literature*, Vol. 13, No. 1/4, Miscellany (Fall-Winter, Spring-Summer 1977–1978), pp. 371–373.
10. Marathe, Sudhakar. Introduction in *Sweet Water and Other Country Stories* by Vyankatesh Madgulkar. Translated into English from the Marathi by Sudhakar Marathe. New Delhi: Sahitya Akademi, 2013. An important critical introduction to Madgulkar in English, along with a generous selection of Madgulkar's stories.
11. Naik, Dnyanada. *Vyankatesh Madgulkar: Lekhak Ani Manus*, ed. Pune: Anubandh Prakashan, 2010. A collection of Marathi articles on Madgulkar written by well-known Marathi writers and critics like M. D. Hatkananglekar, R. G. Jadhav, Arvind Gokhale, Aruna Dhere, G. M. Pawar, Gangadhar Gadgil and Vinay Hardikar and edited by Madgulkar's daughter and Marathi writer Dnyanada Naik. A volume to commemorate Madgulkar's 83rd birthday, most of the articles are personal reminiscences. The interview with Vidyadhar Pundalik and the essay by Vasant Sarawate are taken from this book.
12. Pawar, Go Ma *Vyankatesh Madgulkar: Sahitya Ani Vyaktitva*. Pune: Hermes Prakashan, 2019. A collection of critical articles on Vyankatesh Madgulkar written by a major Marathi critic. It also has interesting letters and interviews. His essay on the representation of Dalit life is his introduction to *Oza*, a collection of Madgulkar's short stories on Dalit life. This essay, in translation, is included in this book.
13. Taralekar, Meera. *Vyankatesh Madgulkar: Bharatiya Sahityache Nirmate*. New Delhi, 2013. A monograph on Madgulkar in Marathi brought out by Sahitya Akademi under the Makers of Indian Literature Series. A useful place to begin reading about Madgulkar in Marathi.
14. Yadav, Anand. *Grameen Sahitya: Swarup Ani Samasya*. Pune: Mehta Publishing, 1979 (2016), 3rd ed. A leading theorist of the *grameen sahitya*, his essay on the language of grameen literature and Madgulkar's place in its development is included in this book in English translation.

Some Marathi Ph.D Thesis on Vyankatesh Madgulkar (found on Shodhganga Inflibnet Website)

1. Atre, Supriya M. "*Vyankatesh Madgulkar: A Critical Study*", Ph.D thesis, SNDT Arts and Commerce College, Pune, 1983.
2. Ghughe, Sangita Ganpatrao. "*Vyankatesh Madgulkar hyanchya sahityacha Lokatatviya Abhyas*", Ph.D thesis, Swami Ramanand Tirth Marathwada University, Nanded, 2003.
3. Jadhav, Bharat Bhimrao. "*Vyankatesh Madgulkar Ani Phanishwarnath Renu hyanchya kadambaryancha taulnik abhya*", Ph.D thesis, Shivaji University, Kolhapur, 2008.
4. Kulkarni, Prajakta Girish. "*Vyankatesh Madgulkar: Vyakti Ani Vangmay-Ek Chikitsak Abhyas*", Ph.D thesis, Department of Marathi, Savitribai Phule University, Pune, 2011.
5. Sutar, Balso Anna. "*Vyankatesh Madgulkar Ani R. K. Narayan yanchya katha sahityacha taulnik abhyas*", Ph.D thesis, Shivaji University, Kolhapur, 2018.

CONTRIBUTORS

Amol Palekar, a much-loved actor and director of Marathi and Hindi films and television serials, started out as a painter before joining the theatre and film industry. He won the *Filmfare* Award and six State awards for Best Actor. His sensitive portrayal of women in films and TV serials that he directed is much appreciated.

Anagha Mandavkar teaches at Ruparel College, Mumbai. Her Ph.D thesis was on "Changing Trends in Marathi Drama." Her publications include research papers, articles for Marathi periodicals, and content for radio programmes and audio CDs. She was a member of the State Marathi Language Committee.

Anand Yadav was one of the pioneers of *grameen sahitya* (rural literature) in Marathi. A well-known writer and critic, with over 40 books to his credit, Dr. Yadav's work covers all literary genres. His most famous work is his autobiography *Zombi* which won the Sahitya Akademi Award, 1990.

Baliram Gaikwad, Principal, KGUC College, Uran, Maharashtra, is an academic, writer and translator. He recently published his translation of Annabhau Sathe's novel *Fakira*. He was the keynote speaker at Dr. Ambedkar's 122nd birth anniversary celebrations at the Indian Embassy in New York.

Bhaskar Laxman Bhole was a leading Marathi political scientist, progressive thinker and translator with more than 30 books to his credit. Besides influential works on Mahatma Jotiba Phule, Dr. Ambedkar, Mahatma Gandhi and Gopal Ganesh Agarkar, he has translated Jose Saramago and Intizar Hussain into Marathi. He retired as professor and head of the Department of Political Science and Public Administration, Nagpur University in 2002.

Chinmay Dharurkar is a linguist and polyglot and teaches at IIT Kanpur. He has co-translated essays from the works of Saussure, Barthes, Foucault,

CONTRIBUTORS

Lefevere, Sontag and Orhan Pamuk's *The Naïve and the Sentimentalist Novelist* into Marathi, written entries for the Marathi Encyclopaedia and contributed to academic journals in English.

Chinmay Ghaisas, Assistant Professor of Marathi, pursuing his Ph.D from Maharaja Sayajirao University, Baroda, India, is a freelance translator and interviewer for All India Radio and Doordarshan. He has won several awards for his contribution to Marathi literature.

Deepak Borgave, is a retired professor of English with a Ph.D in Translation Studies. He has translated several texts from and into Marathi and English and published about a dozen books. His Marathi articles aim to introduce Western Literature, criticism and discourses to Marathi readers.

Dnyanada Naik, like her father Vyankatesh Madgulkar, is a writer of books for children, and was a long time editor of the reputed children's magazine *Kishore*. She has also been a consultant for TV and Radio channels.

Go Ma Pawar, a highly respected teacher, writer and authoritative literary critic, has several books and critical reviews to his credit. His major work on the 20th-century social reformer and critic, Vithal Ramji Shinde won many awards. It was translated into Hindi, and Sudhakar Marathe rendered it into English.

Keerti Ramachandra is a freelance translator of fiction and non fiction from Marathi, Hindi and Kannada. She has edited over a hundred books for all leading publishers, besides teaching and conducting translation workshops.

Madhuri Dixit, Professor of English, editor of the periodical *Pariwartanacha Watsaru*, is a translator from and into Marathi, English and Hindi. Her critical essays and cultural analysis of Marathi theatre, films, caste politics and media production from the perspective of gender and caste have appeared in international academic journals.

Manali Sharma, a bilingual translator, is studying to become a Language Educator and an Expressive Arts therapist for children. She has a keen interest in theatre arts, Hindustani classical music and poetry.

Medha Kale is a Pune-based author, translator and activist working in the field of women and health. She has been a lecturer and ELT trainer and is currently the Marathi Translations editor at People's Archive of Rural India.

Meera Marathe has been a teacher, teacher-trainer, ELT instructor and has taught English in India, Canada, Bangor and Wales and also Hindi to immigrant children in Canada. She translates from Marathi into English and writes articles for academic books and journals.

CONTRIBUTORS

Nadeem Khan, an award-winning translator, has translated the Marathi novels of Bhau Padhye, Vishwas Patil and Avadhoot Dongre and Hindi short stories by Doodnath Singh, Ram Kumar and Jangarh Singh Shyam into English. Also, Sathya Saran's *My Daughter My Shakti* from English to Hindi.

Punit Pathak is currently pursuing his Ph.D in English from The Maharaja Sayajirao University of Baroda, on diasporic literature. He is also an Assistant Professor of English at Auro University, Surat.

Rajanish Joshi is a journalist with the Daily SAKAL, Solapur. He has written 12 books on diverse subjects, 9 plays and 19 one-act plays. He is the recipient of many awards. At present, he is working on his Ph.D, his subject being Water Culture (Jal Sanskruti) in Literature by Vyankatesh Madgulkar.

Ravi Mukul is an award-winning cover designer and a writer. He has designed the covers of books by most leading writers in Marathi. Vyankatesh Madgulkar was to him a dear friend and an inspiration as a writer.

Ravindra Kimbahune retired as a professor and head of the Department of English, Dr. Babasaheb Ambedkar Marathwada University, Aurangabad. He was a well-known literary critic, translator and editor who wrote in English and Marathi. He also edited a renowned Marathi periodical, *Pratishthan.*

Sachin Ketkar is Professor of English at the Maharaja Sayajirao University, Baroda. A bilingual translator and writer, he has contributed papers to several academic journals and participated in seminars on Indian and world literature.

Shanta Gokhale, a Mumbai-based bilingual writer, translator, playwright, screenplay writer, editor, theatre historian and award-winning novelist, is the recipient of the Sangeet Natak Akademi award for overall contribution to the performing arts, the Sahitya Akademi Award for Translation and the Tata Literature Live! Lifetime Achievement Award.

Sudha Joshi is a respected critic, writer and editor and an authority on the short story form in Marathi.

Sudhakar Marathe was a renowned academic, established scholar in English literary studies, teacher-trainer, author, translator and theatre director. He taught in India and abroad and has a voluminous body of publications to his credit. A recipient of several awards, he was a member of the Sahitya Akademi Translation Prize Committee.

Suhas Pujari is Head, Department of Marathi, Sangameshwar College (Autonomous), Solapur. An accomplished scholar, orator and research guide, his Ph.D thesis was on "Marathi Lalit Gadyatil Nisarga Chitran". Among his critical books, some are related to Nature literature. He has contributed to journals and the Marathi Encyclopaedia. He has received awards for his service to Marathi literature. He is the ex-president of Maharashtra Sahitya Parishad, Solapur Chapter.

Usha Tambe is a respected reviewer and critic and an award-winning writer of fiction and non-fiction. She has translated works of major writers from English into Marathi. Actively associated with the Mumbai Sahitya Sangha, she is the President of the Akhil Bharatiya Marathi Sahitya Mahamandal.

Vandana Bokil-Kulkarni is an academic, author, editor, translator, interviewer and presenter. She has numerous articles in renowned books and periodicals, scripts for stage shows and documentaries, profiles of several literary stalwarts and a biography of dancer Rohini Bhate to her credit.

Vasant Sarawate was an eminent cartoonist and writer who illustrated books by well-known Marathi writers and created covers for all Diwali issues of *Lalit* magazine. The Indian Institute of Cartoonists honoured him with a Lifetime Achievement Award in 2009.

Vidyadhar Pundalik was a Professor of Social Sciences but is well known as a short story writer and playwright and wrote extensively for children. He received many awards, including the Soviet Land Nehru Award.

Vikram Bhagwat is an award-winning Marathi playwright, screenplay writer and novelist. His plays have been directed and produced by eminent theatre personalities. Besides ten novels, he has written several scripts for TV serials on Doordarshan.

Vinay Hardikar is 74 years old and has been doing his due in the socio-cultural domain for over five decades.

Vrushali Deshpande, an M.Sc in Bio Science, is a translator, copywriter, content writer, anchor, compere, script writer and director. She has published four books in translation, articles and poems and was a speaker at various national and regional literary conventions.

Wandana Sonalkar is an Indian economist, author and translator. Her research on gender and caste in India led to her translation of several books by Dalit authors from Marathi into English. Her autobiography, *Why I am Not a Hindu Woman*, received much critical acclaim.

INDEX

Note: **Bold** and *italicized* page locators denote drawings/illustrations/paintings

Aadit, Madgulkar 170, 180, 182, 194
Aalanhalli, Shri Krishna 253
abhangas 215
Abhiruchi, journal 8, 14, 98, 211, 250, 255
actors 105, 162–163, 165, 235
adaptations 10, 105, 158–160, 163–164, 210, 253
Adhuniktawadi literature, Gujarati 6
Adiga, Gopalkrishna 6
Adivasis 15–16, 107, 119, 200
"African New Writings" 8
Agarkar, Gopal Ganesh 2, 228
Ahana, Madgulkar 173
Akher Akanya Ghari Ala, Madgulkar 170, 172, 182, 203–204
Akhil Bharatiya Marathi Sahitya Sammelan, as President of 253
Akka 42–43, 130
'Akṣhar' 230–231
All India Radio/Akashvani 10, 105–106, 118, 159, 163, 208, 225, 253; *Kunacha Kunala Mel Nahi* - folk play in 251
Ambedkar, Babasaheb 3, 16, 35–36, 39, 179–180
Ambedkarite Dalit ideology 18
Ambedkarite movement 205
Amitabh 184
Anantha Murthy, U. R. 6
animals 12, 27, 45–46, 48–51, 128, 130–131, 143, 206, 209–213, 215, 220–222
anti-Brahmin: movement 3; riots 8, 250, 252
Apex Colour Lab 230

Apte, Hari Narayan 4, 99, 112, 249
Apte, Narayan Hari 249
"Arabian Nights" 99, 225
Ardra nakshatra (*Betelgeuse star*) 216
art 115, 124, 128, 131
'Art for Art' 3, 8
artist/artists 7–8, 14, 20, 108, 110, 115, 124–126, 129–132, 165–166, 204, 209, 233
Asa Lai Baghithlyath, Madgulkar 175
Ase Chalalele Ahey, Madgulkar 172
ati-Maharashtriya 148
Atre, P. K. 13
Audumber Sahitya Sammelan, as President 253
Australia: radio stations in 105; visit to 252; *see also* All India Radio/Akashvani
award: D. Litt by Tilak Vidyapeeth 254; Ga. Di. Madgulkar Award for Marathi Cinema contribution 254; for *Gavakadchya Goshti* 251; *Jambhlache Divasis* by Government of Maharashtra 252; *Karunashtak*, N.C. Kelkar 253; Sahitya Kala Akademi 209, *242*, 253; from Sharad Pawar *244*; *Tu Veda Kumbhar*-play, Madgulkar 252; *Umbarthais*, Madgulkar, by Government of Maharashtra 252

"Back from the Market", translated by Ian Raeside 252
Bagul, Baburao 13, 169, 184
bahushrut 17, 97
Balzac 106

263

INDEX

Bandhumadhav 17, 185
Bangarwadi: ("The Village Had No Walls"), Madgulkar 1, 9, 63, 66, 111, 116–117, 203, 208, 210, 233–234, 236, 251, 257; cover of German translation 243; Danish translation of 252; directed by Bhalba Kelkar 252; First Prize in Literature 251; Maharashtra Gaurav Puraskar for 240; in *Mouj* 251; NBT translations on 252; screened at Karlovy Vary International Film Festival 237
Bansidhar!, Mate 184
Bara Balutedar tradition 216
Barthes, Roland 15
Barve, Sunil 166
Bazaarachi Vaat "Way To The Bazaar", Madgulkar 53, 186, 190
Bedekar, Maltibai (earlier Balutai Khare with pseudonym "Vibhavari Shiroorkar') 4, 9
Bedekar, Vishram 4, 8, 250
Bet, Madgulkar 170, 178
Bhagwat, Durga 219
Bhagwat, Pu. 233
Bhat, Suresh 192
Bhattacharya, Basu 236
Bhavamudra, Bhagwat 219
Bhave, P. B. 5, 8, 226, 250
Bhavsar, Ravindra 220
Bhole, Bhaskar 18, 21
"Big City Little Boy", Komro 211
Bikat Vaat Vahivaat: directed by Sai Paranjape 253; Madgulkar 10
Binbhintichi shala ("A School without Walls"), Madgulkar 230
Bin Biyanche Jhaad- play, Madgulkar 9, 158–159, 163, 251
Bitta Kaka, Madgulkar 114
"Black-Faced One" (*Kalya~*tondachi), Madgulkar 8, 12, 20, 27, 98, 141, 221, 250
Bombay 100, 126, 141
Borade, R. R. 13–14
Borkar, B. B. 226
Braque 125, 131
brother 9, 29, 42, 109–110, 129–130, 136, 146, 175, 217, 254; Anna as older 110, 121
Burton 105, 228

Caldwell 101, 114
Camus, Albert 225
caricatures 126, 129, 210; *see also* illustrations
caste/castes 3, 7, 18, 21, 35, 111, 113, 145, 148, 152, 170, 175–178, 183–184, 193–195, 199–201; artisan 145, 172, 199–200; Balsantosh 9, 17, 97; Balutedar 19, 32, 168–169, 172, 183, 199; barbers 13, 32, 96, 111, 159, 169, 172; Bharadi 9, 17, 97; Bhorpis 9, 97; blacksmiths 169; Brahman/Brahmins/Bamans/Bamna 33, 35, 67–68, 111, 168, 172–173, 176, 178, 182, 194–195, 200–201; carpenters 32, 43, 96, 111, 147, 169; Chambhar 35, 145, 169, 208; Dalits 1, 3, 15–16, 18–20, 103, 146, 169–170, 172–176, 192–195, 200, 204–206; Dhangar 9; discrimination 7, 16, 143, 193–195; Gondhalis 17, 97; intermediate 16; Jagars 17, 97; Joshis 121; Kulkarnis 36, 38, 111, 121, 172, 178, 202, 220; Kumbhars 96, 145; Lalits 17, 97; lower classes (*bahujans*) 201; Mahars 9, 18, 32–35, 38–39, 42–43, 96, 111, 120, 145, 169–173, 176–177, 180–182; Mangs 18, 43, 120, 145, 169–170, 172–173, 176, 193, 195; Momins 9, 96, 203; Mulanis 9, 96, 146; Nhavis 9, 96, 111, 159; nomadic 18, 175–176, 184; Ramdasi 9, 17, 97; *savarna* 170–172, 174, 176, 205; scheduled 17, 194; *sutars* 96, 111; *tamasha* 17, 97, 177; untouchable 9, 13, 19, 168–170, 172, 174, 176, 178, 182–184, 199, 205; Vadar 170; Vaghye 9; Vani 33, 171; Vasudev 9, 17, 97; Vhalars 145, 170
Census of 1911 2
Cezanne 131
Chaudhary, Bahinabai 103
Chekhov 228

264

INDEX

childhood 9, 110–111, 114, 122, 129–130, 194, 215, 220, 228, 230; companions 120
Chiplunkar, Vishnu Shashtri 2
Chitampalli, Maruti 219, 221
Chitrakatha, Madgulkar" 7, 20, 114–115, 166, 233; Madgulkar, Art Studio *238*
'Chitrakathi', 7, 20, 166, 233; as Madgulkar's Art Studio *238*
Chitre, Dilip 4
Chitre Ani Charitre 125, 130, 132
Chokhamela 16
Chorghade, Vaman K. 4
Chota Jawan-film, Madgulkar 252
city-centric mindset 156
class 3, 16, 112, 118, 148, 154, 193, 206
classification 16, 20, 103
Clifford, William 252
composition 128–130, 160, 164, 198, 227
Corbett, Jim 12, 209–210
Cotts, Surgeon 95
creative: powers 124; writing 20, 95, 179, 227
creativity 98, 148, 166, 179–181
critical reception 15–20
critics 4, 6, 20, 95, 108, 141, 153, 164, 168–169, 178–179
cultural: dissemination 105; heritage 156–157; history 8–9, 15, 21, 151
culture 2, 7, 13, 15–16, 20–21, 105–107, 116, 118, 142, 153, 216–217; Marathi 251
Cummings, E. E. 11

Dahanukar, Sharadini 219
Dalit: authors 185, 205; life 18, 168–170, 173–174, 178, 184–185, 193, 199, 205; literature 17–18, 20, 104, 169, 205; stories 18, 185; writers 18, 169
Dalvi Art Institute 124
Dalvi, Jaywant 165
Dalwai, Hamid 111
Dandavate, Vrundavan 166
Dandawate, Asha 166, 253
Dandekar, G. N. 219
Das, Jibanananda 5
D'Britto, Francis, Fr. 220
Dénglé 229

Descartes 225
Deshmukh, Ram 251–252
Deshpande, Kusumavati 219
Deshpande, P. L. 226, 251
Devaajine Karunaa Keli, Madgulkar 10
Devachya Kathila Avaj Nahi, Madgulkar 10
Devajine Karuna Keli, Madgulkar 16, 158, 160; play directed by Vijaya Mehta 253
Deva Satva Mahar, Madgulkar 32, 36, 39, 146–147, 170, 175, 179–180, 194, 204, 211, 250
dhangars (itinerant shepherds) 1, 9, 13, 100, 164, 250
Dhar, Madgulkar 190
Dharma Ramoshi, Madgulkar 20, 40, 44, 100, 146, 170, 173, 178, 182, 188, 194
Dharwadkar, Vinay 5
Dhasal, Namdeo 13
Dhere, Aruna 8, 220
"The Diary of an Untouchable" (*Eka Asprushtachi Diary*), Mate 13
Dickens 105
didacticism 3, 13
Dighe, R. S. 19
Dighe, R. V. 141
Doha, Kulkarni 219
Dohateel Savalya, Madgulkar 216, 253
Doordarshan 105–106
Dostoevsky 114, 118
drama 115, 161, 165, 191, 197
drawing/sketches 127; animal 131–132; categories of 128; line 128, 131–132; nature 131 (*see also* caricature; illustrations)
dreams 81, 104, 108, 122, 125, 147–148, 199, 221, 235
Dubala, Madgulkar 160, 253

ecocriticism 12, 21
education 2, 7, 16, 101, 152–153, 156, 169, 177, 251
Eka Asprushyachya Diarythil Paana, Mate 184
Ek Ekar ("One Acre"), Madgulkar 231
English Literature 114, 219
epithets 185, 221
essay/essays 6, 8, 19–21, 158, 166, 209, 224; Bhole 18; Pawar on 18
European literature 114

INDEX

Fakira, Sathe 192–195
farmers 13, 64–65, 168–169, 172, 199, 216, 232; *see also grameen; village*
father (Tatya) 34–35, 37, 41–42, 89, 110, 112, 121–122, 129–130, 187, 189–190, 208, 213–214, 224–229, 232, 234–237; letters to 230; with lunch box 225; as story teller 9
Faulkner, William 11
feminist 15–16
festivals 95–96, 104, 195, 203, 215; Bendur 32, 39, 96, 120; *Champa Shashthi* 216; Dasara 96; Makar Sankranti 222; 'Navy-achi Punav' 96; summelan as language of 118; village congregations 96
fiction: rural 6, 153; short 1–2
Fiddler on the Roof 164, 253
films 114, 116, 127, 159, 165, 220, 225, 233, 235–237, 250–251, 254
Flaherty, Liam O 101
folk: arts 17, 97, 165; dramas 159, 161, 163; music 115; performances 17, 97; performers 97; plays (*loknatya*) 1, 10, 143, 158–159; songs 115, 215; tales 159; theatre 10, 160, 165
folklore 10, 159, 164, 211
"Folks Of Mandesh" 1, 9, 100
France 106, 125, 127–128, 130; Anatole 20, 101, 106; visit to 252
freedom 101–102, 149
freedom movement 16, 72, 124, 164
Freud 3
Friedman, Susan Stanford 2

Gadgil, Bal 252
Gadgil, Gangadhar 5, 8, 13–14, 114, 116, 142, 211, 213, 226, 250
Gadima, older brother 214, 232
Gadkari, Ram Ganesh 4, 98
Gaikwad, Baliram xv, 19, 21, 192
Gaikwad, Kondiba 147, 208
Gajarawala, Toral 3, 9
Gana Mahar, Madgullkar 170, 177
Gandhianism 3

Gandhi, Indira 16
Gandhi M. K. 2–3, 35, 194, 200, 250; assassination of 8, 147, 194, 198, 200–201, 203, 206, 208, 213, 250; freedom struggle under 3; Quit India Movement 7
Garja Jayajayakar, Kusumagraj 103
Gauguin 131
Gaurai, Madgulkar 10, 158
Gavakadchya Goshti ("Stories from the Village")-short story collections), Madgulkar 9, 100, 146, 199, 203, 231, 251, 255
Gavakade ("Towards the Village"), Madgulkar 170, 250
gender 19, 21, 183, 193; discrimination 7, 16
Global South 12, 21
Gode Pani ("Sweet Water"), Madgulkar 146, 170–171, 180, 182, 188, 194, 216
Gogol 8, 14
Gokhale, Arvind 5, 13–14, 147, 204, 252
Gomantakiya Marathi Literary Meet 13, 95
Gomantak Sahitya Sammelan, as President of 253
Goodall, Jane 12, 228
The Good Woman of Setzuan, Brecht 253
Gorky, Maxim 8, 114, 228
Government of India Act 1935 2
Grameen Sahitya Sammelan, as President of 253
grameen see rural (*grameen*)
grandmother 129–130
Grapes of Wrath, Steinbeck 116
Grazia, Deledda 113
Grozimek, Bernard 211, 253
Grozimek, Michael 211, 253
Gurjar, Vitthal S. 3–4

Hardikar, Vinay 21
Hastacha Paus ("Hasta Rain"), Madgulkar 117, 199, 217, 221
Hatim Tai 99, 112
headmaster 98; *see also* single-teacher school
Hemingway, Ernest 141
He Paap Kutha Fedu? Madgulkar 170
Hindu Mahasabha 3

INDEX

Hiralal 236
Hitopadesha 249
Hoval, Waman 184
Hubbs, Jolene 11
humanism 164, 193
humanity 12, 20, 101–102, 142, 189, 200, 227
humour 6, 163
hunger 38, 42, 80, 101, 115, 173, 195, 213
hunt/hunting 9, 12, 20, 101, 111, 118–121, 209, 220, 226, 236; *shikari* 1, 45, 101, 118, 202, 209, 236, 241
Huyssen, Andreas 2

Ibsenian realist techniques 10, 165
identitarian movements 15, 18
illustrations 7, 21, 127, 129–130, 249; *Kaziranga 133*
Inamdarancha Balu, Madhav 99
innovations 103, 155, 159; *see also* creativity

Jadhav, Kishor 6
Jambhalache Divas, Madgulkar 186, 251
Janabai 16
Jananayak 233
Janar Kuthe-play Madgulkar, performed by, Progressive Dramatic Association 251; also as "Tu Veda Kumbhar" ("Oh You Silly Potter!"), Madgulkar 158, 160
Janglatil Divas, Madgulkar 12, 131, 253
Joshi, Sudha 15, 21
Joshi, Suresh 6
Julian *see* Patwardhan, Madhav T.

Kaay Sudik Gela Nhai 203
Kadamba, Bhagwat 219
Kadu Ani Gode, Gadgil 211
Kahi Kavita, Maradhekar 4
Kairee ("Raw Mango"), Kulkarni 236
Kalabarobar Chalaspeaks play, Madgulkar 159
Kalagati, Madgulkar 170
Kalal, Sakha 13, 124
Kale, Pramod 253
Kali Aai 231, 255

Kalya Tondachi ("The Black-faced One"), as first short story 8, 98, 117, 141, 221, 250
Kamat, Gajanan 8, 250
Kamleshwar 6
Karani, Madgulkar 202
Karlovy Vary International Film Festival 237
Karnik, Madhu Mangesh 219
Karunashtak, Madgulkar 110, 129–130, 188–189, 253
Karve, Irawati 9, 251
Katkari, Govinda 18, 177, 183
Kaviraj, Sudipta 16
Kenkare, Vijay 162, 164–166
Keshavsut 4, 98, 101, 109
Ketkar, S. V. 6, 148
Khandekar, V. S. 3–4
Khare, Balutai 3–4; *see also* Vibhavari Shiroorkar
Khatri, Jayant 6
Khel, Madgulkar 170
Khude, Saavala Dharma 217
Kinhai 99, 111, 249
Kirloskar magazine 124, 209
Kishore magazine for youth 228
Kolatkar, Arun 4
Kolhapur 7, 126, 141, 250
Kolhatkar, Shripad Krishna 4
Komro, Manuel 211
Kothawale, R. R. 122
Kovale Divas ("The Tender Days"), Madgulkar 7, 70, 72, 115, 126, 199, 232
Krushnakathcha Ramvanshi, Mate 184
Kulkarni, B. S. 220
Kulkarni, G. A. 236
Kulkarni, Shrinivas 219
Kumpanapalikadche Shet ("A farm outside the fence") 253
Kunacha Kunala Mel Nahi-play, Madgulkar 158–159, 251–252, 256
Kunbi 33, 96, 111
Kunte, Krishnamegh 220
Kusum agraj 103

labels/labelling 16, 168–169, 210
La Deshpande, Pu 213
La Fontaine 71, 105

INDEX

language/languages xi–xii, 1–2, 5–6, 12, 17–19, 101–102, 104–105, 115, 130, 155, 182, 195, 212, 220; of city 149–151, 153–156; of community 151; Madgulkar on 11; modernity in South Asian 1–2; nomadic 18; Parushi 195; pure-profane polarity of 152; South Asian 1, 6; southern 19; standard 19, 151–154, 163; theatrical 165; urban 153, 156; village 155–156
La Rochefoucauld 105
Larousse 106
Lautrec 106, 125
Lekhandarshan ("A Glimpse of Writing") 129, 212
libraries 99, 104–106
literary: expression 154–155, 164; works 11, 110, 143, 154, 166, 178, 197–199, 228
literature 101–106, 117, 198; *grameen* 14, 19; imaginative 198; Indian 1, 12, 209, 215; modernist 2, 15
litterateurs 95, 102, 109, 118, 155
livelihood 42, 101, 124, 126, 170, 175
Logan, Bob 106
'Lokahitwadi' Deshmukh Gopal Hari 2
Londhe, Lakshman 220
London yethil Badya Lokanchi Gupta Krutye 249
Lopez 104
lyrics 2, 5

Maaza Guni Janawar ("My Virtous Beast"), Madgulkar 221
Madgul 110–111, 192
Madgulkar G. D. (elder brother) 9, 136, 225, 232, 249–251
Madgulkar-Mirasdar-Patil generation 149, 152
Madgulkar, Sitaram Eknath 146, 251
Madgulkar, Vyankatesh Digambar (VYAMA)/Tatya 1, 5: with Amol Palekar 244; birth of 249; conversation with Pundalik 110; death of 233; fiction 13, 15, 21, 142, 148, 170; horoscope in Marathi 245; legacy of 15–20; life and works of 7–15; and Marathi modernism 4–5; marrying Vimal Mystry 250;

modernist vision 6, 15; novels 13; Palekar on 235; photo on book cover 239, *239*; plays 10, 158–162, 164–166; prose 183; short stories 13; as teacher 9, 249
Madhav, Nath 99, 112, 249
Magar Ani Vanar ("Junglatil Divas") 222
Maharashtra 2, 6, 8–9, 12, 15, 18, 105, 107, 164, 170, 208, 213, 252–253
Maison de la culture de Grenoble 107
Malshe, S. G. 251
Manasollasa 7
Mancharkar, R. B. 15–17
Mandavkar, Anagha xv, 10, 21, 158; classification of plays 10
Mandesh, *karma bhoomi* as 1, 6, 8–10, 100, 142, 161–163, 184, 186, 192, 195, 208, 211, 214–216
Mandeshi Manasa (The People of Mandesh/"The Folks of Mandesh"), Madgulkar 1, 9, 44, 100, 111, 127, 146, 168, 184, 186–187; serialized in Maujand 250
Mandhre, Chandrakant 236
Mangeshkar, Hridaynath 237
Manini-film, Madgulkar 254
Marathas 19, 145, 171, 176, 183
Marathi 1–3, 8, 13–17, 20–21, 141, 143–144, 156, 158, 195, 197, 209, 211, 219–220, 250, 252; discovering books of 249; fiction 3, 13; literary culture 15–16; society 2, 7, 12, 126; theatre 10, 158, 160–161, 165; translations into 12; village 9–10
Marathi literature 1–3, 5–6, 9, 15, 17, 19, 165, 168–169, 171, 192, 197–198, 219–220, 222; modernity in 2–4, 15; precolonial 2
Marathi Sahitya Akademi, as Member of Advisory Board 253
Marathi Sahitya Sammelan 110
Marathi *Shabd Ratnakar* 107
Marathwada 95
Mardhekar, B. S. 4–5, 8, 13, 113, 210, 250
Marquez, G. 228

INDEX

Marut Raya, Madgulkar 12
Marxism 3
Mate, S. M. 13–14, 19, 112–113, 141, 184, 250
Mate-Thokal generation 19
Matisse 125, 131
Maupassant, Guy de 8, 228
Maza Baap 188
Mazya Likhanamagachi Kalsutre, "The Formulas behind my Writing" 199
Meshram, Keshav 184
Mhaiskar, Vidyadhar 220
middle class 10, 20, 103, 112, 119, 161, 165, 206, 235
Milton, Daniel L. 252
Mirasdar 14, 153–154
"Misery", Chekhov 14
Mistry, Vimal 250
modernism 1–2, 4–5, 19, 21, 148; Anglo-American 5; casteless 3, 9; geographies of 2, 21; realistic 15; rural 11–12
modernity 1–4, 9, 15–16, 21, 160, 197
modernization 5, 147
Mohanty, Gopinath 253
Mokashi, D. B. 5, 226
"The Monkey God", translated by Ram Deshmukh 252
Montague-Chelmsford Government of India Act 1919 2
Morley Minto reforms 2
Moropant 249
Morvanchikar, R. S. 217
mother (Aai) Vahini 111, 124, 130; death of 228–229; sketches of 130; stories from 9
Mouj, periodical 8, 14, 251
movements 15–19, 102, 117, 143, 213, 222
Mrugapakshishastra 219
Mukkam Post Dhebewadi, Madgulkar scripting for 252, 254
Mukul, Ravi 8, 21, 234
Murakami 235
Murthy, Anantha 5–6
music 101–102, 160, 166
Muslims 9, 15, 96, 111, 120, 146, 168, 177
My Life as A Hunter: with gun *241*; Madgulkar 119

"*nagar bhasha*" 149
Nagzira, Madgulkar 12, 219–220, 222, 253
Naik, Dnyanada, Ms 220, 224
Naik, Meena 166
Naik, Rajeev 158, 164–166
Nama Master, Madgulkar 170
Nama Satpute 10, 158–163, 253
Namdeo/ Namdev 16, 228
narration 15, 19–20, 141–142, 149, 153, 179–182, 199, 202, 206, 213, 221; style 195; third-person 153; in *Vavtal* 203
Nath, Phanishwar 'Renu' 6
National Book Trust 105, 252
National Center for the Performing Arts theatre, Mumbai 237
National Film Development Corporation (NFDC) 237
nationalism 2–3, 5, 250; anti-colonial 2
National Literary Form 113
native village 194, 215
nature xiv, 11–13, 15–16, 101, 117–118, 123, 128–131, 141–142, 145, 189, 194–195, 201–204, 209–210, 217, 219–220, 222, 227–228, 235–236
navakavya 2, 8; movement 5
navina movement 6
nav katha (modernist short fiction/new short story) 1–2, 4–5, 8, 14–15, 126, 141, 148
nav katha/navina/nayi kahani movement 5, 14
nav/nava kathakar 17, 168
navyathe movement 6
Nehru, Jawaharlal 16, 35, 200
Nemade, Bhalchandra 16, 183
newspapers 104–105, 117
New Woman 3
Nisargotsav, Bhagwat 219
nomadic tribes 9, 121, 176, 199–200
novels 1–3, 7–9, 12–14, 99–100, 105, 112–113, 115–116, 188–190, 192–195, 198, 200–201, 203–204, 206, 209, 211–215, 230, 236–237, 250–253; semi-autobiographical 7, 252
Nyay, Madgulkar 170

INDEX

O'Connor, Frank 14
O'Flaherty, Liam 8, 104, 228
Oh, The Husband Has Gone To Kathewadi (*Pati Gele Ga Kathewadi*), Madgulkar 87
oil paintings 98, 249; *see also* drawing/sketches
Ojha ("Burden"), Madgulkar 194
"On the Trail of the Tiger", Madgulkar 12, 209, 252
oral: communication 151; tradition 114, 143, 159
Orwell, George 210
Overcoat, Gogol 112
ovis 103, 215, 217
Oza, Pawar 146, 186, 188, 199

Padaka Khopata, Madgulkar 170, 174
Pai, Shirish 219
painters 7, 11, 106–107, 126, 146, 235–236, 249–250
paintings 7, 27, 98, 102–103, 107, 115, 124–126, 131, 209, 231, 252; *see also* drawing/sketches
Palekar, Amol 21, 235, 244, 254
Pande, Satish 220
Pandhari Mendhe Hiravi Kurane 211
Pandharpur 38, 125
Pandharyavar Kale ("Black on White"), Madgulkar 128–129, 131
Pantavane, G. V. 13
Paranjape, Raja 251
Paranjape, Sai 253
Paritoshik, Madgulkar 216
Parjanyaat anna-sambhav, Madgulkar 216
Partition of India 4
Parvacha 210
Patel, Jabbar 10, 160, 164–166
Patel, Pannalal 6
Pati Gele Ga Kathewadi ("The Husband has gone to Kathewadi") - comic, Madgulkar 9–10, 87, 158–162, 164, 166
Patil, Anand 17, 185
Patil, Shankar 13–14
patriotism 193, 251
Patwardhan, Madhav T., alias 'Madhav Julian' 4
Paus, Madgulkar 216

Pawar, G. M. (Go Ma Pawar) 17–18, 21, 146, 199, 204
PDA Theatre Academy 227
Pendse, N. S. 6
Pendse, S. N. 165
"The People of Mandesh" Madgulkar 17, 100, 127, 142, 184–185, 216
Phadke, N. S. 3–4
Phanishwarnath 'Renu' 12
Phule, Mahatma Jotiba 2–3, 177
Picasso 125, 131
Pinge, Ravindra 219
Pirandello, Luigi 4
planetary modernisms 2, 21
"Planning a Feast", translated by Bal Gadgil 252
plays 1, 9–10, 20, 106, 116, 143, 158–167, 205, 209, 225, 227; performative aspects of 165
playwriting 10, 164–166
poetry 2, 4–5, 98, 103, 143, 150–151, 163, 211, 250
"The Poisoned Bread", Madgulkar 18
polemical tracts 2
The Portrait of a Desert 118
portraits 124, 126, 128–130, 166, 249
poverty 7, 13–14, 107, 113, 174, 177, 182, 188, 195, 200, 208
power struggle 201–202, 205–206, 222
'*Pradesh sakalyacha* (the Province of Totality) 101
"*praman bhasha*" 149, 151–154; *see also* language
Pravas Eka Lekhakacha, Madgulkar 254
Presidential Addresses 9, 13, 17, 19–20, 95
Priestley 225
protest 69, 204–206
Pudhacha Paul, Madgulkar 204, 250–251
Pujari, Suhas 12–13, 21
Pundalik, Vidyadhar 20, 220
Pune 8, 84–86, 95, 100, 105–106, 194, 204, 209–210, 230, 235–237, 243, 250, 252
Purandare, Kiran 220
Purohit, K. J. 'Shantaram' 5

Quit India Movement 7, 99, 199, 250, 252

Rajwade 228
Rakesh, Mohan 6

INDEX

Rama Mailkuli, Madgulkar 170, 173–174, 177
Ramayanas, by Moropant 249
Ramdas 228
Ramoshis (nomadic tribes) 9, 29, 70, 121, 169, 172, 176–177, 249; settlement 119; *wada* 41, 96, 110
Ranmeva, Madgulkar 12, 253
Rasal, Sudhir 220
Rashtra Seva Dal 159, 164, 252
Ratricha Divas, Mardhekar 5
Ravi Kiran Mandal (group of poets) 4
readers 104–105, 141
reading 101, 104–105, 111, 114, 249
realism 5, 15, 20, 104, 131, 145
"The Red and the Black." Stendhal 107
Rege, Sadanand 5, 8, 250
region 3, 5–6, 101, 104
religion 3, 85, 101, 143, 150, 195, 205
Rembrandt 106
Renault 106
Renoir 131
Reynolds, G. W. M. 249
riots 194, 198, 200–201, 206; *see also* anti-Brahmin riots
rituals 96, 150, 170, 178, 195, 236
Rituchakra, Bhagwat 219
Rodin 125
romanticism 5–6, 13, 164
"The Rose Tattoo" Williams 253
Rousseau, Henri 108, 131
rural (*grameen*) 1, 6, 14–17, 20, 141, 152–153, 155, 169, 184; bhasha 152, 154–155; community 151, 215; *kathakar* 210; katha/story 142, 150, 210; language 149–157; life 11, 13, 116–117, 145–147, 155–156, 168–170, 175–176, 194–195, 198, 200, 204, 210–211, 217; literature 104, 149–151, 154–157, 169; sahitya 6; stories 149, 153–154; writers 19, 154; writing 6, 19
Russell 225
Russian: literature 112; revolution 2–3
Rye, Madhu 6

'Sadashiv Pethis' 6
Sagar, Charuta 13, 175, 184, 237
Sahasey, Ashi Mansey Ashi 221
Saheb, Alauddin Khan 125

Sahitya Sanskriti Mandal, nomination for 254
Sahitya Sanskruti Mandal 105–106, 253
Sahni, Bhisham 6
saints 17, 56, 97, 118
Samikshak, journal 250
Samyukta Maharashtra Movement 6
Sangatye Aika-film, Madgulkar 254
Sangli literary meet 13
Sangte Aikawhich (1959), written by Madgulkar 251
Sanskrit literature 157, 211
Sant, Prakash 124
Santa Namdev (1949) 250
Sapre, Avinash 222
Sartre, Jean-Paul 225
Sarveswaran, Vidya 12
Sathe, Anna Bhau 19, 192–195
Sathe, Makarand 159
Sati - plays - comic, Madgulkar 9–10, 20, 84, 115, 158–159, 161–162, 164, 253
Sattantar ("Transfer of Power") 1, 12–13, 20, 73, 130–132, 200–201, 206, 211, 213, 220, 229
Satyakatha, journal 8, 14, 17, 185, 250
Savarkar, Vinayak D. 3
Sayajirao, Maharaja 105
Scheduled Tribes 194
School Inspection, translated by Ian Raeside 252
Schopenhauer 225
screenplay writer 10, 237
"The Sculptor and his Sculpture" 108
sculpture 102–103, 108, 125
"Serengeti Shall Not Die", Bernard and Grzimek 211; as *Sinhachya Deshat* 253
Service Motar, Madgulkar 147, 160
Shantaram, V. 236
Shejwalkar, T. S. 9, 251
Shelke, Shanta 219
Shelke, Udhav 14
Shida Chambhar, Madgulkar 172
Shipayi, Mithu 18, 176–177
Shirdhankar, Bhanu 4, 209
short stories 2–6, 8, 13–14, 141, 143–144, 146, 148, 158–159, 162, 168–169, 198–199, 209, 250–251, 253; modern Marathi 252; rural reality in 145
simplicity 10, 165, 184, 227

INDEX

The Sindbad Voyages 210
single-teacher school 9, 249–250
Sinhachya Deshat, Madgulkar 130, 253
Sishiragam, Mardhekar 4
Sitaram 251
sketches 12, 103, 125, 127–130, 132, 209–210, 226, 230, 233, 253; of Bittakaka 127; forest animals 132
slavery 103, 205–206
Slovic, Scott 12
Sobti, Krishna 253
social: awakening 193; changes 18, 151, 169, 198, 204; communication 115, 151; obligations 101–102
socialism 3
social structure 145, 147, 169, 212; as water-centric 217
social system 147, 173, 203; *alutedar-balutedar* 9
society 10, 13–14, 16, 20, 101, 111, 113–114, 117–118, 143, 155, 168, 198, 200–201
"The Soil below the Soil" Anand Patil 185
Solapur District Literary Meet 95
Sontheimer, Gunther 253
Sonyacha Pimpal, Kulkarni 219
Soper, Eileen 132
Stage Directions 163
State Textbook Bureau 228
Steinbeck, John 8, 101, 114
Stendhal 107
story teller 7, 9, 115, 142–143, 236
story telling 143, 179
superstitions 14, 146, 170, 194–195, 216, 221
Surve, Narayan 13
Swarnalatha Rangarajan 12
Symbolism 198

'Tagore Syndrome' 5
Talyachya Paali 147
teacher 249; *see also* single-teacher school
theatre 10, 161, 237
Thiong'o, Ngugi Wa 197
Thokal, G. L. 19
Thompson, Ralph 132
Thoreau, Henry David 100, 220, 228
Thurber, James 124

Tilak, Bal Gangadhar 2, 228
Tilak, Jayantrao 123
Times Literary Supplement 105
trade union movement 3, 7
translations xi–xiii, 1, 19–20, 105, 211, 249, 253, 256
travelogues 2, 143, 211
tribes (nomadic communities) 28, 30, 119, 121, 170, 175–176, 183; Gadavi Sonar 170; Gosavi 170; Katkaris 49, 170, 209; Makadwales 170; Nandiwales 170; Paradhis 170, 175–176, 183; Phashe Pardhis 119; vaidu 28, 30, 119, 121, 170
Tu Atha Kuthey re Jasheel?, Mate 184
Tukaram 38, 108, 164, 228
Turgenev 14, 112
Tu Veda Kumbhar ("Oh You Silly Potter!")-play, Madgulkar 9–10, 79, 158–164, 251–253

Umbartha, Madgulkar 252
untouchability 9, 13, 19, 168–170, 172–174, 176, 178, 182–184, 199, 201, 205; *see also under* caste/castes
Upanishads 228
upper-caste villagers 172–173, 180
urbanization 2, 7, 16, 147

Vadarvadichya Vastith, Madgulkar 170, 174, 183, 187, 194
Vaghachya Magavar ("On the Trail of the Tiger"), Madgulkar 12, 122, 209, 252
Vaghe 17, 97
Vahana, Madgulkar 170
Vaid, Bhau 18
value system 195
Van Gogh, Vincent 125–126, 130–131, 252
Varghade, Sureshchandra 220
Vari, Madgulkar 170, 183
Vavtal ("Whirlwind"), Madgulkar 8, 67, 192, 194–195, 200–201, 203, 206, 212, 250, 252; into Russian 253
Veer Dhaval - novel, Madhav 99, 249
Verma, Nirmal 6
Vibhavari Shiroorkar, Balutai Khare as 3

INDEX

village 6–9, 13, 32–33, 37–41, 53–55, 57–58, 63–68, 70–72, 79, 95–100, 119–121, 145–147, 150–153, 155–157, 169–171, 176–177, 184–188, 193–195, 203–204, 249–250; depiction of 13; *see also* rural (*grameen*)
Vimalabai 232
violence 13, 147, 194, 212–213; *see also* anti-Brahmin riots; riots
Viparit Kahi Ghadale, Madgulkar 186
Viprit Ghadale Nahi, Madgulkar 170, 183
Vishari Bhakri ("Poisoned Bread"), Madgulkar 185
visual artist 7, 20, 127
Vyaghri, Madgulkar 45
Vyankatesh Madgulkar yanchi Katha, Gokhale 252
Vyankatesh Madgulkar yanchya daha katha, Malshe 251

wada (mansion) 43, 68, 84, 87, 89, 111, 172, 187
Waghmare, Yogiraj 184
water-culture 13, 215–217

western plays, adaptations of 10, 163–164
"Wheatfield with Crows", Van Gogh 126
wildlife 12, 101, 105, 143, 145, 163, 253
Williams, Tennessee 163, 253
"The Winds of Fire", translated by Kale 253
Wordsworth 99
World War II 2, 4–8, 13, 97, 141, 147
writers 1, 3–6, 11–14, 16–19, 99–102, 104–107, 114–115, 129, 132, 141–142, 149, 152–156, 164–165, 169, 219–220, 225–226, 249–250; country-story 141; Madgulkar-Mirasdar-Patil generation 152; on nature 220
writing/writings 108, 116–117, 127–129, 145, 149, 185, 217; on art 124, 131; for films 250

Yadav, A. 19
Yeats, W. B. 141

Zilla Sahitya Sammelan, as President of 251
Zola 106

Printed in the United States
by Baker & Taylor Publisher Services